European History and European Lives: 1715 to 1914

Part I

Professor Jonathan Steinberg

THE TEACHING COMPANY ®

PUBLISHED BY:

THE TEACHING COMPANY
4151 Lafayette Center Drive, Suite 100
Chantilly, Virginia 20151-1232
1-800-TEACH-12
Fax—703-378-3819
www.teach12.com

ISBN 1-56585-759-3

Jonathan Steinberg, Ph.D.

Professor of History, University of Pennsylvania

Jonathan Steinberg is the Walter H. Annenberg Professor of Modern European History at the University of Pennsylvania and Chair of the Department of History. He was born in New York in 1934, graduated from Harvard in 1955, and was immediately drafted into the U.S. Army, where he served two years in the Medical Corps. After a period in investment banking, he took his doctorate at Cambridge and was University Lecturer (from 1993, Reader) in European History; Fellow of Trinity Hall, Cambridge, from 1966 to 1999; and Vice-Master from 1990 to 1994. From January 1, 1991, to December 31, 2000, he co-edited *The Historical Journal* (Cambridge University Press). In 1992, he served as an expert witness in a Commonwealth of Australia war crimes prosecution.

In December 1997, Professor Steinberg was appointed to the Historical Commission of the Deutsche Bank AG, Frankfurt am Main, set up to look into the bank's activities under the Nazis, and was principal author of the commission's report. He gave the biennial Leslie Stephen lecture on November 25, 1999, in the Senate House of the University of Cambridge with the title "Leslie Stephen and Derivative Immortality." Previous Leslie Stephen lecturers include A. E. Housman, Sir Isaiah Berlin, Iris Murdoch, and Seamus Heaney.

Professor Steinberg is the author of *Yesterday's Deterrent: Tirpitz and the Birth of the German Battle Fleet* (1965), *Why Switzerland?* (1976; paperback, 1980; 2nd ed., 1996), and *All or Nothing: The Axis and the Holocaust, 1941 to 1943* (1990; paperback, 1992; second edition 2002; also available in German- and Italian-language translations). *All or Nothing* tries to explain why Fascist Italy in its zones of occupation in Greece, Croatia, and southern France systematically refused to assist Nazi Germany, its nominal ally, in the extermination of the Jews. By using German and Italian sources, Professor Steinberg attempts to compare the two faces of fascism. He has also translated Margaret Boveri, *Treason in the Twentieth Century* (London, 1961), and Friedrich Heer, *Intellectual History of Europe* (London, 1965), from German and Pino Arlacchi, *Mafia, Peasants and Great Estates: Society in Traditional Calabria* (Cambridge, 1983), from Italian.

From 1979 to 1987, Professor Steinberg wrote a monthly column in *New Society*, and he has reviewed for *The London Review of Books*, *The Evening Standard, The Financial Times*, and *The Times Literary Supplement*. He has written radio and TV documentaries and talks, including BBC Radio Four's salute to the U.S. Constitution on the 200th anniversary of its signing. During his years at Cambridge, he lectured regularly at the Royal College of Defence Studies, the Joint Services Staff College, and continues to lecture at the IBM Cambridge summer school. Professor Steinberg is also a member of the Board of Trustees, Franklin College, Lugano, Switzerland, and of the Presidential Advisory Commission on Holocaust Assets.

Table of Contents

European History and European Lives: 1715 to 1914
Part I

European History and European Lives: 1715 to 1914

Scope:

This course of thirty-six lectures is an experiment. In my forty years in the business of teaching history, I have never done anything like it. I don't think anyone has. The idea is simple: to use individual lives to explain a great historical transformation. That sounds easy but is not. The great historical transformation I have in mind is no small matter: How did the world of lord and serf, horse and carriage, superstition and disease, turn into the world of boss and worker, steam and steel, science and medicine? In other words, how and why did what we call the modern world come about? Why did it start in the Europe of lord and serf in the 18th century and end in the world of boss and worker by 1914? How and why did Europe by the end of the 19th century come to control all the ancient empires of the globe? The trick in this series will be to see these great transformations by looking at the lives of those who made them happen. Most of the lives will be those of great figures—kings, queens, generals, artists, thinkers, and entrepreneurs—but one lecture, that on the Irish famine, will have no single biography. The Irish people of the 1840s will be the actors.

The course falls into two clear sections: Section 1 covers the years 1715 to 1815, from the end of the attempt by one French monarch to dominate Europe—Louis XIV—to the final defeat of another—Napoleon. Its principal transformation is the French Revolution or the democratic transformation. Section 2 takes the story from 1815 to 1914, from the end of the Napoleonic war to the beginning of the first of two terrible world wars of the 20th century. In this period, the main transformation is the Industrial Revolution, with the accompanying explosion of science and technology.

To lecture on lives raises a serious problem of method. Much of what happened in the years 1715 to 1914 depends on the lives and activities of ordinary people whose struggle for existence and happiness makes up the great story of modern history. Changes in population, disease, famine, immigration and emigration, factory labor, strikes and trade unionism, literacy, emancipation of women, armies, and empires are mass phenomena, not individual ones. No single life can remotely express these huge forces. Much of the time, those then living had no way of knowing the things we now know. What justifies the biographical approach?

First of all, it is fun. It is in our nature to be interested in one another. The people whom we shall study are among the most interesting people who have ever lived. That's why we remember them, and the rest have been forgotten. Telling the stories of their lives helps us to understand what it is to be human and to grasp the idea that even the "self" has a history that changes over time.

Second, it is way to look at the great changes. If we see the times in which our figures lived as a kind of lens or magnifying glass, we can look for the background, as well as the foreground. We know what they could not: what happens next. Their future is our past. We know what they had no words to describe or tools to measure.

Third, it is a way to educate ourselves, using the meaning for the Latin verb *e-ducere*, which means, according to my ancient Latin dictionary, "to lead or draw out." In other words, education does not mean "stuffing the mind with information" but drawing out our awareness of ourselves and our world. By looking at what even the greatest of the actors of the past could not see or understand, we get a glimpse of what we may be missing in our own thinking. After all, the things we take for granted are rarely conscious and never written down. When we observe the way people in the past seemed unaware of great changes now obvious to us, we have a useful moment of self-doubt. What are we missing in our world? We become one degree less self-confident that we know what is going on. That touch of humility, that creative moment of hesitation, that openness to the possibility that we might be wrong, those are the signs of a real historical education.

Lecture One
History as a "Soft" Science

Scope:

This lecture provides a road map of the course. The basic idea is to tell the history of Europe, from the aristocratic early 18th century to the outbreak of the First World War, through the lives of the colorful personalities who traversed its landscape. Each life, in a highly distinctive way, helped shape the 18th century and the "long 19th century." This course looks at 35 such individuals. Though roughly biographical in scope, the course concerns itself more with how each of these lives embodied a specific, critical stage in Europe's development or represented new and powerful ideas that propelled the Continent toward modernity. These two centuries are crucial in European development. They begin with a world of privilege, poverty, disease, and inequality, the so-called *Old Regime*, whose way of life was not that different from that of the Romans or the Chinese Empire, and end with cities, technology, a new kind of state, and modern mass society. At the end of this period in 1914, Europe is like our own world, and a new self, set in a new social reality, has become the dominant actor.

The lives we study affect that process. We will look at monarchs and politicians; those who affected the economy; gender relations, industry, and science; along with philosophers, writers, and artists. In one lecture, we analyze the disaster of a whole people in the Irish famine. Our challenge is to discover whether lives can embody the great forces and factors that historians often describe as impersonal. Is biography a way to see the whole story through the optic of one individual?

Outline

I. A great transformation takes place in Europe between 1715 and 1914—from the Old Regime to modern mass society. The *Old Regime* is a term invented after the French Revolution to describe a lost world of privilege, aristocracy, serfdom, and poverty. How does it become the modern regime of cities, technology, mass movement, and increasing equality?

A. The sudden explosion of European culture and power in the 18th and 19th centuries is a general trend of the period, and there are great shifts in power.

    1. Huge new empires grow up after 1715. The British and the French are new players, replacing Spain and Portugal.

    2. Between 1715 and 1914, the growth of European supremacy becomes obvious. By 1914, Europe (together with the English-speaking former colonies), the United States, and Japan enjoy a near monopoly on high technology. The gunboat of *gunboat diplomacy* is the symbol of this supremacy.

B. A second change is the rise of the secular state.

    1. A state founded on reason and *natural laws* begins to emerge. It is the end of the *divine right* of kings. The social contract is the great revolutionary experiment: The state can be conceived as reformer and provider of welfare, education, and so on.

    2. The belief in the "yoke of sin," the conviction of the sinfulness of humanity, gives way in these two centuries to the idea that human nature is good and can be shaped by the activity of the state.

    3. The great Enlightenment project begins between 1715 and the 1760s. The idea was to use human tools to perfect human nature. This attempt links 1789 to 1989. All the ideologies of the modern era (fascism, communism, liberalism, nationalism) believed they knew how to make us happy and virtuous.

C. A third change comes about through the exploitation of science and technology.

    1. An agricultural revolution brings new crops and crop rotation systems. After 1848, for the first time in history, famine ceases to be a threat in Europe.

    2. New technology is developed, such as the steam engine, which multiplies the capacity of labor by multiples of *horsepower* and, by the 1830s, produces a transportation revolution. The telegraph, invented in 1833, offers instant communication.

    3. A new technology of measurement is seen in the developments in statistics, data filing, and surveying, giving political authorities new sources of power. The state "knows" about its citizens.

D. Industrialization applies new technology and new machinery to human work. The factory embodies the multiplication of human power by assembly lines and mechanized, simplified production systems.

　1. New products and new consumers develop. Traditional marketplaces give way to shops. The English become "a nation of shopkeepers" in Adam Smith's phrase. The shop represents specialization of trade and distribution, and the *consumer* is born.

　2. Why England was first to industrialize is a complicated question. Trade produced capital accumulation. The new financial institutions allowed for modern investment and speculation. People collected in factory towns, and new social problems arose.

　3. Economics developed as a way of understanding these new realities. We will examine the greatest economics textbook ever written, Adam Smith's *The Wealth of Nations* (1776) in Lecture Thirteen.

E. Demographic changes are reflected in the sudden growth in European populations around 1700.

　1. Epidemics decline, and medicine, health, and nutrition improve.

　2. As a consequence, humanity in our period faces the problems of overpopulation for the first time. In fact, gains in productivity, as well as agriculture and industry, made these fears groundless.

F. War is prominent and has far-reaching effects on society.

　1. The 18th-century war was a military chess game. Professional soldiers used fixed maneuvers and stylized tactics. Armies enjoyed long winter pauses, and most ordinary people were not involved.

　2. The French Revolution transformed war because it transformed society. The revolutionary wars of the 1790s introduced the war of masses. People were drafted, and the French waged a "people's war" against "enemies of the people." Democratic war is much more destructive than old professional warfare. From 1789 to the trenches of the western front, there is a direct connection.

G. The transformation of art and the *public sphere* has no parallel in other eras.

    1. Before 1715, the arts represented the crown and altar. The arts served patrons who had political or religious power (for example, Michaelangelo and the ceiling of the Sistine Chapel).

    2. After 1750 (roughly), art became a commodity for sale to the "public" (a new phenomenon in human history).

    3. The new artist was genius, critic, and salesman at the same time.

II. There are advantages and limits in using biography as a way to understand these changes.

    A. We see the types of changes embodied in the lives studied.

        1. Frederick the Great or Joseph II tried to create the new type of state. We see the king as state-builder and reformer from above. Although these kings were *absolute despots*, they ran into limits.

        2. Biography helps us to see the modern self emerge. By studying the lives of Hume, the philosopher and skeptic; Rousseau, the self-confessor; Mary Wollstonecraft or George Eliot, as "new" women; Goethe, the artistic genius as himself a work of art, we watch the emergence of our own selves.

        3. Robert Walpole, Adam Smith, or Nathan Meyer Rothschild illustrate the emergence of capitalism and the first stages of globalization.

        4. The Krupp family represents the new kind of heavy industry.

        5. The new public sphere involved the sale of art works and the mass marketing of culture, but it also produced a new sort of religion of art. Samuel Johnson and C.P.E. Bach represent the 18th-century stage of this change. The painter Goya marks the transition from court to popular painter. Wagner and Tolstoy represent the cult of art in an industrial society.

        6. Robespierre, Mazzini, Karl Marx, and Friedrich Engels represent the new type of revolutionary. Metternich,

Edmund Burke, and Pope Pius IX embody the conservative reaction to the new revolutionaries. Wagner is a pivotal figure who started off as a revolutionary but turned into the prophet of a new conservatism that both fueled Nazism and created a powerful artistic cult.

7. Pasteur and Darwin embody the role of science, and the politician David Lloyd George represents the new kind of politics of reform.

8. The "Jewish problem" is represented by Nathan Meyer Rothschild and Alfred Dreyfus, whose lives embody the problems of Jewish emancipation on the road to modernity in Europe.

9. Two aristocrats in a modern world—Otto von Bismarck, the German statesman who unified Germany, and Queen Victoria, the monarch who embodied a kind of democratization of English politics—allow us to see two different strategies for dealing with the emergence of mass society.

B. The lectures tend to be divided into two parts: the biography of the individual and the social context of his or her life and achievement. Thus, the lives are a way to understand the changes of the period.

C. There are disadvantages in using biography as a way to understand history.

1. *Hard* history and *soft* history are my terms for distinguishing two domains of historical evidence. Hard history covers demography and quantitative history. Human beings are both subject and objects; as objects, they can be counted or, as consumers, their aggregate behavior is measurable. Statistics and computerized research provide something close to "objective" knowledge.

2. Soft history deals with biography, politics, and society, where the evidence cannot be measured and, in a sense, it "talks back."

3. Certain problems are not easily understood through a single life, which is why one lecture offers the biography of a mass of people, the generation of the Irish who suffered the 1840s potato blight.

4. The long-run elements (Keynes: "In the long run we are all dead") are not likely to be covered well by biography. No life can cover a long enough span. Certain phenomena (population, nutrition, industrialization) will be hard to catch in this course.

D. The return of biography as a method of study and of selling books is a striking phenomenon of the last 15 years.

1. In the 1950s, 1960s, and 1970s, serious historians studied large-scale forces and factors and used social scientific techniques. Biography was not done by "real professionals."

2. Biography as a technique has become popular and produced some of the best-selling books of our time, such as *Benjamin Franklin* by Edmund S. Morgan, *John Adams* by David McCullough, *Winston Churchill* by Roy Jenkins.

3. There are several possible reasons for the return of biography. The most important is the decline in prestige of social scientific models, brought on by the fall of communism. The explosion of religious fundamentalism in all the world's major religions was not predicted by social scientists, which further reduced their claims.

4. An advantage of biography as a means of explanation is that it tells a story. The life can be set in an analytical framework; for example, the life of Frederick the Great can be compared to the "model" of absolute despotism. We must be aware of the constraints on the actor and the choices open to him or her. The human dimensions of a problem come clear when the life is seen as emblematic.

III. The objective of this course is to provide a means of historical reflection.

A. Are there "lessons of history"?

1. History offers lessons, such as "Things rarely work out as planned" or "What most people think most of the time is going to happen turns out to be wrong," but those are not what the public really wants from historians.

2. The public and politicians want specific lessons, such as "Resistance to communism in Vietnam in 1968 was the same as resisting Nazism in Europe in 1938." It wasn't.

B. The comparative approach is useful as an alternative to a laboratory.

    1. Comparison is an essential element in this course because the types of lives have been chosen to be compared.

    2. We can draw modest lessons by comparing phenomena.

C. Studying biography provides enjoyment and enlightenment.

    1. The great lives are interesting in themselves. Theodor Fontane (1819 to 1898), the best German novelist of the 19th century, wrote: "When Bismarck sneezes or makes a toast, I find it more interesting than the wise speeches of six members of Parliament."

    2. These lives show us the greatest examples of what it is like to be human, and that exercise alone is deeply pleasurable.

Essential Reading:

Mary Fulbrook, *Historical Theory: Ways of Imagining the Past.*

Questions to Consider:

1. In what ways does your life "embody" certain identifiable changes in a wider historical context?

2. Why do you think historical biographies have become bestsellers lately?

Lecture One—Transcript
History as a "Soft" Science

Welcome to this new course of lectures, *European History and European Lives*. The course begins in September 1715 with the death of Louis XIV, and it ends on August the 3, 1914 when Sir Edward Grey said, "The lights went out all over Europe, and the great guns begin to destroy human lives in a mass industrial slaughter never seen before."

Now, in this lecture what I want to do is provide a kind of roadmap for the course. The basic idea of the course is to tell the history of Europe from the aristocratic early 18th century to the outbreak of the First World War through the lives of colorful personalities who traversed its landscape. Each life, in a highly distinctive way, helped shape the 18th century and what I think of as "the long 19th century," the period from the French Revolution to the outbreak of the First World War. This course looks at 35 such individuals. Though it is biographical in scope, the object and aim of the course is to explain how each of these lives embodied a critical specific stage in European development, or represented new and powerful ideas that propelled the continent toward modernity.

These two centuries are absolutely crucial in European development. They begin with a world of privilege, poverty, disease and inequality, the so-called Old Regime, whose way of life and standard of living were not much different from that of the Romans or the Chinese Empire, and it ends with cities, technology, a new kind of state, and mass modern society. At the end of this period, in 1914, Europe is like our own world, and a new human self set in a new social reality has become the dominant actor.

The lives we study affect and create this process. Some are monarchs, some are politicians, some affect the economy, some have to do with gender relations, some have to do with industry, banking or science. There are philosophers, writers, and artists. In one lecture, we shall look at the disaster of a whole people, the Irish Famine. They are the actors, and that generation is the biography, the collective biography for that lecture.

Now, this course is frankly an experiment, I have never done it before and I have never seen anybody crazy enough to try it either. This is simply something that nobody's done before. The basic questions are: Can you do it? Can lives embody the great forces and factors that historians often describe as impersonal? Is biography a way to see the whole story through the optic of an individual? That's the challenge for lecturer and student alike.

Now, what is this great transformation of Europe about, the transformation from the Old Regime to mass society? The term itself "Old Regime" is a historic artifact. It was invented after the French Revolution to describe what went before. It describes a lost world of privilege, aristocracy, serfdom, and poverty.

Now, how does it become the modern world of cities, technology, mass movements, and equality? The main features of the transformation I'd like now just to outline very briefly. There's a sudden explosion of power, European power, in the period that we're looking at, between 1715 to 1914, Europe becomes supreme in the world. It becomes obvious, by 1914, that Europe, together with the English-speaking former colonies, the United States and Japan, enjoyed a near monopoly on high technology. You can think of a symbol of it in something like the gunboat of "gunboat diplomacy." A small European state like Belgium could send a gunboat up the Congo and subdue great empires and tribes.

A second change which we take for granted now but is fundamental is the rise of the secular state in Europe. For the first time in human history, a state founded on reason and natural law grows up. It ends the divine right of kings and the whole traditional way of seeing kingship and rule, and in this there is a kind of social contract, a great revolutionary experiment.

The state is the "creation of the people," as the Constitution of the United States says, the people's contract, so to speak, to construct their new authority. This new state expresses the people's will. It can be conceived as a reformer, it can provide welfare, it can provide education, it can provide public health, clean water, whatever the citizens want it to do.

Now, with that change the belief in the "yoke of sin," the conviction that mankind is born in sin, gives way in those two centuries that we shall be studying, to the idea that human nature is fundamentally good, and that it can be shaped by our own efforts and indeed by the activity of the state. The great Enlightenment project begins between 1715 and the 1760s. Its idea was to use human tools to perfect human nature, and this Enlightenment project continues, really, I suppose, until the collapse of the Berlin Wall and the end of communism, for all the modern "isms" (fascism, communism, liberalism, nationalism), believed they knew how to make us happy and virtuous by human devices.

A third feature of this great transformation, something we again sort of take for granted but need to think about, is the exploitation of science and technology. There is an agricultural revolution which brings new crops and new rotations, and for the first time in human history, famine disappears. It happens in our period, after 1848.

There is new technology. The steam engine multiplies the capacity of labor by multiples measured in horsepower, and by the 1830s produces a transportation revolution in the railroad. The telegraph, invented in 1833, offers instant communication. There is also, and this is much less noticed, a new technology of measurement, a development in statistics, data filing. The card file is invented in 1774. The surveying of roads, and all these kinds of techniques give the political authorities new sources of power.

The state knows about its citizens in a way which has never been possible before, and this process, of course, continues in our own lives. It is now possible with smart cards to have everything about us available to the state, from our blood group to our income tax category.

Industrialization is another phenomenal and important change which takes place in the two centuries that we shall be studying. The new technology, the new science, and the new machinery are applied to human work. The factory embodies the multiplication of human power by assembly lines and mechanized simplified production systems. You get new products and new markets, and the traditional old-fashioned market gives way to the shop. England becomes "a nation of shopkeepers," in Adam Smith's famous phrase. When you think about it, a shop represents specialization of trade, specialization of distribution. You need wholesalers; you need a whole system, whereas the traditional market is just a place where people bring their wares. The consumer is born in our period.

Now, why England was the first to industrialize is a really complicated problem. Historians don't agree and we don't have to solve the problem, but what we will look at in Lecture Three when we look at Sir Robert Walpole and the first bubble economy of the modern period, great crash of the South Sea "bubble" in 1720, that trade produced a huge amount of capital accumulation in Great Britain. No doubt the slave trade was an important element in that. New financial institutions, banks, and stock exchange, began to grow up which allowed for the investment to move around and for speculation to occur. People began to collect where employment grew up, in the so-called factory towns, and with them you get new kinds of problems, new kinds of slums that had also never been seen before.

In addition, although people forget it, economics itself, the idea that there is a thing called "the economy," which can be studied by theory, is a product of this era. We shall look in Lecture 14 at the greatest economic textbook ever written, Adam Smith's *The Wealth of Nations,* which is one of the three revolutionary events of 1776; it could be argued that Adam Smith's textbook is at least as important as the American Declaration of Independence.

Then there's demographic change. At around 1700, for reasons which are still not entirely clear, there's a sudden growth in European population. Epidemics decline, medicine and health improve, nutrition and diet also improve, and here too demographers are not certain how or why it happened. There are consequences, though. For the first time in our period humanity faces the problem of over-population, but not, in fact, the starvation which is expected. As we shall see, the general view was that this population could not be fed. Malthus published his great book in our period, in 1798, and we shall talk about that later.

There's a fantastic change in the nature of war in society. In the 18th century, war was a military chess game. Professional soldiers used fixed maneuvers and stylized tactics, armies enjoyed long winter pauses, and most of the ordinary people were not involved. In fact, Frederick the Great used to say that when he went to war, he wanted his citizens not even to know that it was happening. The French Revolution, which ushers the modern world, transformed war, because it transformed the whole of society. When we look in Lecture 16 at what Robespierre and the French Revolutionaries actually did, they introduced the "war of the people" because they created citizens, they transformed the whole nature of war.

The people were drafted; everybody was drafted in the French Revolutionary War, including animals and old people They all had jobs to do, in the people's war against the enemies of the people. That too, was something absolutely new which had never seen before. It wasn't true in the Roman Empire, and it wasn't true in the Chinese Empire, this vast mass of people fighting against its enemies.

It turned out, and is still the case, that democratic war is much more destructive than the old professional elite war. The old war of the elites responded very much to the needs of other elites. You didn't destroy your enemy, but when democracy was unleashed there was no limit to war, and we end our lectures on the eve of the great destruction of the peoples in the trenches in the First World War, the beginning of the tragedies of the 20th century of the industrialized mass killing, which of course ends in the holocaust.

Then, there was another change in our period which is very remarkable, and so far as I know, again, has no real parallel. That is the transformation of art and the public sphere. Before 1715, the arts represented the crown or the altar. The arts served a patron who had a political or religious power, or a political or religious message to send. I mean, take the case of Michelangelo painting the Sistine Chapel. He was a great artist; he had already had an international reputation, but his patrons were people who had political or other needs. He was painting the Sistine Chapel for Pope Sixtus as part of the pope's glorification.

After about 1750 something really odd happens, and this is, I think, new. Art becomes a commodity for sale to the public. "The public" is a new phenomenon in the whole of human history. It's again something we take for granted; an anonymous public, armed with its pocketbooks, can go out and buy art, and there are all sorts of consequences of this transformation with which we are of course still living. The new artist was no longer a servant, was no longer somebody who wore livery like Haydn did in his entire political career, he was just a servant of Prince Esterhazy.

The new artist was a genius; the new artist was selling the products of his or her soul to the public, and the artist was sometimes critical, but you also need critics to tell the public what to buy. Sometimes the artists sell their own things, and sometimes other people sell them. In Lecture Nine, we'll look at the music of Carl Philipp

Emanuel Bach, the son of the great father, who actually was one of the first people to sell music. His father, perhaps the greatest musician of all time, never sold a piece of music. It wasn't part of Johann Sebastian Bach's world. He worked for either a prince or he worked most of his life for the Church; it wasn't part of his art to be sold.

We have a whole series of enormous changes here, and I would argue that the sum of these changes makes Europe itself exceptional in the history of the world, and created the modern world in which we now live. Now, I'm going to pause for a minute, and think with you about the advantages and limits of biography as a way to understand these changes. How is this course actually going to work? I hope what will happen is that you will see in each life a principle or a set of practices or some long-term trend which is embodied.

For example, let's take the two enlightened despots of the 18th century whom we shall be looking at, Frederick the Great and Joseph II. They were more or less contemporary, and both were imbued with an idea that you could make the state more efficient, more productive, more useful in war, by applying the laws of reason. That's why we speak of them as "enlightened," because they read the philosophers, they read the new theoreticians about how society should be organized, and thought, "Right, we can apply this and make our societies much more productive."

What we see, then, is the king as a state-builder, because after all, the state itself is a creation of the period we're looking at. There wasn't a state before. When Louis XIV was asked, "What is the State?" he said, *"L'état c'est moi!"* "It's me." Frederick the Great said, "I am the first servant of the state." That is, out there, there is some entity, some structure now which is not the king's personal property.

Thus, we see the king as state-builder and reformer from above, and although both kings were absolute despots, they ran into the limits of their projects. As we shall see, Frederick the Great was caught in a dilemma which he could not solve. There is no way that an absolute despot can actually run an absolute state rationally, because he's absolute and everybody's scared of him, so they will lie to him; Frederick was caught in the coils of his own absolutism.

Joseph, who was even more extreme, ran up against limits which have to do, I think, with human nature. People could not be made better by reformers from above, another way in which biography should help us to see the modern self emerge. When we look at the lives of somebody like Hume, the philosopher and skeptic in Lecture Eight, or Rousseau, the first person to confess his true inner life, including his sexual life, I think in the whole of human history, or Mary Wollstonecraft in Lecture 17, the founder of feminism, who took enlightened principles and applied them to women for the first time. There is also George Eliot, who not only made women the heroines, often, of her books, (and we shall look at *Middlemarch* which I think is her greatest novel) but was herself a new woman. Or Goethe, the artistic genius, who converted himself into a work of art, we watch something mysterious but recognizable, that is the birth of a new subjectivity, the new human self, the kind of people that you and I actually are.

Then, if we look at three different figures: Robert Walpole, Adam Smith or Nathan Meyer Rothschild, we see the emergence of capitalism, and the first stages of globalization and the emerging capitalist society. Walpole was the first person in modern society to experience, although the Dutch sometimes claim this, the first bubble economy and how it was solved. Adam Smith wrote the textbook for modern capitalism. Adam Smith could not be refuted, and never has been refuted, although what his message was, as I shall suggest, was not what most people today think it was. The Adam Smith society doesn't read the master carefully enough.

When we come to Nathan Meyer Rothschild, we come to an absolutely amazing phenomenon. Here was someone who, though not poverty stricken, was a Jew from the ghetto, born in the 1770s, and who in 25 years, was the richest man in the world. As we shall see, Rothschild's fortune relative to his age was much greater than Bill Gates's is to ours. Rothschild was so unbelievably rich because he had invented the international capital market.

Then, we look at the Krupp family in Lecture 32. They represent a new kind of industry, the great iron, coal and steel industry, the world of the Vanderbilts and the Rockefellers and the American robber barons who become the representatives of the new military industrial complex in Germany in the 19th century.

When we look at the new public sphere and the sale of artworks and the mass marketing of culture, we also notice something very remarkable, and that is that it produced a new sort of religion of art.

We're going to follow this in two stages. In Lecture Six, we're going to look at the life of Dr. Samuel Johnson, the first English literary figure to live without a patron, and C.P. Bach, whom I've already mentioned. These two represent the 18th-century stage of our great change. The painter Goya marks the transition from court painter to popular painter. Wagner in Lecture 27 and Tolstoy in Lecture 34 represent the cult of art in an industrialized society.

Then, we're going to look at several kinds of revolutionaries and their opponents. Robespierre, the great French Revolutionary, the head of the Committee of Public Safety, who genuinely believed it was possible, by introducing a new political structure, to make human beings virtuous. When they were not virtuous, it was not because the people were not good, but because spies and evil people were suborning them. He began the first modern mass execution and invented modern terrorism, (in the sense that the Great Terror is the political model from which all subsequent terrorists come). Mazzini, the enlightened nationalist, believed that nationality would make people free. Karl Marx and Friedrich Engels believed that the abolition of private property would make people free and virtuous. They represent three new types of revolutionaries not seen before in human history.

Then we'll look at various types of conservatives. Prince Metternich represents the old-fashioned conservative, who sees things from the top. Edmond Burke invented modern conservatism of a traditional kind, in that it's history, not ideas, that really matter. No human ideas will ever be able to solve our problems.

We'll look at Pius IX, the greatest pope of the 19th century, and perhaps the greatest pope of modern times. He condemned absolutely everything to do with liberal society, and we shall try to understand the logic which made Pope Pius IX believe that everything that liberalism represented was an error as he described it in the "Syllabus of Errors."

Then, in a kind of odd way, in Lecture 27 we're going to look at Wagner, who was a pivotal figure. He started as a revolutionary, fought in 1848 on the barricades, ended as a reactionary. At the same time, he created the greatest cult of an artist and an art form in modern times, the Wagnerian Cult, which we shall look at, at its Temple of the Arts in Bayreuth.

Scientists and reformers come next. Pasteur and Charles Darwin embody the new prestige of science. Along with Adam Smith's *The Wealth Of Nations*, the *Origin Of Species* is certainly one of the most important books ever written. We'll look at both Pasteur and Darwin in the relationship between science and society, and then we'll look at David Lloyd George, who represents the modern politician, the new demi-god, in the name of social reform.

I want also to look at the Jewish problem in modern history, because after all, European history, I suppose in some sense, comes to its end in the smoking ruins of Berlin in 1945, and in the piles of corpses lying inside and outside the great concentration camps.

Nathan Meyer Rothschild and Alfred Dreyfus, Lectures 20 and 35, represent two lives on the stage of Jewish emancipation on the road to modernity. As we shall see, both, in different ways, embodied certain profound kinds of anti-Semitism in the modern world.

Then, we shall look at the way certain old elites deal with the old world. The lecture on Otto von Bismarck, one of my favorite characters, the German statesman who unified Germany, and Queen Victoria, who allowed the democratization of English politics, permits us to see two different strategies for dealing with the emergence of mass society. Bismarck, a kind of reactionary revolutionary, played the democratic card to get around all his opponents, but for reactionary ends, to make sure that the power of the King of Prussia stayed intact. Victoria, in a very mysterious way, allowed her monarchical powers to erode slowly and gently over 60 years.

Now, all of these lectures will try to set the individual into a social context of his or her life and to achieve this kind of unity, so the lives should be a way to understand the changes of the period. For me, preparing these lectures has been a voyage of discovery. I have learned an amazing amount that I did not know. Goya, for example was new to me in all sorts of ways, but much more important I learned to see connections which I didn't know existed.

Now, let me just say a quick word or two about the limits of biography. There are I think, roughly speaking, two ways of thinking about the past, what I think of as hard history and soft history, my private terms for distinguishing two domains of historical evidence. Hard history covers demography, quantitative history, economic history, all those things that you can count. Since people are both subjects and objects, as objects they can be counted as consumers; their aggregate behavior is measurable. Statistics and computerized research provides something close to what you might call objective knowledge about the past.

Soft history deals with biography, politics and society where the evidence can't be measured and where in a sense the evidence talks back. All of our actors will speak to us in their own words during this course of lectures, and that's the most important single thing I will be bringing you, the fact that you will hear them speaking in their own voices. As a consequence, certain problems are not easily understood through a single life, which is why Lecture 24 offers the biography of a large mass of people, that generation of Irish who suffered the potato blight of the 1840s.

In addition, the long-run elements and what Kane said, "In the long run we are all dead," are not likely to be well-covered by biography. No one life, even Queen Victoria's, is long enough as a span to cover all the great phenomena like population growth, nutrition change, and industrialization. I shall try to point these trends out as we go on, but I'd like you to keep them in mind also.

Another thing which is worth noticing is that biography has returned as a method of study and of selling books. In the 50s and in the 60s, when I began my career, serious historians did not do biography, and they would never remotely have conceived of doing a course like this. A proper historian did forces and factors, all those model-building exercises which seem to be so much more scientific. Biography was left to amateurs, most of whom were women.

Biography is back, though. Biography as a technique has become very popular, and has produced some of the best-selling books of our time. Just think of them: *Ben Franklin* by Edmund Morgan, or *John Adams* by David McCullough, a whopping bestseller. Robert Caro's big study of Lyndon Johnson, *Theodore Rex* by Edmund Morris, *Winston Churchill* by Roy Jenkins, the two volume history of Hitler by Ian Kershaw, and *Mussolini* by Richard Bosworth.

Now, there are all sorts of reasons for the return of biography, and it's not clear why these things happen. It is quite a recent phenomenon, one I suppose is the declining prestige of the social scientific models. The fall of communism dragged the social scientific approach down with it. The explosion of religious fundamentalism across the world was unexpected and not predicted by social scientists either, who thought the world was becoming more secular.

Biography has come back, and it has certain advantages; it tells a story. A life is inevitably lived on a timeline, and hence, the historian must use the narrative techniques to describe it. The teacher and student have to be aware of these real constraints, and the real choice is open to them.

Thus, we begin a process of reconstruction, of what it might look like from the actor's position. The human dimensions of the problem come near when life is seen as emblematic. The forces and factors combine in a human life.

Now, a final quick word on the objects of the course. Are there lessons of history? Well, not exactly. The problems of history are mostly too complicated to be packaged in little lessons, although politicians and people in public do ask us often for it. For example, Vietnam in 1968 was the same as resisting Nazism in Europe in 1938, though it wasn't the comparison that led to all kinds of catastrophic decisions. The comparative approach which I'm going to develop in these lectures, though, is a useful alternative to the laboratory of historical science which doesn't exist. We cannot re-run the past with the variables altered. What we can do is compare tightly marked comparisons and see how the different sorts of phenomena operate. We can draw certain modest lessons by comparing the phenomena.

I hope, though, that the most important thing about this course is that it will actually be fun, these lives are really interesting. Theodore Fontana, my favorite German novelist, the best novelist, I think, of the 19th century, wrote, "When Bismarck sneezes or makes a toast I find it more interesting than the wise speeches of six members of Parliament." Now, these are great lives. These are lives of fascinating people; these are lives which I think show us the greatest example of what it is like to be human, and looking at these lives and understanding them is deeply pleasurable. To listen to their voices is, I think, the greatest single joy of this course, and I hope very much that *European History and European Lives* will ultimately be more than anything else a tremendous amount of fun. Thank you.

Lecture Two
Augustus the Strong—Princely Consumption

Scope:

Augustus the Strong, duke of Saxony and king of Poland (1670–1733, r. 1694–1733), is our first subject. He had a large frame and even larger appetites. He consumed art, money, and women with gargantuan gusto. He built palaces, collected art, founded the famous Meissen china works, and made himself into the king of Poland. He ruled the richest of the many German states and nearly exhausted the royal treasury. Yet Augustus and the huge wastefulness of his life cannot be understood without knowing the system in which he operated. His conspicuous consumption grew from the needs of his state in an extremely expensive competition among states. He was not unique in his age, and his life is a way to understand the lost world of Old Regime Europe. As we shall see in Lecture Four, the Prussian kings made another choice: to save money and build an army. That choice, unusual in its time, determined the rest of European history to our own day. Yet to explain the Old Regime, we must begin with certain features that made Europe unique in world history.

Outline

I. The nature of Europe itself explains some of the continent's amazing vitality and the character of Augustus's world. From the fall of the Roman Empire to the adoption of the Euro nearly 16 centuries later, all attempts to impose uniformity from above have failed. From Charlemagne to Hitler, the dream of unity has resisted all those who tried to impose it.

II. The peculiar combination of Roman, Christian, and feudal inheritance made Europe unlike any other part of the world.

   A. The first legacy is the Roman inheritance.

      1. When the Roman Empire disintegrated, it left an unusual legacy: the image of a world empire that was also a city, a *polis*, an entity composed of citizens who had laws, votes, plebiscites, senates, consuls, and all the rest of Roman republican paraphernalia.

2. No other world empire had those features. Roman law embodied them and passed it to us today through the conduit of Latin Christianity and humanist scholarship.

3. Most of the words in our political vocabulary, starting with the words *political* and *vocabulary* themselves, can be traced back to the Roman Republic or its predecessor, the Greek city-state.

4. The civic practice of free Romans rested on slavery. Citizens belonged to a privileged minority who depended on institutional inequalities to enjoy the *otium*, or leisure, that the *res publica* required.

B. Cutting across and, in many ways, undermining the Roman inheritance is the Judaeo-Christian inheritance.

1. In its later years, the Roman inheritance got mixed up with the very different values of the Judaeo-Christian prophecies. The Old Testament prophets condemned "those that oppress the hireling in his wages." The prophet Malachi asked, "Have we not all one father? Hath not one God created us?" (Malachi 3.5 and 2.10).

2. This message of the equality of all men became one of the central precepts of the "good news" of Jesus Christ, that the last shall be first, that the poor are particularly blessed, and that in a famous simile, "It is easier for a camel to go through the eye of a needle, than for a rich man to enter the Kingdom of God."

3. The Roman Catholic Church, which survived and preserved the Roman civic inheritance, transmitted the revolutionary egalitarianism of Jewish and Christian prophesy to Europe. "When Adam delved and Eve span, who was then the gentleman?" asked the peasants who rebelled in England in 1381.

4. Judaeo-Christian egalitarianism planted a ticking bomb at the base of every European authority, whether religious or secular. St. Francis; Savonarola; Martin Luther; the Anabaptists; the *enragés* of 1792; the utopians of the 19th century; the anarchists, communists, hippies, and demonstrators outside the IMF of our own time continue in varying ways to try to fulfill that ancient prophesy, where indeed the last shall be first.

C. The final peculiarity of European history is feudalism, that curious disintegration of central authority that occurred only in ninth- and 10th-century Europe and early-modern Japan and nowhere else.

  1. The two feudal systems in Europe and Japan arose when the emperor's authority fell into bits. Great lords took chunks of imperial power and, to sustain their new authority, made deals with lesser lords and they, in turn, with even lesser lords and so on.

  2. In the Latin West, but not in the Greek or Russian Orthodox East, there emerged a thicket of rights, privileges, exemptions, and contractual agreements out of which the Swiss cantons and other European polities emerged.

  3. The struggle to regain central control over the disintegrated imperial possessions, the battles between princes and their *Stände* ("estates"), between cities and their guilds, between churches and their tenants, between peasant communities and their lords became the structural reality of Europe from the 11th century to last week. These struggles used the language of Roman law and civic individualism but also of Christian justice and egalitarianism.

III. The balance between unity and diversity is the key to European history.

  A. The vitality of the smallest European political entity is rooted in Roman law and Christian ideas of justice. Every entity had rights and privileges, yet rulers tried to suppress the liberties of the little units.

  B. In this frame, Augustus the Strong, electoral duke of Saxony and king of Poland, lived his life.

IV. At the core of the Old Regime was an astonishing institution, the Holy Roman Empire.

  A. The empire is impossible to understand. Even its greatest expert, Johann Jakob Moser, threw up his hands in trying to describe it.

  B. The empire was structured to include an elected emperor and a kind of parliament.

1. The Imperial Assembly, or Diet (*Reichstag*) consisted of three councils: those of the electors, princes, and the free cities or imperial cities (*Freistädte oder Reichsstädte*).
2. The electors were, initially, many princes who claimed the right to elect a head of the empire. The Golden Bull of 1356, however, restricted this right to seven ecclesiastical and secular princes, who were called prince-electors (*Kurfürsten*).
3. Augustus of Saxony was one of seven electoral princes as duke of electoral Saxony. Not all Saxony was electoral, nor were all his territories inside the empire.
4. The smaller princes, free cities, archbishoprics, and so on had their own names and titles. For example, the Margrave of Ansbach held the titles duke, prince, count, and lord over more than 30 territories. He actually ruled only in a part of the Sayn County, but he had grandiose and absurd claims to all the rest.
5. Hundreds of these small princes were "sovereign" in their territories. The free cities and the ecclesiastical princes were also numerous. The prince archbishops, like the pope today, were sovereigns of territories; monasteries also often were sovereign.
6. The map was a crazy jigsaw puzzle of overlapping jurisdictions and states, semi-states, or possessions of local lords.

V. This map serves as the backdrop for the life of Augustus the Strong.

   A. An aspiring prince, Augustus was born into the Wettin "family," a great European dynasty.
1. All politics in this world were, in some sense, family politics. The family was a political structure. Princes and princesses were there to produce heirs and heirs were to be married to other important dynasties to solidify claims. Marriages were acts of state.
2. Frederick Augustus, born May 12, 1670, was a younger son and faced the problem of inheritance and status. His grandfather was an electoral duke, but he would have had no chance if plague, smallpox, and pneumonia had not wiped out his father, older brother, and many others. Augustus, who was physically quite strong, survived.

B. In 1694, Augustus inherited the throne. His education was limited, and his main ambition was to acquire *Ruhm* ("fame" or "glory").

    1. In this period, all princes had the ambition to be "glorious."

    2. Augustus spent $50,000 a month (in today's money) on his "grand tour" as a young prince; he had a "Turkish costume" covered in diamonds; and kept three or four mistresses at a time.

    3. His court was "the proudest and most expensive in Germany" (1695), and his main maxim was *Pracht macht Kunde* ("Splendor makes news!").

C. Augustus's capital city was Dresden.

    1. Electoral Saxony had two great cities, Leipzig and Dresden, but Augustus preferred Dresden to sober, hard-working Leipzig.

    2. He built an astonishing array of buildings in Dresden, aspiring to make it the "Paris of the North," and spared no expense on his glass and tableware and the importation of famous artworks for museums he founded—all to show the greatness of the elector.

D. Its population, industries, and famous mines gave the electoral state of Saxony its great wealth.

    1. The population of the capital, Dresden, in 1733 was about 50,000, and of the duchy, about 1 million.

    2. In its wealth and variety, Leipzig was the second city.

    3. Johann Sebastian Bach was organist at the Thomaskirche in Leipzig. Its special Protestant industriousness in fact made Leipzig richer than Dresden but less showy.

E. The politics of the early-modern royal state were very simple. It rested on the practice of absolutism (the duke rules absolutely), but there were ancient rights (ancient privileges of the nobility, towns, corporations, and so on) that clashed with the duke's claims to be absolute.

1. Almost all the smaller princes had the same ambitions as Augustus, to be mini-magnates; all lesser princes in Germany (and there were thousands) imitated Louis XIV's *absolutism* and his style of life—building mini-Versailles palaces—with disastrous consequences for the state treasury and the population.

2. Politics in Saxony and elsewhere (except Prussia) revolved around the battle between the prince, in this case, Augustus, and his *Stände* ("estates"). The estates voted the money; the prince spent it.

F. Augustus wanted desperately to earn the title of king, marry above his station, marry his children to the greatest princes and kings, win a war, and become glorious. He did not think that the welfare of the subjects mattered very much. The grand stage of Europe gave Augustus a chance.

1. To the east was the kingdom of Poland, the biggest state in Europe, where the government had become completely anarchic.

2. In the struggle between king and estates, the estates had won. Any Polish nobleman could exercise the *liberum veto* in parliament.

3. Because the Polish parliament, or *Sejm*, elected the king, Augustus had a chance. All the candidates bribed the members lavishly.

4. Unfortunately for Augustus, Poland was Catholic; he hurriedly converted to Catholicism in 1697.

5. His misfortune was that his attempt to get himself elected king in 1733 provoked the War of the Polish Succession over the rival claims of Augustus and the Polish prince Stanislaus Leszcynski to the throne of Poland. Stanislaus was backed by France, Spain, and Piedmont-Sardinia; Augustus, by Russia and Austria.

6. Poland was a buffer state, an area with weak government surrounded by others who wanted to intervene. Thus, Augustus had spent a fortune to become a king without a real country.

G. Europe was moving from the period of small states and variety to an era of great states with greater uniformity.

1. The emergence of Russia as a great power threatened Poland, as did the growth of the power of Prussia.

2. Poland and Saxony were doomed to be squeezed between Russia and Prussia.

3. Augustus's ambitions did not fit reality. He was playing in a league too high for him and for his successors.

VI. Augustus the Strong stands as an example of the old version of rule. Louis XIV said, *"L'etat c'est moi"* ("I am the state"). That was already wrong in 1700 but not yet clear. Augustus's failures arose partly from his personal characteristics but really reflected change in the structure of authority in the state itself.

Essential Reading:

Charles W. Ingrao, *The Habsburg Monarchy, 1618–1815.*

Supplementary Reading:

Helen Watanabe-O'Kelly, *Court Culture in Dresden.*

Questions to Consider:

1. Is it possible to imagine what *glory* meant for a prince in the 18th century?

2. How do you explain the fact that Augustus's bad morals, many mistresses, and lack of education seem to have been irrelevant to his functioning as a prince?

Lecture Two—Transcript
Augustus the Strong—Princely Consumption

In the last lecture in this series, *European History and European Lives*, I tried to set out the great themes of European development from 1715 to 1914. This lecture begins with our first life, and it's a life that probably most of you will not know, but it's necessary to set the stage for the old world. It is the life of Augustus the Strong, duke of Saxony and king of Poland, who lived from 1694 to 1733.

Now, why have I chosen Augustus? Well, he represents all of the Old Regime features, which I think are most characteristic of the Old Regime state. It's a world that we've lost and it's very, very difficult to recapture. I think, of all the lectures I'm going to be setting before you, this is probably the one that requires the most imagination. Even the terminology these people used doesn't make much sense to us now.

As in every lecture, though, I want to start with a context. You won't be able to understand Augustus the Strong unless you understand certain features about European history, its uniqueness which constrained his world. I think that the very nature of Europe itself explains some of the continent's amazing vitality and the peculiar problem of Augustus's rule.

The first characteristic I want to put to you is that from the fall of the Roman Empire to the adoption of the Euro, or the expansion of the European Union to new members, in nearly 16 centuries, all attempts to impose uniformity from above have failed. From Charlemagne to Hitler, the dream of unity in Europe has resisted everybody who tried to impose it.

Now, why is this? It's because European culture rests on a very peculiar combination of Roman, Christian and feudal inheritances, and it's the interaction of these three which give Europe its peculiar character and make it unlike any other part of the world.

First, the Roman inheritance. When the Roman Empire disintegrated in the fifth century, it left an unusual legacy, the image of a world empire which was at the same time a city, a *polis*; an entity composed of citizens who had laws, votes, plebiscites, senates, consuls, and all of the rest of Roman republican paraphernalia. No other world empire had those features, not the Chinese, not the Inca, not the Maya, not the Mogul, not the Egyptian. The empire was a city. Roman law, which spread with the empire, embodied all these characteristics, and passed them to us today through the conduit of Latin Christianity and humanist scholarship.

There is scarcely a word in our political vocabulary, starting with the words "political" and "vocabulary," which cannot be traced back either to the Roman Republic or to its predecessor, the Greek city-state. Now, the civic practice of free Romans and free Greeks rested on slavery and citizens. Those to whom Socrates put hard questions and Cicero made great speeches belonged to a privileged minority; they depended on the institutional inequalities to enjoy what was called in the Roman Republic *otium*, or leisure, which the *res publica* required.

That's the first legacy. Cutting across that, and in many ways undermining it, is the Judeo-Christian legacy. In its later years, the Roman inheritance got mixed up with the very, very different values of the Judeo-Christian prophecies. The Old Testament prophets condemned "those that oppress the hireling in his wages." The prophet Malachi said, "Have we not all one father, hath not one God created us?" This message of the equality of all men became one of the central precepts of the "good news" of Jesus Christ, that the last shall be first, that the poor are particularly blessed, that, in a famous simile, "It is easier for a camel to go through the eye of a needle than for a rich man to enter the Kingdom of God"?

Now, the Roman Catholic Church, which survived the fall of the Roman Empire and preserved Roman civic inheritance transmitted this revolutionary egalitarianism of Jewish and Christian prophecy to Europe. "When Adam delved and Eve span, who was then the gentle man?" asked the peasants who rebelled in England in 1381. Judeo-Christian egalitarianism planted a ticking bomb at the base of every European authority, whether religious or secular. Saint Francis, Savonarola, Martin Luther, the Anabaptists, the *enragés* of 1792, the extreme radicals in the French Revolution, the utopians of the 19th century, the anarchists, communists, hippies and demonstrators outside the International Monetary Fund of our own time, continue in varying ways to fulfill that ancient prophecy where indeed the last shall be first.

The third legacy is feudalism. This is a final peculiarity of European history. It's that curious disintegration of central authority, which occurred only in ninth- and tenth-century Europe and early modern Japan and nowhere else. The two feudal systems in Europe arose when the emperor's authority fell into bits, great lords took chunks of imperial power, and in order to sustain their authority had to make deals with lesser lords and they in turn with even lesser lords down to the base of society.

In the Latin West but not in the Greek or Russian Orthodox East, something we shall see when we look at the life of Catharine the Great and the life of Tolstoy, there emerged in the West a thicket of rights, privileges, exemptions, and contractual agreements out of which the Swiss cantons emerged and the other European polities. Now, the struggle to regain central control over the disintegrated imperial possessions, the battle between princes and their *Stände* or estates, between cities and their guilds, between churches and their tenants, between peasant communities and their lords, between the structural reality of Europe from the 11th century to last week and the desire to unify things, these struggles used the language of Roman law and civic individualism, but also Christian justice and egalitarianism.

Now, I believe that the balance between unity and diversity is the key to European history. The vitality of even the smallest European political entity is rooted in Roman law and Christian ideals of justice. For example, the European Union and expansion depends on plebiscites in places like Malta, Slovenia and Estonia, whose population together does not amount to the population of the greater metropolitan area of some place like Washington. Every entity, no matter how small, has its rights and privileges; kings and emperors tried to suppress the liberties of little units.

Now, it's in this frame that Augustus the Strong, electoral duke of Saxony and king of Poland lived his life; in other words, the great generalizations of European history focus down each of the actual daily struggles of a prince-like Augustus the Strong, who had to deal with the fact that his realm was nothing but a thicket of rights, privileges, exemptions, claims and so on, and which he wanted to suppress.

Now, at the core of Old Regime Europe was an astonishing institution called the Holy Roman Empire, which, as Voltaire once said, "Is not holy, is not Roman, is not an empire." Indeed, it's almost impossible to describe what it actually was. It is literally impossible to understand conceptually, even its greatest expert wasn't able to understand it.

The most detailed description of the Imperial Constitution can be founded in two books, *A German State Right* and *New German State Right*, written by a lawyer called Johann Jakob Moser, who lived between 1701 and 1785. Moser threw up his hands when he tried to describe it, and I love this passage, so let me just quote it to you: "We have various kinds of lands, various forms of governments, with estates and without them, imperial towns, a nobility, some of whom are immediate," (that is to say, people who can appeal directly to the emperor), "subjects of all different sorts, and a thousand of other such things, to think for oneself what good is it here, not the slightest. What can the philosopher do about it? Not the slightest. These are plain facts that I must accept. I must accept them as they are, unless I want to deform and ruin our German Empire."

As we will see, that particular view was very hateful to the theorists of unity and reform in the Enlightenment. We'll come back to that in a later lecture. Now, what was the structure of this crazy patchwork of rights? It had an emperor who was elected, and it had a kind of Parliament. The Imperial Assembly or Diet, the so-called *Reichstag*, consisted of three councils, a council of electors, a council of princes and a council of free or imperial cities.

Now, I want to focus on the electors. The electors were a group of people, many of whom had claimed the right to elect the head of the empire. However, a Golden Bull, that is an agreement of the empire, in 1356, restricted this right to seven ecclesiastical and secular princes. I hope you're still with me, because it gets worse.

These were called prince-electors, *Kurfürsten*. According to the Golden Bull, the council of electors consisted of seven members: The king of Bohemia; the archbishop of Mainz; the archbishop of Trier; the archbishop of Cologne; the duke of Saxony-Wittenberg, (that's our Augustus, he had that right); the margrave of Brandenburg, (who later was the king of Prussia, we'll come to him in Lecture Four); and count Palatine of the Rhine.

Augustus of Saxony was one of seven electoral princes as duke of electoral Saxony. Now, of course it wouldn't have been the Holy

Roman Empire without a lot of inconsistencies. Not all Saxony was "electoral," and not all of his territories were inside the empire, which was a jigsaw puzzle of miscellaneous authorities.

The smaller princes, the princes who were represented in the council of the princes, the free cities, the archbishops, etc., had their own names and titles. I want just to choose one case I like, the margrave of Ansbach, who in 1791 actually sold his principality because he couldn't support his English mistress. He moved to London and bought himself a nice house there to get out of the Holy Roman Empire. Here are the titles of this tin-pot little prince whose territory would be a quarter of the size of say, a typical American county. This is what he called himself, the margrave of Brandenburg, duke in Prussia, duke of Silesia, duke of Magdeburg, duke of Jülich, duke of Kleve, duke of Berg, duke of Stettin, duke of Pomerania, duke of the Kashubes, and Wendes, of Mecklenburg, and Krossen, burgrave of Nuremburg, prince of Halberstadt, Minden, Kammin, of the Wendes, Schwerin, Ratzeburg and so on, pages of titles, some of which were real, most of which were not.

From this long list, he actually ruled only in a part of Sayn County, as I say, a tiny territory, a postage stamp size, but he had these grandiose and absurd claims to all the rest. All of these princes did; they all had these kinds of claims, long lists of titles.

Now, the hundreds of small princes were quote, "sovereign" in their territories, they had nobody above them except the emperor. Inside their territories these sovereign princes had smaller princes who were not free to appeal directly to the emperor, but had their overlords in these particular princes like the margrave of Ansbach. It's a bit like these Russian dolls: Inside the Russian doll is a smaller Russian doll, and then a smaller Russian doll, and a smaller one.

Now, every one of these entities had rights; they were free cities, and when we're talking about cities we're often talking about communities with maybe three hundred people, but what made them free was that the local prince couldn't tax them; the emperor could. Imagine this thicket of rights and responsibilities. Then, you may have noticed that three of the electors were archbishops: The archbishop of Mainz, the archbishop of Trier, and the archbishop of Cologne.

Now, these were ruling prelates. They were like mini-popes. The Archbishop of Cologne was exactly like the pope is Vatican City today, or as he was in the 19th century, when the pope was a great territorial ruler. They were the princes of Cologne, or Trier, or Mainz and you had entities in which an abbot, for example, the prince-abbot of Fulda was the ruler of the territory of Fulda, it's just absolutely amazing.

What did the map look like? The map was a crazy jigsaw puzzle, and if you look, for example at the map of the Duchy of Baden or the Duchy of Wittenberg it actually does look like a jigsaw puzzle. If one looked at it carefully, one would see that there are bits which are green, and there are bits which are light green, and there are bits which are pink, and there are bits which are orange, and all of these bits represent the fact that even down to tiny towns, some of these towns, although they were in the Grand Duchy of Baden, were not part of the Grand Duchy of Baden.

You can see if you look at any map of the 18th century what the political problem was of a typical German prince. He ruled over a map which looked like a jigsaw puzzle of states, entities, abbeys, free cities and so on which were not his. They weren't part of his territory, and what does a prince want? A prince wants to unify the whole thing.

Now, let's turn against that background to the life of Augustus the Strong. Augustus came from one of the greater of German families, the Wettin family, they were a great European dynasty like the Habsburgs and the Hohenzollerns, not a small one like the margrave of Ansbach. All politics in Augustus's world were in some sense family politics, the family was the political structure, if you married the right prince you added that princely kingdom to your title, so you became Anhalt-Dessau Koburg Sayn by marriage, and so politics really did resolve around the question of whether you could produce male heirs, and whether these heirs could be married to important dynasties to solidify the claims.

Marriage, therefore, was an act of state, as was, indeed, I have to say, we'll come to this later on, sexual acts, which were observed, often very publicly by the members of the court, and of course the bearing of children. Now Frederick Augustus, the later electoral duke of Saxony was born on May the 12, 1670, he was, unfortunately for him, a younger son, and he therefore had the problems of an inheritance and status, his grandfather was an electoral duke but he would've had no chance if plague, smallpox and pneumonia had not wiped out his father, his older brother and many others in the entourage. Augustus was very strong physically, that's why he was known as *Augustus das Physisch Stärke*, Augustus the Physically Strong. On a visit to Prussia as a prince, he bent an iron bar to the amazement of the court in Berlin. Physical strength, as we shall see when we look at the career of somebody like Maria Theresa or Catherine the Great, was a really important aspect in the 18th century. You had to be strong to survive the infectious diseases of the age.

In 1694, when disease had wiped out everybody in sight Augustus inherited the throne. Now Augustus had almost no education. He wrote German phonetically; he wrote exactly the way it sounded and so it really is funny to look at. Education was absolutely irrelevant; education is after all, a middle class, not an aristocratic virtue. Augustus's main aim was to acclaim glory, *Ruhm* in German, fame. In the period we're looking at, it was the ambition of all princes, and that includes Frederick the Great, to be glorious.

Now, I just find it very hard to grasp what that might have meant in those days, but we can see the signs of glory in the really colossal spending, in vast portraits. There isn't a palace in the old Holy Roman Empire, that you don't go into, and there is some great dome, and you see the electoral prince or the prince abbot surrounded by portraits of Jupiter and all the other gods. The throne is being held up by angels, a vast inflation of the reality of what these little princes were about.

Now, some examples from Augustus's life will illustrate how you might pursue glory, and one of the things you did as a young prince is that you went on a grand tour. I did some reckoning, and it's not very reliable, but I reckon that it cost $50,000 in modern terms a month for the electoral prince or the future electoral prince to take his grand tour. He also had a Turkish costume made which was covered in diamonds; I reckon the costume alone was worth eight million dollars today, just for one court robe.

He had the reputation of having hundreds of mistresses, he certainly had three or four at a time, and there is a wonderful chronicler, Liselotte von der Pfalz, who was married to the French Dauphin, a German lady who kept a diary, and she was very much impressed with the fact that Augustus the Strong managed to arrange his affairs in such a way that his wife and his mistress both had children a week apart, and she wrote in her diary that he clearly had "lead in his pencil," I like that.

The British ambassador said that some of the electoral duke's mistresses were so inconsiderable that it even wasn't worth bribing them. His court, and he was proud of this, was quote "the proudest and most expensive in all Germany." In other words, the more money you spent, the greater your glory. In 1695, he was the most expensive German prince, and that made him glorious.

His advisor, Jakob Heinrich von Flemming, said that the prince was famous alike for his virtues and his vices, and he went on to argue that Augustus put his pleasures even before his princely ambitions. And the maxim of Von Flemming was *Pracht macht Kunde*, "splendor makes news," or "splendor advertises you," I think we could perhaps translate it. *Kunde* or *Kundschaft* is the German word for "passing information around," if you make something *Kunde* you've made it public.

Now the king had a capital city, Dresden. Electoral Saxony had two great cities, Leipzig and Dresden, but Augustus preferred Dresden to sober, bourgeois, hardworking Leipzig. He built an astonishing array of buildings in his capital Dresden. His ambition was to make Dresden the "Paris of the North." No expense was spared on his glass or tableware. He imported famous artworks, he founded museums, he brought about the establishment, by the way, of the famous Meissen porcelain works, all of that was done to make the king glorious. If you go into any museum of 18th century art, you'll see stuff from Augustus's collection. All of this fantastic, what shall we call it, conspicuous consumption, *Pracht macht Kunde*, to use Von Flemming's phrase, was to show the greatness of the elector, splendor makes you newsworthy, it makes you glorious.

Now, electoral Saxony, luckily for him, was a relatively rich and quite large German state. Its population, its industries, and its famous mines gave it great wealth. The population of its capital Dresden in 1733 was about 50,000. Let's not forget that the biggest American city in the 18th century, Boston, had 20,000 in 1790, so 50,000 is a lot of people, and the duchy had nearly a million.

In its wealth and variety, Leipzig was the second city, and we shall come back to Leipzig in a later lecture. The great Johann Sebastian Bach was the organist at the Thomaskirsche in Leipzig. But its special Protestant industriousness and thrift made Leipzig probably richer than Dresden, although there are no figures, but it wasn't so showy.

Now, the politics of the early modern state were very simple, and if you think of that jigsaw puzzle map of a typical German state you can see why. In principle, what the duke wanted to be was absolute; the duke rules absolutely and his word is law, but there were a huge number of ancient rights and privileges: Ancient privileges of the local nobility, towns and corporations and abbeys which clashed with the duke's claims to be absolute. Almost all of the smaller princes had the same ambitions as Augustus, to be mini-magnates. All of the princes in Germany, and there were thousands, imitated Louis XIV's absolutism and his style of life, with disastrous consequences for the state treasury and the population; they all built mini-Versailles palaces, even the prince-archbishop of Trier, or the prince-abbot of Fulda.

Politics in Saxony and everywhere except Prussia, as we shall see in Lecture Four, revolved around the battle between the prince, in this case Augustus, and his estates, a sort of parliament. Now there's a problem of translation here, English has no history of *Stände* or estates, and hence doesn't have a word for it, but the estates in effect were like a kind of feudal parliament, they voted the money or not, and the prince spent it or not and usually the prince spent it whether they voted it or not.

Now, the object of all this princely politics was that Augustus wanted to raise the glory of his family by marrying his many children to the greatest princes and kings. He wanted desperately to earn the title of "king" and marry above his station, win a war and become glorious. He did not think that the welfare of his subjects mattered very much to him. Karl Friedrich, the Grand Duke of Baden, said, "My neighbor of Wittenberg does his best to ruin his lands; I do my best to improve mine and neither of us succeeds."

Now, the grand stage of Europe gave Augustus a chance. To his east there was a place called the kingdom of Poland. Now the government of Poland had literally become completely anarchic, in the struggle between the king and the estates, the estates had won. In the Polish parliament or S*ejm*, any nobleman could exercise the co-called "liberal veto;" any nobleman could veto the procedures of parliament, so of course nothing got done. The Polish parliament elected the king, so here was a chance for Augustus to become a king.

Now, how did you do this in a parliament so anarchic? Obviously by bribes. As a candidate, you bribed as many Polish noblemen as you possibly could, and as richly as you could, and you hoped that when bribed they stayed bribed, which was the definition of an honest congressman in the 19th century, a congressman who when bribed stayed bribed, and then you got this kingdom.

Poland in 1700 was the biggest state in Europe. It was bigger than Russia; its territories extended from the Baltic to the Black Sea, so although it was chaotic, it was a real prize. Now, Poland was unfortunately Catholic, and so Augustus hurriedly converted to Catholicism in 1697. His misfortune was that his attempt to get himself elected king in 1733 was successful. He became king of Poland, and in that success provoked the War of the Polish Succession, over the rival claims of Augustus and the Polish Prince Stanislaus Leszczynski to the throne of Poland.

Now, because Poland was a buffer state, something I shall get to in a second, it mattered to all the great powers who was in it. Thus, the great powers who had backed Augustus went to war against the great powers who had backed Stanislaus Leszczynski. Stanislaus was backed by France and Spain (the Bourbons), and Piedmont-Sardinia (the House of Savoy), and Augustus by the Romanoffs and by the Habsburgs in Austria. We'll come back to this in a later lecture, because it matters in the reign of Maria Theresa; it sets the stage this war.

Augustus found himself caught up in conflicts among the great powers in which he was a ludicrous if extremely expensive pawn. All his attempts to lead the Saxon armies were fiascos; he was no general. He got in the way of the serious soldiers, and people pushed him around, but in the end, the powers of Russia and Austria, who were nearer and had more at stake, succeeded in putting Augustus on the throne.

Now a word about Poland as a buffer state. Europe in the *ancien regime*, of course, was composed, so to speak, of almost nothing but buffer states, but Poland was an important one. It was a buffer state as an area, with weak government, surrounded by others who wanted to intervene. Now, if you think about contemporary Afghanistan, Afghanistan is now and has been for quite a long time a buffer state, and it was the vacuum in Afghanistan which sucked the Russians in, in the late 1970s. This was the disaster really which brought down the Soviet Empire. Whenever there's a power vacuum between other powers, there's a constant temptation of the other powers to get in there and get control of that buffer, and that is still the problem of Afghanistan today.

What Augustus had done is he had spent a fortune to become a king without a real country, because what was happening was that to the east, as we shall see when we look at the rise of Catherine the Great and the emergence of modern Russia, and to the west in Prussia, which we shall look at in Lecture Four, new states were emerging which were not states like Augustus's or the margrave of Ansbach, but real states which could mobilize forces. The emergence of Russia as a great power, and the emergence of Prussia as a great power threatened Augustus's rule.

Europe was moving from a period of small states and variety to an era of great states with greater uniformity. Poland and Saxony were doomed to be squeezed between Russia and Prussia, and indeed, when we come to Maria Theresa we shall discuss the eradication of Poland from the map in the three great partitions of 1772, 1793 and 1795.

Augustus's ambitions simply did not fit reality, he was playing in a league too high for him and for his successors. Augustus the Strong is an example of the old version of rule, and that's why I put him at the beginning of our course. Louis XIV said the state, "*c'est moi,*" "it's me." It was already wrong in 1700, but not yet clear.

Augustus's failures arose partly from his personal characteristics, but really reflected the changes in the structure of state authority which were beginning to transform Europe. The example of Augustus helps us to understand how remarkable Prussia was and how great Frederick the Great really was. His brilliance and his frugality combined to make Prussia a unique European state. The fact that Frederick did not spend money like Augustus of Saxony, the fact that he wore an old blue soldier's tunic and had almost no hobbies, was one of the keys to the rise of Prussia as a great power, and as we shall see, it was Prussia around which the great German Empire was formed which transformed Europe in the 20th century. Thank you very much.

Lecture Three
Robert Walpole—Politics of Corruption

This lecture is dedicated to Sir John Plumb (1911–2001)
who taught me how to understand Georgian England.

Scope:

Sir Robert Walpole (1676–1745), who served as prime minister for more than 20 years, was older than Augustus the Strong but seems somehow modern to us. Why? Georgian Britain differed from every continental country. As English speakers, we look back on 18th-century Britain as "normal" because the Anglo-American way of life and politics has become the world standard and, therefore, seems inevitable and progressive. Very little of that could have been foreseen in the early 18th century, when France dominated European politics, culture, and minds. Foreign visitors noticed with amazement that Britain looked richer, freer, more urban, and more literate than any continental European country but could not, of course, imagine that the British were inventing the modern middle class, the Industrial Revolution, and representative government. Walpole, the first modern prime minister, made his name in the South Sea Bubble scandal, a financial crash uncannily like the dot-com meltdown. We can see our world beginning to take shape as we look at the age of Robert Walpole. Yet, like Augustus, Walpole belonged to an aristocratic, premodern social order, not to ours. The growth of political stability in Britain, which had suffered a terrible civil war (1640–1660), beheaded one king (1649) and deposed another (1688), and was invaded twice by would-be kings (1715 and 1745), occurred under Walpole's shrewd, corrupt, and comfortable administration.

Outline

I. My peculiar experience of England is an element in this story. For more than 30 years, I lived in a relic of Walpole's world, Trinity Hall, but was never allowed to lecture on it. The "Yank" in Cambridge was kept safely in European (that is, across-the-channel) history. Thus, this lecture is my first ever on 18th-century England.

II. In some respects, England is unique in Europe, and that uniqueness presents a problem.

  A. Each society is unique in some sense, but the English case is odd. English culture has become world culture. On Sundays in Philadelphia, for example, West Indians dressed in white play cricket in Fairmount Park. Pakistani officers have British uniforms and wear mustaches, and their "batmen" polish the regimental silver. Such examples are numerous.

  B. My central hypothesis is that the United Kingdom is an "exception" in modern Europe and, by extension, the United States and English-speaking countries are also exceptions.

   1. Britain's history was determined by geography, the island kingdoms. The continental "state" arose as a function of the expense of defense. England developed in relative safety.

   2. The United Kingdom is a multinational state composed of four nationalities: English, Scots, Welsh, and Irish. The term *British* applies to all four nations.

III. There are several special features of English development without which one cannot understand Walpole.

  A. Religious pluralism characterized 18th-century England.

   1. Eighteenth-century England had an established Anglican Church but also non-conformists (Wesleyans, Baptists, Congregationalists, and so on), as well as Catholics and Jews.

   2. Its degree of tolerance was unusual in Europe (in contrast with the Netherlands, for example), and the sheer variety of religious sects and churches was unique to England (Scotland was more uniform).

  B. Mercantile capitalism had evolved with the corresponding growth of economic institutions.

   1. The English had developed a set of modern financial institutions. The Bank of England was founded in 1694. The brokers were making markets in coffeehouses by 1700. The English common law was effective and uniform.

   2. Commercial values were compatible with noble status.

C. There was no state in the continental sense.

    1. There was a peculiar absence of state control. Law was decentralized: Note the role of the justice of the peace in the country or medieval corporations in the towns (the so-called *livery companies*).

    2. There was no standing army, which had serious long-term implications.

    3. There was almost no domestic control of personal activity.

    4. There was, on the other hand, the uniformity of the *king's justice* from the 15th century, and there was equality before the law.

D. An urban middle class had evolved, the members of which met in coffeehouses and shops.

    1. The coffeehouse was the meeting place of a new public, where the aristocracy mixed with others of lower standing. Social mobility was possible.

    2. Primogeniture was important. For example, the grandson of a duke is only a Mr. (for example, *Mr.* Winston S. Churchill).

    3. English "public schools" blurred social boundaries but produced a type of person unique in Europe: the "gentleman."

E. Britain was a relatively wealthy nation. One contemporary observer noted that some merchants in Britain were wealthier than European nobility, and Daniel Defoe commented that the standard of living of ordinary workers was comparatively comfortable.

F. The British were very pleased with themselves. There was a high level of patriotism and jingoism. Britain was best.

G. In politics, the monarchy was weaker than it was on the Continent.

    1. One legacy of the English civil war was a reduction in the power of the Crown. This was a real contrast with the Continent: Louis XIV of France, who ruled from 1643 to 1713, created absolute government, and German and Italian princes imitated him. (See Lecture Four on Frederick the Great.)

2. The "Protestant succession" of 1688 was both a religious and a political arrangement. Parliament (Lords and Commons) was embedded in ancient "rights," but these were not written down.

3. Political parties emerged. In the English debates between 1688 and 1750, the battle between *Whig* and *Tory* was central. Neither of these were parties in our sense but embodied currents of opinion or clusters of attitudes. Whigs were Protestant, anti-Catholic, anti-French, and pro-German (that is, the Hanoverian dynasty after 1714); Tories supported "Church and King" and were anti-London, anti-commercial, and anti-Hanoverian. Some were pro-Stuart; some, pro-Catholic; and so on.

4. The structure of rule was such that the king's patronage was crucial: All jobs were *his* to grant. The key to government was the favor of the king, the queen, or occasionally, the Prince of Wales as crown prince.

5. The peculiar situation in the United Kingdom in 1714 was that the new King George I (1660–1727), king of Great Britain and Ireland, was a German prince. In 1698, he became elector of Hanover. He was exactly like Augustus the Strong (see Lecture Two), but he was the heir of the last Stuart, Queen Anne, who died in 1714.

6. The career of Walpole was entirely dependent on King George I and George II, the "German" kings. There was constant conflict between the king and Prince of Wales (the later George II). Walpole's skill lay in winning both father and son. Thus, the most successful prime minister of the 18th century fell because of a royal family quarrel. Britain was still operating under the Old Regime.

IV. The social structures of 18th-century England also influence our understanding of Walpole.

A. In the countryside, there was the high aristocracy, great landlords, such as the duke of Newcastle, duke of Bedford, and others. There was also a large squirearchy: A country squire was a gentleman who was often without title but had an estate, a grand house with a name.

B. The boundaries were blurry (as always in England) between aristocracy and gentry. The Walpoles were simply squires in

Norfolk, that is, gentry, not aristocracy; they were socially commoners.

C. Parliament was one of the instruments of gentry rule; it was a closed corporation, and voting was limited. The tiny numbers of voters were distributed by history, not population. For example, Old Sarum had no voters left, but it still had a parliamentary constituency with a seat. It was easy for a grand local lord or well-to-do gentleman to buy the seat.

D. The oligarchic character of the institutions plus the system of patron and client meant that parties were essentially bought and paid "factions" tied to a great lord or powerful member of the House of Commons.

   1. Corruption was essential to reward and punish. Many obsolete offices were intentionally maintained, for example, the Board of the Green Cloth, with four members, each paid £500 a year for doing nothing but voting correctly.

   2. Big jobs meant big money. Walpole was paymaster general from August 3, 1714, to October 1717. Over £100,000 passed through his hands (more than £10 million in today's money); much of it ended up in Walpole's account.

   3. Walpole had a huge income and huge expenditures. He was involved in turning his country seat at Houghton in the county of Norfolk into a palace, in buying up local office-holders, and investing in farms in Norfolk and Suffolk.

   4. Walpole was a big man physically (over 250 pounds) and in politics.

V. Walpole was born August 26, 1676, at Houghton, Norfolk, into a family with origins as simple country squires.

A. The early death of his two older brothers and his father ended Walpole's education.

B. At 17, he was now head of the household and soon married to Catherine Shorter, a wealthy heiress to a merchant fortune.

C. At age 25, he entered Parliament as MP for Castle Rising, then for King's Lynn, a Norfolk port.

D. His skill was very much "internal" to the House of Commons, that is, not in public oratory. Walpole was an expert on finances and a manager of men.

E. His role in covering up scandal earned him the title of "Skreen Master General." His technique was: "to skin the wound over rather than probe it" (Plumb, 1956, p. 333).

F. Walpole had a reputation for cynicism, among other traits.

   1. The Earl of Chesterfield described him as "good-natured, chearful, social; inelegant in his manners, loose in his morals. He had a coarse, strong wit, which he was too free of for a man in his station, as it is always inconsistent with dignity" (Stanhope, Augustan Reprint Society, nos. 259–260, 1990).

   2. His policy was to preserve peace with France. He had contempt for those who easily advocated war.

   3. He had the virtues of the cynical, shrewd manager of men and affairs. He had no need to raise emotions or stir crowds. Crowds had no votes. He used skill, efficiency, corruption, and cynicism, both in his own interest and that of the nation.

G. His financial policy was the key to his success.

   1. His reputation was made as a financial wizard. He invented the *sinking fund* for the national debt, a fund into which a certain amount of government revenue is paid for the purpose of redeeming the national debt.

   2. Walpole began the fund in 1717, and by 1727, the national debt was reduced from £54 million to £47.5 million.

H. The South Sea Bubble was the first modern stock market boom; the craze affected the highest ranges of society.

1. Walpole was also involved but, luckily, had to sell his stock in January 1720 to buy farms. His banker saved him by a delay in executing his orders to get back into the overheated market in August/September 1720.

2. Walpole lost a lot but escaped the blame. His calm defense of the directors of the South Sea Company, who were his political enemies, was a model of restraint. He prevented a witch-hunt and protected the royal family, who had also been involved. He accumulated much good will and increased his reputation.

3. The sudden death of his main rival, Charles Spencer, third earl of Sunderland, allowed Walpole, now First Lord of the Treasury, to exercise undisputed political supremacy.

VI. Walpole was both modern and not modern. The political machine was fueled by greed and oiled by money and position. A tiny oligarchical ruling elite was more easily run than a modern mass democracy. Walpole's power was a function of the antiquated arrangements of the House of Commons, local government, and other institutions, yet the type is recognizable; he was an aristocratic Boss Tweed or Boss Crump.

A. His corruption, vast debts, mania for collecting art and books, and conspicuous consumption were no less flamboyant than those of Augustus the Strong.

B. Walpole's third son and an 18th-century wit, Horace Walpole, defended his father, noting that the "Grand Corrupter" ran his country in peace and prosperity for 20 years. We might ask ourselves if we point fingers at the corrupter because we dislike how easily corrupted we ourselves are.

Essential Reading:

John Merriman, *A History of Modern Europe,* pp. 255–274, 354–398.

J. H. Plumb, *Sir Robert Walpole: The Making of a Statesman.*

Questions to Consider:

1. Walpole used corruption to maintain political stability. Was that justified? Was England to be ruled in any other way?

2. Is it acceptable to use the word *modern* in the context of Walpole's England?

Lecture Three—Transcript
Robert Walpole—Politics of Corruption

In my last lecture, I considered Augustus the Strong, who was an example of princely conspicuous consumption in Germany. In this lecture, I want to look at Sir Robert Walpole, who was six years younger than Augustus. He was born in 1676 and he died in 1745, and he was the first modern British prime minister.

Before I do that, I want to say a word about my own experience of Walpole's world, because it's an element in this story, since for me history is thinking about the past and not the past itself, the identity of the thinker matters. From 1961 to 1999, I lived in Cambridge, England. I did my Ph.D. and taught there. I was fellow tutor, and, at the end, vice master of the Cambridge College, Trinity Hall. Trinity Hall was founded in 1350, when it was modernized by Sir Nathaniel Lloyd, who lived from 1669 to 1741, and was master from 1710 to 1735, precisely in the period of Walpole.

Lloyd was a perfect example of an 18th-century successful life. He was a wealthy civil lawyer, that is, practicing Roman law. He held a mastership at Trinity Hall without giving up his fellowship, his college, Oxford or his London practice. It didn't matter that he had three jobs. That was fine in those days. Later in the century, Lord North made his 28-year-old brother a bishop. And the colleagues said, "Surely my Lord your brother is a little young to be a bishop." Lord Mourth replied, "When he is older he will not have a brother who is a prime minister." That is the world of the 18th century.

Lloyd's world was corrupt, full of abuse and privilege. Lloyd was a shameless pluralist. He gathered up offices and stipends with that unembarrassed greed, which made Dr. Johnson, a newer contemporary in the subject of Lecture Six, observe that, "a man is never so innocently employed as when he's making money." He left legacies to the college, did our Sir Nathaniel as a large monument in Trinity Hall Chapel, which he had inscribed in Latin. It says, "Epitaph should be truthful. Telling lies is wicked. This place is holy. Go outside and tell lies."

Lloyd was rich enough to pay £4,000 for a modernized front court. I reckon that was £3,840,000 pounds in today's money, or about $5.5 million. It had a neo-classical Front Court and a new dining hall, which was light and airy. It had a modern fireplace equipped with a good draft. The ceiling was white and curled with all those vines and tendrils and sheaves of grain, so beloved of the 18th century. It was an expression of the "Age of Reason." Its length was twice its width, as indeed was the layout, which fortunately Lloyd bequeathed to the college, and which the college actually never carried out. It was a thoroughly modern donation.

Lloyd took a very robust and modern view of giving. He had been an undergraduate at Lincoln College, Oxford, and in 1735 gave them the sum of £250. In his will, he wrote, "It is not being used as I directed, so no more for me." Thus, for over 30 years I lived in a relic of Walpole's world, but was never allowed to lecture on it. The "Yank" in Cambridge was kept safely in European history, by which the English mean things that happen across the channel to the east. This is, therefore, my first ever lecture on 18th-century England, and I am looking forward to it hugely.

Now, if Europe is unique, England is unique in Europe. The problem of uniqueness is of course that each society is unique in some sense, but the English case I think is really odd. English culture has become a world culture. On Sundays, today, in Philadelphia, West Indians play cricket in Fairmont Park dressed in whites. Pakistani officers wear British uniforms, have mustaches and they have "batmen" who polished the regimental silver.

First, the central hypothesis I want to put to you is that the UK is an exception in modern Europe, and by extension the United States and all English-speaking countries are also exceptions in the development of European state and society.

England's history was determined by its geography as the "Island Kingdom." The continental state, like Prussia, which we shall see in the next lecture, arose as a function of the expensive defense. England developed in relative safety. Here, there is a parallel in the United States; September 11 was the first time in history that American citizens felt unsafe at home. By contrast, by the 20th century, the UK was already unsafe in World War I, and more so in World War II. The British were bombed at home. Think of the London Blitz, the V2 rockets, etc.

Second, the United Kingdom is a multi-national state composed of four nationalities: English, Scots, Welsh, and Irish. The term

"British" applies to all four nations. English is England; Scottish is Scotland.

Now, there are special features of English development without which you can't understand Walpole. First, there is religious pluralism. Eighteenth-century England had an established Anglican Church, but it also had that array of religious groups, the non-conformists (the Wesleyans, the Baptists, the Congregationalists, the Quakers). You also had Catholics and Jews. Its degree of tolerance was unusual in Europe, by contrast even with the Netherlands, and the sheer variety of religious sects in churches was unique to England. Scotland was much more uniformed.

Second, mercantile capitalism had evolved with the corresponding growth of economic institutions. The English had developed a set of modern financial institutions. The Bank of England was founded in 1694. Brokers were making markets in coffeehouses by 1700. The English Common Law was effective and uniform. Commercial values were compatible with noble status, which they were not on the Continent.

Third, and this is very true of America still today, there was not a state in the continental sense. There was a peculiar absence of state control. Law was decentralized. The role of the justice of the peace in the country or medieval corporations in the towns replaced them. There was no standing army, which had very serious long-term ramifications. There was almost no domestic control of personal activity, but there was, on the other hand, and this was unique in Europe, a uniformity of king's justice from the 15th century, and there was equality before the law.

In regard to class, there was an urban middle class, which met in the coffeehouses and shops. In 1711, *The Spectator* wrote, and I quote, "The club of which I am a member is very luckily composed of such persons as are engaged in different ways of life and deputed as it were out of the most conspicuous classes of mankind…My readers, too, have the satisfaction to find out that there is no rank or degree among them who have not their representative in this club."

Now the coffeehouse was the meeting place of a new public, where the aristocracy mixed with a lower standing. Social mobility was possible. Then you had, again, uniquely in England, the importance of primogeniture. The grandson of the duke is only a mister (Mr.).

Mr. Winston S. Churchill was the grandson of the duke of Marlborough. English public schools blurred social distinctions but produced a type of person unique in Europe, the gentleman.

An eyewitness from Switzerland, Cesar de Saussure noticed in 1727, "Some merchants are certainly far wealthier than many sovereign princes of Germany and Italy. They live in great state. Their houses are richly furnished, their tables spread with delicacies." The prince of Anhalt-Dessau lived in a country house built in the 1690s.

By comparison with the great houses of English merchants, it was a cottage. Daniel Defoe commented on the standard of the living of ordinary folk in 1728: "They eat well and they drink well, even those we call poor people. Journeymen working, and painstaking people do thus. They lie warm, live in plenty, work hard and need no want."

Now, here are some numbers. Robert C. Allen of Oxford University compared wages in European cities using a gram of silver as a base. London building craftsmen were paid 14.7 grams per day. Amsterdam was in second place with 11.8 grams. De Saussure and Defoe were both right. Middle class people, lawyers and merchants were richer than princes of Germany. With this wealth went a self-image. The British were very pleased with themselves. De Saussure wrote, "I do not think there is a people more prejudiced in its own favor than the British people, they allowed this to appear in their talk and manners. They look on foreigners in general with contempt, and think nothing is well done elsewhere as in their own country."

It was a high level of patriotism and jingoism. Now, politics are tricky. The monarchy was weaker than it was on the Continent. One legacy of the English civil war in the 17th century was a reduction in the power of the Crown. Here, there was a real contrast with the continent. Louis XIV of France, who ruled from 1643 to 1713, created absolute government, and German and Italian princes imitated him (as we saw in Lecture Two and we see again when we get to Frederic the Great).

This was not true of the monarchy in England. The "Protestant succession" of 1688 was both a religious and a political arrangement. Parliament (Lords and Commons) were embedded in ancient "rights," but not written down. If we compare this to Augustus the Strong, it was the estates who won and the princes who lost.

Then, you had the emergence of political parties. In the English debates between 1688 and 1750 the battle between Whig and Tory is central, but these are not parties in our sense of the word. They were more currents of opinion, clusters of attitude. Whigs were Protestant, anti-Catholic, anti-French, and pro-German. That is, they supported the Hanovarian dynasty after 1714. Tory supported "Church and King." They were more Catholic. They were anti-London. They were anti-commercial. They were anti-Hanovarian. Some were still pro-Stuart and actively pro-Catholic.

The structure of rule was also a regime. There was a king and he had a court. The king's patronage was crucial. All jobs were his to grant. The key to government was the favor of the king or the queen, or occasionally the Prince of Wales as crowned prince.

Fifth, you got the fact that this dynasty that Walpole manipulated was a foreign dynasty. The peculiar situation of the United Kingdom in 1714 was that the new king, King George I, who lived from 1660 to 1727, although king of Britain and Ireland, was a German prince. In 1698, he became elector of Hanover, which is what Augustus the Strong was. He was elector of Saxony, so they were of the same rank. He was exactly like Augustus the Strong, but he was lucky.

He was the heir of the last Stuart, Queen Anne, who died in 1714, and he became a real king, which Augustus did not. Thus, the career of Walpole was entirely dependent on King George I and King George II, the two German kings. There was constant conflict between the king and the Prince of Wales (the later George II), and Walpole's skill lay in winning both father and son. Thus, the more successful prime minister of the 18th century fell because of a royal family quarrel. It was still the Old Regime.

Now, we need to think a little bit about the social structure, because you can't understand Walpole without placing him precisely in 18th-century English society. There was an aristocracy and there was also a uniquely English category known as the "gentry." In the countryside there was the high aristocracy, great landlords such as the duke of Newcastle or the duke of Bedford. There was also a large squirearchy, a gentry, as well. A country squire was a gentleman often without a title, but an estate and a grant house with a name. Mr. Darcy's Pemberton Hall in Jane Austin's *Pride and Prejudice* is a good example. He's not "Sir," he's just "Mr. Darcy." With £10,000 a year, though, he's a very, very, rich man in deed, a millionaire.

Now, in regard to social distinction between the nobility and the gentry, the boundaries were blurry as they always are in England. It's one of its secrets. Between aristocracy and gentry there was no fixed line. The Walpoles were simply squires in Norfolk—gentry, not aristocracy. They were commoners.

Gentry rule worked in the following way. Parliament was a closed corporation, and voting was very limited. The tiny number of voters was distributed by history and not population. Old Sarum, for example was a ghost town. It had no voters left, but it still had a parliamentary constituency with a seat. It was easy for a grand local lord, a well-to-do gentleman to buy the seat. The duke of Newcastle said in October of 1719, and I quote, "I will take the liberty to say that I myself make the difference of 16 votes." In other words, the duke of Newcastle actually owned 16 parliamentary seats.

Now we come to the role of corruption. The oligarchic character of these institutions (that is to say, they were a closed corporation in which a small number of people were involved), plus the system of patron and client, meant that parties were essentially "bought and paid" factions tied to a great lord or a powerful member of the House of Commons. Now, corruption was essential to reward and to punish. Many obsolete offices were not abolished on purpose, for example, the Board of the Green Cloth with four members each paid £500 for doing nothing but voting right.

Big jobs meant big money. Walpole was paymaster general from August 3, 1714 to October 1719: £109,208 pounds passed through his hands (the equivalent of £10,483,000 in today's money, or $15 million. Much of it ended up in Walpole's account. He had a huge income, but he had also had huge expenditures. He was always in debt. He was involved in turning his country seat at Houghton, in the county of Norfolk, into a palace, in buying up local office-holders and investing in farms in Norfolk and Suffolk. I meant to say, by the way, that Houghton is much bigger than the princely houses of any of these medium-sized German princes. It's bigger than Augustus the Strong's palace in Dresden. Walpole was a big man, over 250 pounds, and a seriously big man in politics.

Now, let's turn to his life. The origins of his family were as simple country squires, and like Augustus the Strong, very characteristic of the 18th century, the early deaths of his two older brothers and father made Walpole head of the house, but it also ended his education. Walpole was as the English say, "Eaton and Kings," which is shorthand for a type of education at two of the most exclusive high schools and colleges. Eaton is the Eaton School. Kings is Kings College Cambridge.

At 17, he was now head of the household, and soon married to Catherine Shorter, a wealthy heiress to a merchant fortune, thereby making him richer. At 25, he entered parliament as MP for Castle Rising in Norfolk, and then for King's Lynn, a Norfolk port. Now, he was still very much "internal" to the House of Commons. He became an expert on finances and as a manager of men. When King George I tried to give him the baronage in June of 1723, Walpole stated, "He rather chose to inherit the highest titles than to wear them," and to pass the title to his son. His role in covering up scandals earned him the title, "Skreen Master General." His technique was, and I quote, "To skin the wound over rather than to probe it."

He had a reputation for cynicism. Archbishop Cox described him: "Flowery oratory he despised. He ascribed to the interested views of themselves or their relatives the declaration of pretended patriots, of whom he said, 'All these men have their price.'" The Earl of Chesterfield describes his character: "In private life he was good-natured, cheerful, social, inelegant in his manners and loose in his morals. He had a coarse, strong wit, which was too free of for a man in his station, as it is always inconsistent with dignity. He was very able as a minister, but without a certain elevation of mind necessary for great good or great mischief."

His policy was to keep the peace and to preserve peace, especially with France. He had great contempt for those who easily advocated war, the so-called "warmongers." I quote, "A patriot, sir? Why, patriots spring up like mushrooms. I could raise 50 of them within 24 hours. I have raised many of them in one night. It is but refusing to ratify an unreasonable or insolent demand and up starts a patriot."

He had the virtues of the cynical shrewd manager of men and affairs. He had no need to raise emotions or stir crowds. Crowds had no votes, no one to emphasize this point. We're dealing here in a period in which the total vote for the House of Commons would be something of the order of 50,000 to 60,000 people. He didn't need to appeal to the public. There was, in Britain at this point, a public already, but it had not yet got the vote. He used his skill, his efficiency, his corruption and his cynicism, both in his own interest and in that of the nation.

Now, his financial policy was the key to his success. His reputation was made as a financial wizard. He invented the sinking fund for the national debt. A sinking fund is the fund into which a certain amount of government revenue is paid for the purpose of redeeming the national debt. In other words, it makes sure that the debt will be paid off, because you put away so much each year. It's what a business does when it amortizes its new equipment. Walpole began the fund in 1717, and by 1727 the national debt was reduced from £54 to £47.5 million, and how modern all this actually does sound to us.

It is in the South Sea Bubble that Walpole really made his reputation, though. Here, he was just simply lucky. This was the first modern stock market boom. The South Sea Company had been given a monopoly on the trade in the Southern Pacific, and it produced prospectuses which said, "This is a place where we will make infinite fortunes." It sold a whole lot of shares, which weren't worth a lot. They were based on promises exactly like dot-com companies in our recent crash, which made huge sums of money on companies which had not only never made any profits but were never likely to make some. This is the first, I think, really modern stock exchange bubble.

Now, the craze affected the highest ranges of society. Everybody who had money was buying shares. In this respect, it really is like what happened in the dot-com boom, and Walpole was also involved; he bought a lot of shares. Luckily, in January of 1720, he needed to buy some farms, and so his banker, Robert Jacombe had to sell him out of some of his very substantial gains.

Now, why was Walpole buying farms? Walpole bought farms because the farms came with farm tenants, and they came with income; he was always desperately in need of income. Some of the villages also actually had parliamentary seats attached to them. So he was, in fact, spending his money both to bolster his income, which was never adequate to his expenditures, and also buying himself more support in the House of Commons. Thus, Walpole missed the great boom up to a point.

By August and September, he was chafing at the bit. He wanted to get back into the market. How many people are there out there in the

United States, and around the world, who made the mistake of getting into the market in the year 2000 like Walpole, who was, in effect about to do in the autumn of 1720?

He was again lucky. His banker, Robert Jacombe, was a very, very clever man, and he had come to the conclusion that the stock market was not going to sustain this any longer. The result was, he delayed carrying out Walpole's orders. In the 18th century, it took weeks for a letter to get from Houghton to London. All Jacombe had to do was basically sit on the letters for a couple of days, and he saved Walpole from putting all his cash back into the market. When the crash came, it was a complete and total crash, of the kind we've just experienced in the dot-com boom.

The South Sea Company was worth basically nothing but promises. The paper that he has been issued was worth nothing at all. A huge number of people lost their money, including members of the royal family and the highest aristocracy.

Now, Walpole escaped the blame. The reason why he escaped the blame was that he had been a backer of the Bank of England, which was founded in 1694, and which also competed for the monopoly, which the South Sea Company wanted to get and lost. That meant that Walpole represented the losers. The South Sea Company were his political enemies. They were mostly Tories. They had done their best to undermine him. They used their vast wealth, which they made during the boom to try to get rid of people who were in Walpole's cabinet.

Now, Walpole was a very, very shrewd political operator. Instead of going after them, which would be the natural instinct of a lesser man, he was a model of restraint. There was, as you can imagine, a huge witch-hunt, similar to the crisis about Enron and Worldcom inquest, very familiar. Who was to blame? Hang these people from the highest lamppost. Punish them. Walpole said, "No, we're not going to do that kind of thing." He prevented a witch-hunt for two reasons. One, because he thought it was wise; you never know, tomorrow you might need your enemy as your friend, and above all, a witch-hunt would expose the investments of the king, the queen, the Prince of Wales, and all kinds of people who had lost a hell of a lot of money, very often in illicit speculation.

What he did was that he accumulated huge goodwill by the way he managed this crisis. Almost nobody went to jail. A few of the directors of the South Sea Company did. He came out of this with increased reputation. And now he was again lucky because his main rival, Charles Spencer, 3rd Earl of Sunderland died suddenly, and Walpole became the first Lord of the Treasury. He suddenly found himself the first person able to exercise undisputed political supremacy.

Now, I want to say a word about what that actually meant. First, Lord of the Treasury became in time the title of the English prime minister, but not the time that Walpole took it on in 1720s. He went on being prime minister for a long time, or "prime minister" is what we call him.

It was still by no means obvious that the House of Commons would ever be the equal of the House of Lords. The House of Lords was full of much greater magnates, much more important people, and the House of Commons was full of people like Walpole himself, squires and gentlemen. They had rights, but the gradual growth of the Commons at the expense of the Lords is one of the themes that we shall follow in the whole course of these lectures, because between Walpole and David Lloyd George, there's a direct lineal connection between the beginning of the 18th century and the beginning of the 20th. There is, in fact, a direct connection. The office, which Walpole did so much to create, was the office which Lloyd George himself eventually inherited. We see here now the beginning of the modern parliamentary system, and it of course operated in this rather peculiar way.

Now, we should stop and pause and reflect on Walpole's career, and draw some conclusions. Walpole was both modern, and one can feel it when one talks about it. There is a modernity there. There is a sense that one is dealing with institutions that we can recognize in a way, which we simply could not see in Lecture Two. The world of Augustus the Strong, the language he uses, the way he spends money, how he behaves is simply alien. It belongs to the Old Regime. Walpole belongs, on the other hand, in part to our world. The art, I think, of studying the early 18th century is not to be guilty of anachronism, not to put back onto Walpole the things which we take for granted in our own world.

I want now just to outline for you the ways in which I think Walpole's world was very different from ours. The first is that the political machine was fueled by greed, and oiled by money and position. Now it is, of course, true that the political machine is still fueled by greed and oiled by money and position. I think I quoted in the previous lecture, but its worth quoting again, that 19th century observation that "an honest congressman is a congressman who once bought, stays bought." There's absolutely no doubt if we look at the operations of the American Congress or any government in the world, influence, money and wealth play an important role. In American politics you can't run for office without assembling money before you start.

What I think is characteristic of Walpole's world, though, was that he was taken for granted. It was simply obvious that you could only operate the system in this way, although there were laws, and when the laws were exceeded you would get caught. A tiny allegorical ruling elite was more easily run than a modern mass democracy. Walpole's power was a function of the antiquated arrangements of the House of Commons, local government etc., yet the type is recognizable. He was an aristocratic Boss Tweed, or Boss Crump. His corruption, his vast debts, his mania for collecting art and books, his conspicuous consumption was no less flamboyant than Augustus the Strong, but it was of course not for Augustus's reasons.

It was not because Walpole used this money to make himself an engine of state. For Walpole, it was not the case of *Pracht macht Kunde*. Walpole collected money as a private man. He collected money the way Bill Gates collects money and uses it to buy artwork, or any of the great millionaires of our age found museums, or buy paintings.

His third son was Horace Walpole, one of my favorite characters, one of the great wits of the 18th century, and I'd like to give him the last word about his father. I quote, "He kept this country in peace for 20 years and it flourished accordingly. He injured no man, was benevolent, good humored, and did nothing but the common necessary business of the state. Ask why his name is not veneration, you would be told from libels and trash that he was the great corrupter."

The problem, I think, is that the truth is too unpleasant. We dislike how easily corrupted we are, so we tend to blame the corrupter rather than ourselves, but in Walpole's case, I think the corruption was simply a way to run this machinery. Walpole knew how to run it almost better than anybody before or since.

Lecture Four
Frederick the Great—Absolute Absolutist

Scope:

Frederick the Great, King of Prussia (1712–1786, r. 1740–1786), embodied the principle of a rational autocracy. He wanted his state to hum like a well-oiled machine. All the parts had specific functions, but only the king could see the whole. Wit, philosopher, expert musician, brilliant general, tireless administrator, he called himself "the first servant of the state," and for 46 years, he served the state with no family, no close friends, no advisors, no confidantes—only his six beautiful greyhounds and a few silent servants. His life shows the limits of and contradictions in the idea of rational autocracy. No human being, no matter how brilliant, can avoid the paradoxes built into our mortality and human nature. The more the great king centralized power, the harder he worked, the more the state evaded his absolute control.

Outline

I. Frederick the Great was a phenomenon recognized as extraordinary in his own lifetime. His peculiar fascination today is in his personality and its link to events.

   A. Frederick was the most interesting, ablest, and most complicated ruler in the 18th century.

   B. His long reign lasted from 1740 to 1786. Longevity was itself a source of stability in an age when the rulers held nearly absolute sway. Longevity brought continuity of policy and direction.

   C. He changed tremendously during the course of his reign.

      1. The young Frederick was a dandy, an aesthete, powdered and covered in jewels. He had long, beautiful hair hanging down both sides in loose curls. His palace as crown prince at Rheinsberg was a literary paradise.

      2. The old Frederick was a fierce, toothless, scarecrow, who wore a filthy blue military coat.

   D. His work habits were phenomenal.

      1. The daily routine of the old Frederick was quite incredible: He was up each morning at 4:00 in summer, 5:00 in winter. Servants had orders to wake him by force with cups of coffee laced with mustard. Frequently, he slept in his day clothes, filthy, snuff-covered waistcoats, and poorly powdered hair.

2. His morning work was dealing with dispatches, reports, and orders—literally every detail was in the king's control.

3. A five-hour break followed for a ride and long lunch. Lunch at the king's table was a terrible ordeal. Guests faced royal monologues and terrible table manners. Beautiful food was ruined by heavy spices.

4. He was in bed by 10:00, read to by his faithful servant, Catt.

E. Music was Frederick's main recreation. His evenings were devoted to music, his only real luxury.

1. He maintained a royal orchestra of the highest standard at all times for himself alone, not for concerts or other purposes.

2. His flute teacher was Johann Joachim Quantz (1697–1773), who also served as conductor.

3. C.P.E. Bach was his keyboard player from 1740–1768 (see Lecture Nine), but the king hated the great composer's music as too modern.

4. The two Graun brothers, Karl Heinrich (1704–1759) and Johann Gottlieb Graun (1702–1771), both famous composers and players, worked in the king's orchestra.

F. Frederick the Great was utterly isolated as a person.

1. He never had children. The queen (Princess Elisabeth Christine of Brunswick-Bevern) was miserable and ignored. It's not clear if they ever had sexual relations, and she certainly never lived with him. He had no favorites, no mistresses, no sex life. He loved his famous greyhounds but no other living thing.

2. His father, Frederick William I, who reigned from 1713 to 1740, was a brutal, violent, puritanical man who lived for his tall soldiers and had contempt for his dandy son. The king beat and humiliated his son unmercifully, as he beat his servants, pastors who preached badly, and his ministers.

3. In 1730, Frederick tried to escape his father's torture, was caught, imprisoned in the fortress of Küstrin, and made to watch the execution of his companion, Lieutenant Hans Hermann von Katte, the young officer who had been his accomplice in the plan.

4. I believe that Frederick William I actually beat Frederick because he was gay and punished him by executing his lover. He next intended to execute Frederick but was talked out of it.

G. Frederick's intellectual interests were wide.

1. His main language of conversation was French, which he spoke perfectly.

2. He composed concerti and sonata, wrote philosophy and history, and engaged in a famous correspondence with Voltaire.

3. He was a great intellectual, as well as a great king.

H. Frederick the Great's legacy was his transformation of Prussia into one of the great powers of Europe, ruled as a *rational state*.

1. Frederick was an outstanding soldier. He was, unlike Augustus the Strong or any other king of his generation, a great general and field commander. He won famous victories in the Seven Years' War (1756–1763). Despite the fact that Prussia was poorer and less populous than Saxony, Frederick's military genius turned it into one of the five great European powers.

2. Prussia's military tradition made it the vehicle around which Bismarck unified Germany. Indeed, it was a Prussian field-marshal, Paul von Hindenburg und Benckendorff, who made Hitler chancellor and other Prussian aristocrats who tried to assassinate Hitler on July 20, 1944.

3. The *rational state* is also part of Frederick's legacy. The king was a genius as an administrator. His domestic genius created a new kind of state, based on absolute authority but religiously indifferent and governed by the will of perhaps the smartest human being ever to rule a great state (Napoleon is the only competitor).

I. The king was a universal genius. To do Frederick justice, two lectures are needed: one on his military and diplomatic brilliance and the other on his domestic political achievements.

II. Frederick was the perfect philosopher-king.

    A. His technique of rule involved the art of concealing his thoughts. He wrote: "The art of concealing your thoughts or 'dissimulation' is indispensable for every man who has the management of weighty affairs."

    B. The king avoided all informal influences. Frederick was the most absolute ruler ever. Nobody influenced him. He had a wife he never saw, no mistress, no family, no friends, no advisors; hence, he was free of corruption or persuasion.

        1. His brilliant mind and commanding personality showed him that he needed no advice.

        2. As a philosopher and historian, he was free of the need for theoretical instruction.

        3. Because he had no religion, he was not influenced by God; his atheism was shocking to his era.

    C. His view of his duty as king was unusual.

        1. Frederick had only one belief—in the power of reason—and one goal—the well-being of the state. He wrote: "The ruler is the first servant of the state. He is paid well, so that he can maintain the dignity of his office, but he is required in return to work effectively for the well-being of the state" (*Political Testament*, 1752).

        2. Frederick was the most absolute of all absolute rulers—Hitler or Stalin were much less absolute than Frederick.

III. The paradoxes of absolutism brought about Frederick's failures.

    A. Even Frederick could not be both a generalist and a specialist, could not know everything. Experts are necessary, and expertise is a form of power; its use allows the expert to escape the king's control.

    B. Further, the dynamics of deception played against the king.

        1. Frederick's anger meant the end of one's career or, worse, one's life. Because nobody wants to tell the king unpleasant truths, lies are built into the system.

        2. Frederick was too smart to be fooled and trusted no one. But if all are liars, how does Frederick know what is really going on? He introduced supervisors to check on his civil servants' performance, but in turn, they lied.

3. Lying is rational if the king is absolute, unforgiving, and quick-tempered.

C. Rule by an absolute absolutist is impossible.

1. The job specifications are incredible; the absolute absolutist must be inhuman.

2. Frederick's lack of normal human relations was unique and terrifying. Every other absolute monarch or dictator was corrupted or affected by some humanity or contact with other beings.

D. Normally, in absolutism, there was a "kitchen cabinet," or *camarilla*.

1. Absolutism in normal hands always leads to a kitchen cabinet, because influence is a function of proximity.

2. There is a parallel in the U.S. presidency. The U.S. president is an enlightened, elected king of the 18th-century variety; the White House staff and the First Family are structures of influence.

IV. Frederick was also affected by the paradox of the rational state.

A. The committee or council is a rational instrument of rule, but consultation inevitably reduces absolutism.

1. Frederick rejected the committee system of his father, believing that committees simply provide opportunities for mutual intrigue and for the introduction of hate and passion into the affairs of state.

2. Frederick regarded his ministers and bureaucrats as *Dummköpfe* ("blockheads"). Hence, all collective decision making was abolished in 1740. The result was that ministers of departments gained strength.

3. The operations of vertical authority came into play. The logic is as follows:

a. Only the king can decide.

b. No committees exist to reconcile differences among ministers.

c. Intrigue to persuade the king to accept one or the other view is inevitable.

d. Hence, the king is rarely in a position to decide using rational criteria.

e. The king is frustrated and angry and acts irrationally.
B. To illustrate, consider the U.S. Constitution as a comparison.
  1. The wisdom of the Founding Fathers was greater. Like Frederick, they were rationalists but with a difference. For Frederick, rationality was a form of thought based on means and ends. For the Founding Fathers, rationality was a device for analyzing reality; hence, the U.S. Constitution rests on observation of human nature, then uses rationality to contain its vices. The object, of course, is the opposite of Frederick's: to prevent the exercise of absolute power.
  2. James Madison's views, for example, reflect the same mechanical rationality as in Frederick's state, but the Madisonian view has one advantage: It starts with human fallibility.
  3. Ambition and self-seeking are universal. Frederick loses his temper at these inevitable human reactions; the Founding Fathers calmly harness ambition for rational ends.
C. What if rationality rests on wrong assumptions?
  1. An example is found in Frederick's finances, which the king oversaw himself.
    a. The state was there to carry out the king's purposes, and war was its main object; hence, financial activity was rationally directed to fill the war chest.
    b. The state treasury was filled with bags of silver, and Prussia was, by far, the best run continental state; it fought two great wars (1740–1748 and 1756–1763) without bankruptcy.
    c. After a generation of war, the Prussian treasury, which held 13.8 million thaler in 1763, had, on Frederick's death in 1786, reached 23.7 million thaler, including the cost of maintaining 87,000 men in a standing army.
  2. Frederick's trade policy was quite successful. He encouraged trade and industry, along with toleration of Jews. He also founded state monopolies in porcelain manufacture, trade, mining, tobacco, coffee, and other industries.

3. Frederick's economic ideas were, however, wrong. Adam Smith wrote in 1776 in *The Wealth of Nations*: "The sole use of money is to circulate consumable goods..." Hoarding silver in bags was deflationary and reduced the wealth of the state.

4. Thus, Frederick the Great fails the test as a rational finance minister, which also involves a paradox. To follow the British model meant freeing the markets from control, which undermined absolutism. The error is not simply wrong knowledge, but is built into the system.

D. The very system of monarchy is irrational.

1. Frederick was not chosen by public examination. It was an accident that he was a genius; his successor, Frederick William II, was a nice cello player but lazy and indecisive. Heredity is not a rational way to select leaders, but organic, biological, and dependent on genetic variation.

2. The family tradition in the House of Hohenzollern was an unusual one.

   a. The great elector (1640–1688), Frederick William I (1713–1740), and Frederick the Great (1740–1786) all had long reigns and great skills.

   b. Prussia was turned into a military state. Like Israel, it had no defensible borders and enemies all around it. Hence, the king had to be, first and foremost, a general.

   c. The rulers spent modest sums on palaces, fancy clothes, or royal display. The court of Prussia was notoriously spartan.

3. Frederick relied on the aristocracy as officers in the army, a second irrationality.

   a. The concept of *Ehre* ("honor") was fundamental.

   b. Frederick was clear that only aristocrats could be proper commanders.

   c. The Prussian *junker* class was a service nobility. It had a monopoly of high office in the army and state in exchange for surrender of feudal rights to resist payment of taxes and other considerations.

     d. The irrational exclusion of men of talent who happen to be commoners reduced the pool of gifted officers.

     e. Again, this irrational outcome shows the limits of the absolute absolutist. Because royal position rests on nobility and both rest on birth and privilege, not reason, the king could not escape this paradox.

V. Frederick the Great was an enlightened prince.

     A. The king was a full-time intellectual, author of theoretical texts and famous letters. He corresponded with great luminaries of the Enlightenment.

     B. His indifference to religion was an essential tenet of the Enlightenment. During the 18th century, no European state or society was religiously homogeneous, but minorities were persecuted.

     C. Frederick encouraged religious tolerance, which meshed with the Enlightenment belief in the right of the autonomous human being to choose a religion on the basis of reason or conscience. Frederick also saw the practical advantages of tolerance for modernizing states, which need new bases for loyalty to the sovereign and to attract immigrants.

     D. The reign of Frederick was a great period of German culture, spawning, among others, Goethe, Schiller, and Immanuel Kant, who paid tribute to Frederick in his famous essay "What Is Enlightenment?" (1784).

     E. By 1786, because of Frederick's fame, Berlin was a capital of enlightened thought and German culture. Prussian prestige in war and in letters was at its highest. Yet Frederick the Great, the idol of the new German intellectuals, spoke only French and disdained the new German culture, another paradox of the absolute absolutist.

Essential Reading:

Gerhard A. Ritter, *Frederick the Great: A Historical Profile*.

Supplementary Reading:

David Fraser, *Frederick the Great*.

John Merriman, *Modern Europe*, chapter 7, "The Age of Absolutism," pp. 274–326.

Questions to Consider:

1. Is it fair to compare the views of Hamilton and Madison to those of Frederick the Great when the aims are so different?

2. What is "honor" and who has it?

Lecture Four—Transcript
Frederick the Great—Absolute Absolutist

In the last lecture, we looked at Robert Walpole, the first modern British prime minister, who was born in 1676. Now, we move up a generation. King Frederick the Great of Prussia was born in 1712, and I'm going to reverse the usual order of these lectures. I want to first introduce the character so you can understand the structural problem that we have to deal with. King Frederick the Great was a phenomenon in his own lifetime, and he had a peculiar fascination. Frederick was the most interesting, ablest and most complicated ruler in the 18th century, and he reigned for a very long time, from 1740 to 1786.

Now, longevity was itself a source of stability in an age when rulers held near-absolute sway. Longevity brought a sort of continuity of policy and direction. He changed tremendously during the course of his reign. The young Frederick was a dandy, an aesthete, beautifully powdered hair, covered in jewels. He had long, beautiful hair hanging down both sides and loose curls. His palace as crowned prince at Rheinsberg was a literary paradise. Baron Bielfeld wrote, I quote: "The days glide by in tranquility seasoned with all the pleasures, which can flatter a reasonable mind. Fare for a king, wine for the gods, music for angels, delightful walks in gardens and woods, parties on the water, the cultivation of letters and the fine arts, spirited and pleasant conversation."

The old Frederick was a fierce, toothless scarecrow who wore a filthy blue military coat. Henriette von Engloffstein remembered seeing him as a young girl in the 1780s in Potsdam, "I'd once put my head out of the window, and saw that this body of cavalry was led by a mummy-like figure of an old man in a shabby uniform. A large plumed hat was jammed at an angle above the face, which was deformed by a huge nose, a small caved in mouth, and great bovine eyes. This frightening creature rode so close to me that his arm literally brushed my turned up nose. The king glanced back and those terrifying eyes bore through me compelling me to draw my head back inside."

His working habits were phenomenal. The old Frederick was quite incredible. He was up each morning at 4:00 a.m. in summer and 5:00 a.m. in winter. Servants had orders to wake him up by force, with cups of coffee laced with mustard. He frequently slept in his day clothes, which were filthy and snuff-covered, and he had poorly powdered hair.

His morning work was dealing with dispatches, reports, orders, government by cabinet order. Literally every detail of the kingdom was in the king's control. A five-hour break followed for a ride and a long lunch. Now, lunch at the king's table was a terrible ordeal. Guests faced royal monologues and really terrible royal table manners. Beautiful food was ruined by heavy spices. One observer wrote, "He scorched his innards daily with dishes laced with condiments of quite incredible ferocity."

The afternoon brought more recreation. Music was his main hobby. His evenings were devoted to music and that was his only real luxury. He maintained a royal orchestra of the highest standard there at all times for himself alone, not for concerts or for other purposes. His flute teacher was the outstanding flutist of the day, who also served as conductor. The great C.P.E Bach, whom we shall be talking about in Lecture Nine, was his keyboard player from 1740 to 1768, but the king hated the great composer's music. He thought it was too modern and it was never played. Karl Heinrich and Johann Gottlieb, both famous composers and players, worked in the king's orchestra. He went to bed by 10, was read to by his faithful servant Catt and went to sleep.

Frederick was utterly isolated as a person. He never had children. The queen, Princess Elisabeth Christine of Brunswick-Bevern was miserable and ignored. It's not clear if he ever had any sexual relations with her, and she certainly never lived with him. He had no favorites, no mistress, no sex life. He loved his famous greyhounds but no other living thing.

His father, Frederick William I, who reigned from 1713 to 1740, was a brutal, violent, puritanical man who lived for his tall soldiers and had contempt for his dandy of a son. The king beat and humiliated his son unmercifully, as he beat his servants, pastors who preached badly (he'd just go up into the pulpit and whack them with his walking stick if he didn't like their sermons) and his ministers.

In 1730, Frederick tried to escape his father's torture, was caught, and imprisoned in the fortress of Küstrin, and made to watch the execution of his companion, Lieutenant Hans Hermann von Katte, the young officer who had been his accomplice to the plan. My guess is, although it's not in the record, that Frederick William I actually beat him because he was gay, and punished him by executing his lover. He next intended to execute his son but was talked out of it.

Frederick had enormous intellectual interests. His main language of conversation was French, which he spoke perfectly. He composed concerti and sonata. He wrote philosophy and history. He engaged in a famous correspondence with Voltaire. He was a great intellectual as well as a great king.

Now, why does Frederick the Great matter? First, Frederick was a remarkable soldier. Unlike Augustus the Strong, whom we talked about in Lecture Two, he really was a great general, a great general and a great field commander. He won famous victories in the Seven Years' War between 1756 and 1763, which Americans called the French and Indian War, and in fact there is a curious memorial to Frederick in the town King of Prussia, Pennsylvania. In King of Prussia there is a really huge mall, and it's always startling to me to listen to them say at "The Court at King of Prussia," meaning the mall, which of course is very different from the court of Frederick the Great.

Yet, Prussia was a kingdom both poor and less populous than Saxony. Frederick's military genius turned it into one of the five great European powers. Prussia and its military tradition made it the vehicle around which Bismarck unified Germany. It was a Prussian field marshal, Von Hindenburg, who made Hitler chancellor, and Prussian aristocrats who tried to assassinate Hitler on July 20, 1944—so Prussia really matters.

Now, Prussia was intended by the king to be a rational state, and the king was a genius as administrator. His domestic genius created a new kind of state, based on absolute authority but religiously indifferent and governed by the will of perhaps the smartest human being (Napoleon is the only exception) ever to rule a great state.

The king was a universal genius and, to do him justice, there are really two lectures needed, one on his military and diplomatic brilliance, and the other on his domestic political achievements, but in this lecture I want to look at the domestic structures.

Now, Frederick considered himself the philosopher king and he had a variety of techniques of rule. The first was to conceal your thoughts. His view was, and I quote: "The art of concealing your thoughts or dissimulation is indispensable for every man who has the management of weighty affairs. The whole army tries to read its fate from the countenance of its commander." There is a famous exchange with his old tutor in 1740, just after he became king, which illustrates Frederick's techniques.

> His tutor, Kalckstein, said: Your Majesty, am I right in thinking there is going to be a war?
>
> Frederick: Who can tell?
>
> Kalckstein: The movement seems to be directed on Silesia. (which in fact it was)
>
> Frederick: Can you keep a secret? (and he took the old man by the hand)
>
> Kalckstein: Oh yes, Your Majesty.
>
> Frederick: Well, so can I

The British ambassador reported to London on the Prussian government, and on November 25, 1761, and I quote: "Consider that there is but one person that knows everything, that he does not choose to talk about disagreeable subjects, and that his rank is such as exempts him from being importuned with questions. As for the general officers, they know only what passes in their own bodies but seem not in the least informed of the general plan of operations."

The king avoided all informal influences. Frederick was the most absolute ruler ever. Nobody influenced him. He had no wife [that he ever saw], no mistress, no family, no friends, no advisors, hence he was completely free of corruption or persuasion. He had a brilliant mind and a commanding personality, and that showed him that he had no need for advice.

As a philosopher and historian he was freed of the need for theoretical instruction. He had no religion, so he was not influenced by God. His atheism was shocking to his era, and it's still I think shocking even to us. In 1752, he wrote: "All religions, when one looks at them closely, are founded on a tissue of lies and are more or less absurd." This is what he said about Christianity in 1768: "Christianity is an old metaphysical fiction stuffed with contradictions and absurdities. It was spawned in the fevered imagination of the Orientals and then spread to our Europe, where some fanatics espoused it, where some intriguers pretended to be convinced by it, and some imbeciles actually believed it."

His view of his duty as a king was very unusual. Frederick had only one belief, the power of reason, and only one goal, the well-being of the state. This is his job description, so to speak, of a monarch's role: "The ruler is the first servant of the state. He is paid well so that he can maintain the dignity of his office, but he is required to work effectively for the well-being of the state."

Now, a note here, he makes no claim to royalty, to tradition, to majesty. The king is simply a well-paid autocratic administrator. There's no glory as in Augustus's sense, as we saw in Lecture Two. Frederick was the most absolute of all absolute rulers ever. Even Hitler or Stalin were much less absolute, that is to say they were much more open to influence than Frederick was.

Now, I want to get to the real paradox of Frederick's reign. The most brilliant person probably ever to rule a great state nevertheless failed in certain important respects. Absolute absolutism is, I think, humanly impossible. Why? Well, there is first of all the problem of the generalist and the specialist. Even a genius like Frederick can't know everything. Experts are necessary, and expertise is a form of power. Every expert diminishes a bit from the king's absolutism. Its use allows the expert to escape the control of the king. "After all, your Majesty, this is the way it is," they say to the king.

A second and more serious factor is the dynamic of deception. The king's anger meant the end of your career or worse, jail or execution. Nobody wants to tell this king unpleasant truths, so lies are built into the system. The king is too smart to be fooled and trusts nobody, but if everybody lies, how does he know what's really going on? Well, he introduces supervisors to check on the performance and they lie, etc. Now, lying is absolutely rational if: 1) the king is absolute; 2) unforgiving; and 3) extremely quick-tempered; and the king was all of those three things. That meant that the king was never told the truth, and this means that rule by an absolute absolutist is in some sense impossible.

Moreover, the job specification that the king gave himself was incredible. The absolute absolutist must be inhuman. It was Frederick's lack of normal human relations, which is both terrifying and unique, which made him so effective. Every other absolute monarch or dictator was corrupted or affected by some humanity or contact with other beings. Frederick had none. Normally, and this is true of most absolutists, there was a *camarilla* or, to use the American term, a "kitchen cabinet." Absolutism in normal hands always leads to a kitchen cabinet since influence is a function of proximity.

There's a parallel in the U.S. presidency. The U.S. presidency goes back to Frederick's time. The Constitution was drafted in 1787, a year after Frederick the Great died, and it presents us with an elected 18th-century enlightened king. The White House staff and the first family are actually structures of influence, and there's a nice anecdote about Pat Buchanan when he was a speechwriter for Richard Nixon, and he ended up getting an office, which was a broom closet, in the White House. Somebody said, "Mr. Buchanan, your office has no windows." He said, "I don't need windows. I'm on the same floor as the office of the president and the vice president. I'm near the Oval Office. Nearness means everything." That, of course, is the key to the kitchen cabinet. Somebody who sees the president everyday, like the president's wife, is an influential person by virtue of her presence.

Frederick had none of that. Nobody influenced him. This brings us to the paradox of the rational state. Now, the committee or council are rational instruments of rule. To have a council of advisors makes sense, but consultation inevitably reduces absolutism, so Frederick's first act in 1740 was to reject the committee system of his father. I quote: "Committees simply provide opportunities for mutual intrigue and for the introduction of hate and passion into the affairs of state." Away with councils. So what's the consequence? Ministers, okay, since Frederick regarded all his bureaucrats as blockheads, he stopped any kind of collective decision-making among them.

The result was that the ministers of departments got stronger, because they didn't have to coordinate their activities with anybody else as long as the king didn't interfere, and that made Frederick angry. He wrote in 1748: "His Majesty has discovered with the greatest displeasure that a kind of hate or animosity of spirit exists among the ministers." Then, thirdly, you have the operations of vertical authority. The logic is this: 1) Only the king decides; 2) No committees exist to reconcile differences among ministers; 3) Intrigue to persuade the king to accept one or the other view is inevitable; 4) The king is rarely in a position to decide on wholly rational criteria, even Frederick the Great; 5) The king gets frustrated and angry and acts irrationally because he's fed up, and you see a lot of that in Frederick's reign.

Now, to illustrate what I mean, let's take a look at the U.S. Constitution as a comparison. The wisdom of the Founding Fathers was in some respects greater. Like Frederick, they too are rationalists, but with this difference. For Frederick, rationality was a form of thought based on means and ends. For the Founding Fathers, rationality was a device for analyzing reality. Hence, the U.S. Constitution rests on observations about human nature, and then uses rationality to contain its vices.

The object, of course, is the opposite of Frederick's, to prevent the exercise of absolute power, and I think the most beautiful passage in the whole of the constitutional literature is James Madison's famous discussion of power in *The Federalist Papers*, No. 51. I want to quote one paragraph:

> Ambition must be made to counteract ambition. The interest of the man must be connected with the constitutional rights of the place. It may be a reflection on human nature, that such devices should be necessary to control the abuses of government. But what is government itself, but the greatest of all reflections on human nature? If men were angels, no government would be necessary. If angels were to govern men, neither external nor internal controls on government would be necessary. In framing a government which is to be administered by men over men, the great difficulty lies in this: you must first enable the government to control the governed; and in the next place oblige it to control itself.

Now, there's the same mechanical rationality in Madison as in Frederick, but the Madisonian view has one enormous advantage. It starts with the assumption that human fallibility, ambition, and self-seeking are normal, universal. What you need to do is to design a mechanical system which will make these forces counteract each other and balance them out. Frederick loses his temper. The Federalist uses ambition for rational ends.

Now, another problem is that rationality is fine provided it rests on the right assumptions, but what if it rests on wrong ones? Let me take some examples. Frederick's finances: Frederick was his own minister of finance. Income and expenditure of the state always remained the king's secret. Now, the state was there to carry out the king's purposes, and war was its main object. So here, financial activity was rationally directed to make sure that you had a really full war chest at all times, and the state treasury was literally filled with bags of silver.

Prussia was by far the best run continental state. It collected taxes. In the 17th century it abolished the estates and had no problem collecting taxes. Everybody was involved. It fought two great series of wars: The war for the Austrian succession between 1740 and 1748, and the Seven Years' War between 1756 to 1763, in which it was nearly destroyed, but it was never bankrupt. Indeed, at the end of a generation of war between 1740 and 1763, the Prussian treasury still had 13.8 million thaler, which I think is the same word as the dollar but it didn't mean of course the same thing in 1763.

In 1786, on his death, the treasury retained 23.7 million thaler and Frederick was still able to support a standing army of 87,000 men. Now, by comparison with any other state in Europe at this time, this was an astonishing achievement. His trade policy was quite successful. He encouraged trade and industry, and he was perfectly prepared to tolerate Jews because they brought trade and commerce with them. He founded state monopolies in porcelain manufacture, trade, and mining. There was a tobacco monopoly. There was a coffee monopoly, and all these monopolies poured money into the state treasury.

His economic ideas were wrong, though. Adam Smith wrote in 1776 in *The Wealth of Nations*, which we shall see when we get to Lecture Thirteen, "The sole use of money is to circulate consumable goods… the whole apparatus of the state is unproductive." Now, hoarding silver in bags in a treasury was deflationary. It took money out of the economy and reduced the productivity. It therefore actually reduced the wealth of Frederick's state, and this was something which observers at the time could see. The British Ambassador Lord Malmesbury wrote of Frederick's policies, and I quote: "A large treasury lying dormant in his coffers impoverishes his kingdom; that riches increase by circulation; that trade cannot subsist without reciprocal profit; that monopolies and exclusive grants put a stop to evolution, and of course, to industry; and in short that the real wealth of a sovereign consists in the ease and affluence of his subjects."

Now, Frederick therefore failed the test as a rational finance minister, and that, too, involves a curious paradox. To follow the British model meant freeing markets from control. Freeing markets from control means freeing your citizens from control. Freeing your citizens from control undermines absolutism. In other words, to do what Adam Smith said was rational, and it was rational, would have been to undermine the whole nature of the absolutist state because free markets go with free people. You can't have them as long as you run the state the way Frederick did. That means that the error is simply not wrong knowledge, but is built into the system.

Then, there is a final paradox of the rational state and that is monarchy itself is an irrational way of choosing a leader. The very system is not rational. Frederick was not chosen by public examination. It was an accident that the whole Hohenzollern dynasty was so able. It was an accident that between 1640 and 1918 there are only 10 Hohenzollern monarchs, and they all reigned for an average of 33 years. It's an accident that Frederick the Great turned out to be a genius. His successor, Frederick William II was a nice cello player, played some really nice music and had some wonderful music written for him by Haydn, but he was lazy and indecisive.

Heredity is not rational, but organic, so to run a state based on these kinds of things is simply not rational. As it happens, the family tradition of the House of Hohenzollern was a very unusual one. The great elector, 1640 to 1688 an elector like Augustus II of Lecture Two, or King Frederick William I, 1713–1740, and Frederick the Great 1740–1786 all had long reigns and great skills. Prussia was turned into a military state. Like Israel today, it had no defensible borders and enemies all around it, hence the king had to be, first and foremost, a general, and the rulers therefore had to save their money for their armies.

The rulers of Prussia, unlike almost every other prince in 18th-century Europe, spent hardly any money on palaces, fancy clothes, or royal displays. The court of Prussia was notorious among the other princes. Duke Carl August of Weimar visited Frederick's Berlin in 1785, and he wrote to a friend: "I shall soon embark on a journey which, however, will not make me freer, but take away from me for a time my personal and particularist freedom. I will go to Berlin for eight days. As soon as possible, I shall flee the sight of the blue slaves." The blue slaves were the blue uniform of the Prussian Army which both king and soldiers wore.

Now, a second irrationality was that Frederick very sensibly relied on the aristocracy as officers in the army and the concept of honor was fundamental. Only a gentleman had honor and only a gentleman could be a proper soldier. Frederick was clear that only aristocrats could be proper commanders. What he did was to offer his nobility the following deal. The Prussian *junker* class was not a very rich noble class, peanuts compared to the English, but it was a service nobility. It was offered a monopoly of high office in the army and state in exchange for the permanent surrender of its feudal rights to resist payments of taxation.

Now, making the aristocracy the sole agent of high office and of command in the army meant that people of talent were irrationally excluded, who just happened to be commoners. You reduce the potential pool of gifted officers and civil servants. Again, this was an irrational outcome and shows the limits of absolute absolutism, although when we get to Joseph II we'll see somebody who tried to push these limits even further, and didn't do what the aristocracy with Frederick the Great did. Since royal position rests on nobility, the king is, so to speak, the greatest noble, and since both rest on birth and privilege, not reason, there's no way the king could escape this paradox.

Now, Frederick was an enlightened prince, and he was famous as enlightened. He was a full-time intellectual, author of theoretical text and famous letters. He corresponded with all the great luminaries of the 18th century and wrote, in French, both poetry and prose. His indifference to religion was an essential tenet of the Enlightenment itself, as we shall see when we come to look at people like Hume. During the 18th century, no European state, other than Britain, was religiously entirely homogenous. Britain was, of course, certainly not religiously homogenous but, like Prussia, it was religiously tolerant at the exact extreme. The free liberal commercial society, polite commercial society of England was religiously tolerant and the extreme absolute autocratic Frederick was tolerant, too.

Now, Frederick was religiously tolerant, because, first of all, he didn't believe in the stuff, as we saw, but he favored tolerance because of the enlightened belief in the right of the autonomous human being to choose a religion on the basis of reason or conscience, and secondly, because it was a pragmatic consideration of modernizing states, which need new basis for loyalty to the sovereign and the need to attract useful immigrants.

Now, Frederick the Great was a great German prince, but he only spoke French to anybody civilized. He spoke German to his servants and didn't even speak German to his dogs. The dogs were addressed in French and they all had French names, so German was a language he didn't use very much, and it's an irony which we shall see when we look at the lecture on Goethe, that it's under Frederick the Great that the great period of German culture begins. Goethe, Schiller, Immanuel Kant, the philosopher who also wrote his great works under Frederick the Great and was indeed a subject of Frederick. In his most famous essay on enlightenment called "What is Enlightenment?" of 1784, Immanuel Kant asked:

> If it is now asked whether we at present live in enlightened age, the answer is no, but we do live in an age of enlightenment. As things are at present, we still have a long way to go before men as a whole can be in a position (or can even be put into a position) of using their own understanding confidently and well in religious matters, without outside guidance…the obstacles to universal enlightenment, to man's emergence from his self-imposed immaturity, are gradually becoming fewer. In this respect our age is the age of enlightenment, the century of Frederick.

In other words, for the greatest philosopher of 18th-century Germany and perhaps one of the greatest philosophers of all time, Frederick's religious tolerance was the key to the liberation of the human spirit from it's self-imposed immaturity, by which Kant meant the belief in a god and religion. The greatest European philosopher paid tribute to Frederick the Great. Here, there's a final paradox. Because of

Frederick's fame as an enlightened ruler, he attracted to Berlin, in spite of the fact that it was a very despotic state, and as we saw Duke Carl August of Weimar wanted to "flee the sight of the blue slaves," he collected an assembly of the most brilliant and talented writers in the German language.

Because Prussia's prestige in war and in letters was at its highest, people were attracted to Berlin, which up until Frederick's time had been a god-forsaken remote garrison state, and that is still the case even today in the new unified Germany, Berlin is miles to the east. It's much, much closer to the Polish border than it is to anything in the west. Frederick the Great became the idol of the new German intellectuals, yet he was utterly disdainful of German culture, and as I said only spoke and read French writers. In one of his wonderful writings he said: "What could I have done for German writers that equaled the advantage I granted them by not bothering with them and not reading their books?"

Thus, we have here a paradoxical figure, a man who created the greatest, what became the greatest European state, Prussia. As I said at the beginning, it becomes the nucleus of the unified Germany of Bismarck in the 19th century, and is the core and by far the largest state in the Germany of the First World War and of Adolf Hitler. Here, we have taken a step on the road to modernity.

Lecture Five
Jean-Jacques Rousseau—A Modern Self

Scope:

Jean-Jacques Rousseau (1712–1778) is, like us, middle class, self-made, and full of self-awareness. He is the first representative of what would become the modern sense of self. Although of humble birth, he joined and influenced the aristocratic elites of Europe. He wrote the first French bestseller, *Julie ou La Nouvelle Héloise*, a story of passion across the lines of class. He wrote works of philosophy, and his *Social Contract* remains one of the most important accounts of democracy ever written. He argued against the prevailing optimism about the progress of civilization and believed that the "noble savage" represented humanity's highest form of morality. He made his private life, loves, and sexual urges public in his *Confessions*. He was a mega-star in 18th-century culture but also a man of his time, born in the same year as Frederick the Great. Rousseau became part of that movement of ideas called the Enlightenment and was effective because of the new "public" that emerged in the 18th century, which had money and leisure to "buy" ideas, literature, and music. Thus, the new structure of society itself was an element in Rousseau's career.

Outline

I. Even today, Switzerland is partially a remnant of medieval Europe.

   A. In Rousseau's time, it was a collection of small valleys and cities with surrounding territories that enjoyed formal independence. These territories were called *republics*, although the term was not used as it is today.

   B. Authority in the republics was not derived from the people but from a small body of nobles. The largest republics had formed leagues to control so-called subject territories.

   C. Geneva, Rousseau's birthplace, was one of these republics but was not yet a member of the Swiss Confederation.

      1. It was an 18th-century Hong Kong, a small, independent, French-speaking state.

2. It was Protestant and the home of Calvinism. Its publishers were free to publish texts forbidden in Catholic France.

D. Geneva's form of government was complicated and oligarchical. The Founding Fathers were aware of Switzerland as a model of how to do things. Geneva was an aristocratic oligarchy of wealthy families, corrupt and undemocratic.

E. Despite that structure, its reputation was unusual.

    1. By the standards of 18th-century Europe, Geneva was "free," a place of "liberty." If we compare Geneva with the absolute despotism of Frederick the Great (see Lecture Four), we understand why Europeans thought so.

    2. Rousseau was always proud to call himself *citoyen du Genève* ("citizen of Geneva") as his title on his works; plain "citizen" was good enough.

F. Only a fraction of the population, less than a quarter, were "citizens" with full rights.

    1. *Citizen* meant full membership in a kind of exclusive club. The rest were either *habitants* ("inhabitants") or *natifs* ("native born" but without rights).

    2. Yet the image of the Roman Republic (see Lecture Two) gave this system prestige as a system of civic virtue. The republic, in theory, rejected the society of title, rank, and hierarchies.

    3. For Rousseau to use the simple title *citoyen* in Old Regime Europe was a form of rebellion in itself.

II. The Enlightenment will occupy us in several lives, including those of Hume (Lecture Eight), Catherine the Great (Lecture 10), Joseph II (Lecture 11), Adam Smith (Lecture 13), and Robespierre (Lecture 16), and is one of the main themes of the first half of this course.

A. The Enlightenment was a movement of ideas and is difficult to define easily.

1. Dictionaries start with the image of "light," receiving mental or spiritual light, but where does the light come from? The traditional answer was that God and his revelation gave us the divine light.

2. The Enlightenment was a revolution in thought: The "light" in the 18th century was no longer the light of revealed truth but the light of human reason. This development was unique to Europe and is an essential element in the evolution of modern society.

3. The implications of this "light of reason" are fundamental:

    a. If all are endowed with natural reason, the world should be better and people should act that way.

    b. The fact that they do not shows that reason is impeded by ignorance and "superstition"; for the Enlightenment, *superstition* meant belief in God.

    c. Education and the elimination (or reduction) of religion were, thus, essential.

B. The new basis of authority was human reason.

1. This meant the authority of individual reason, best expressed in the admonition of the great philosopher Immanuel Kant: "Have courage to use your own understanding!" ("What Is Enlightenment?" 1784).

2. Enlightenment was an extension of the Protestant conscience and Martin Luther's notion of the priesthood of all believers (1520).

3. The Enlightenment replaced faith with reason, and the results were a fundamental milestone on the road to modernity. One view was that God is reason; hence, the world must be a reasonable machine.

4. The other view was that there is no God. The universe is simply a great machine governed by laws of nature.

5. The Enlightenment, which was European in scope, was a spectrum of views on the role of reason, God, the nature of man, the just society, the causes of inequality, and the problem of luxury. Scotland, England, Germany, Italy, and Spain all experienced their own versions of the Enlightenment.

C. The Enlightenment sparked the growth of the new public sphere.

1. Economic growth and ideas played a part in the Enlightenment: Money and mobility transformed social structures. Wealth ignores social hierarchies and ancient distinctions; money brings society into movement.

2. Jürgen Habermas developed the idea of the bourgeois *public sphere*. Habermas, born in 1929, is a German philosopher and emeritus professor at the University of Frankfurt. Habermas thought that the 18th century was a period in which a new space emerged, both beyond and alongside the court, the closed corporation, and the family.

3. The public sphere is real and can also be imaginary, as expressed in literary works. The public sphere was a function of the growth of towns, printing presses, and literacy.

4. The market for goods and services developed, and new consumption goods spread, such as coffee. The coffeehouse was the perfect institution of the public sphere; it was open to all, irrespective of rank in society, and it offered newspapers and conversation to all.

5. The French version of the coffeehouse was the *salon*, an open house in the apartments of a prince or wealthy aristocrat. Careers were made and broken at salons, which were frequently run by women, as they, too, entered the new public sphere.

6. An encyclopedia, such as the one compiled by Diderot, was the most important physical expression of the Enlightenment. It represented the systems of knowledge, the rational explanation of that knowledge, and its availability to anybody who could read.

7. A generation of intellectuals was now able to live by its wits. Careers were open to all, great or humble in social standing, if they were smart and could shine in the salons.

III. Jean-Jacques Rousseau was born in 1712 in Geneva. His father was a watchmaker, and his mother died soon after his birth.

A. His father left Geneva when Jean-Jacques was only 10, and Rousseau was apprenticed at the age of 13, first to a notary, then to a coppersmith, but after three years, he ran away.

B. After several days of wandering, he was directed to the household of the wealthy and charitable Madame Louise de Warens in Savoy; she would become his first lover and his tutor in arts and letters.

C. From that point on, Rousseau's life was influenced by his relationship to women (was he looking for his lost mother?), characterized by a succession of mistresses, patronesses, lovers, and one wife. They all appear in the *Confessions* and are described quite literally.

D. His sexual appetites were strong but rather specialized. His ideal was what we would now call the dominatrix.

E. In his *Confessions*, he also describes the way he came to write his novel, *Julie ou la Nouvelle Héloïse* (published in 1761). The relationship between the hero and heroine, St. Preux and Julie, was autobiographical. The hero is a middle-class tutor; the heroine, a noble lady. Again, Rousseau expresses the theme of sexual domination.

F. It was not so much what Rousseau did, but the fact that he talked about it. Rousseau's private life and sex life became public. In 1771, he began public readings of his *Confessions*. The new modern "self" was born in Rousseau's life and was a literary and personal creation.

IV. Paris and its salons were the stage for Rousseau's dramatic career.

A. In 1742, Rousseau moved to Paris to make a career as a musician and composer. His opera *Les muses galantes* made his reputation. He met Diderot, Condillac, and other stars of Parisian intellectual society and entered the salon world.

B. In 1750, he made his great philosophical breakthrough in an essay competition of the Academy of Dijon. The issue to be addressed was "if the reestablishment of the sciences and arts has contributed to the purification of customs."

C. Rousseau answered with a resounding no: "It is thus that dissolution of morals, a necessary consequence of luxury, brings with it in its turn the corruption of taste."

1. The essay was signed, not "Rousseau," but "A Citizen."
2. The discourse was a sensation. It attacked the Enlightenment's view of progress and urban life. Rousseau argued that luxury and city life destroy morals.
3. Man is essentially good, a "noble savage" when in the "state of nature," but society is "artificial" and "corrupt."
4. Rousseau was ambivalent about Paris and city life, yet paradoxically depended on it. His career was a creation of the new Parisian world, yet he ostentatiously and noisily rejected it.
5. The new Rousseau was still a "citizen" but had now become a hermit, a prophet of the natural and savage, though, of course, making sure that Paris was watching him in his country hideaway.
6. In *A Dissertation on the Origin and Foundation of the Inequality of Mankind* (1755), he launched an attack on society, which "for the advantage of a few ambitious individuals, subjected all mankind to perpetual labour, slavery and wretchedness."

D. Rousseau was also one of the most important philosophers of all time.

1. Between 1750 and 1762, he published "The First Discourse," *Whether the Restoration of the Arts and Sciences has assisted the purification of morals* (1750); "The Second Discourse," *A Discourse upon the Origin and the Foundation of the Inequality among Mankind* (1754); *Julie ou la Nouvelle Héloïse* (1761); *The Social Contract* (1762); and *Émile, ou l'education* (1762).
2. This was an astonishing achievement—any one of these books would have been enough to make him immortal.
3. *Émile ou l'education* is the least known of his great works. Immanuel Kant considered its publication an event comparable to the French Revolution.

4. *The Social Contract* is an exploration of the dilemma of pure democracy: How can the citizen be free if his or her will is subjected to the will of the majority? The first chapter begins with one of the most famous phrases ever written: "Man is born free; and everywhere he is in chains."

5. The *Volonté générale*, or *General Will*, is deeply controversial; the problems, which Rousseau simply denies, are as follows:

    a. How can protection be ensured against the tyranny of the majority?

    b. What happens if the general will is wrong?

    c. How justified is Rousseau's assumption of the similarity and equality of citizens?

    d. Are there limits on the power of the sovereign general will?

E. Twentieth-century critics have condemned Rousseau as the father of totalitarian democracy, the inspiration of Jacobins and Communists. The *Social Contract* was precisely what the Founding Fathers rejected, and the Constitution of 1787 was designed to prevent democracy, not encourage it.

V. Rousseau was the first to plot the evolution of the modern self, to be that self, and to write the theory of that self's philosophical basis, how that self was to be incorporated into the community and how the new community was to operate. He was the first to ask, a generation before the U.S. Constitution was drafted, what is the meaning of democracy and the "will" of the people? He was also the first exponent of romantic love as the source of self and the first modern advocate for the importance of women. His contribution was to foresee the outlines of our world.

Essential Reading:

Jean-Jacques Rousseau, *Rousseau: 'The Social Contract' and Other Later Political Writings*, Victor Gourevitch, ed.

Supplementary Reading:

Jonathan Steinberg, *Why Switzerland?* 2nd edition.

Questions to Consider:

1. Do you agree with Rousseau that modern, city life corrupts morals?

2. To what extent do we need protection in our democracy today against what Rousseau called "the General Will" or what we might call "majority opinion"?

Lecture Five—Transcript
Jean-Jacques Rousseau—A Modern Self

In the last lecture, we looked at the very strange person of Frederick the Great, an absolute despot with almost no human interaction. In this, we look at Jean-Jacques Rousseau, who was born in the same year and was a direct contemporary of Frederick the Great's, but whom could not be more different. To begin with, Rousseau was Swiss, and he came from that particular Swiss world which was a collection of small valleys, cities and surrounding territories, all of which enjoyed formal independence. "Republic" was the term used to describe them, but not in our modern sense.

James Madison, one of the Founding Fathers, indeed all the Founding Fathers, was very interested in Switzerland as an example, and republics in particular. And in *The Federalist Papers*, No. 39, he says:

> What, then, are the distinctive characters of the republican form? Were an answer to the question to be sought, not by recurring to principles, but in the application of the term by political writers, to the constitution of different States, no satisfactory one would ever be found. Holland, in which no particle of the supreme authority is derived from the people, has passed almost universally under the denomination of a republic. The same title has been bestowed on Venice, where absolute power over the great body of the people is exercised, in a most absolute manner, by a small body of hereditary nobles.

Now, Switzerland itself was a confederation of republics in exactly that sense. The largest republics formed leagues to control some so-called subject territories. In 1796, the Bern aristocrat Karl-Viktor von Bonstetten reported on Lugano, then a subject territory, under the control of the 13 cantons of the Old Confederation (the entire region was very badly governed). He wrote: it's "organized ideally for evil, where good is impossible." The Landvogt or Bailiff "was the judge of life and death. Uncountable are the abuses of such a regime. In no corner of Europe, no matter how dismal, has torture raged so wildly as in Italian Switzerland. The Landvogt who had no salary, had to live off fines (that is, pecuniary punishments) and with these he compensated for…the corruptions with which his office had been purchased."

Now, Geneva, which was Rousseau's birthplace, was not yet a member of the Swiss Confederation, but it was allied to it. It was a sort of 18th-century Hong Kong, a small independent French-speaking state, but it was Protestant, and the home of the Calvinist religion. Its publishers were free to publish texts forbidden in Catholic France.

In structures, Geneva's form of government was complicated and oligarchical. The Founding Fathers were aware of the Swiss model and how not to do things. This is what John Adams wrote about Geneva. I quote:

> In the republic of Geneva, the sovereignty resides in the general council, lawfully convened, which comprehends all the orders of the state, and is composed of four sindics, chiefs of the republic, presidents of all the councils; of the lesser council of twenty-five; of the grand council of two hundred, though it consists of two hundred and fifty when it is complete; and of all the citizens of twenty-five years of age. The rights and attributes of all these orders of the state are fixed by the laws. The history of this city deserves to be studied with anxious attention by every American citizen. The principles of government, the necessity of various orders, and the fatal effects of an imperfect balance, appear no where in a stronger light. The fatal slumbers of the people, their invincible attachment to a few families, and the cool deliberate rage of those families, if such an expression may be allowed, to grasp all authority into their own hands, when they are not controuled or over-awed by a power above them in a first magistrate, are written on every page.

It was an aristocratic oligarchy of wealthy families, corrupt and undemocratic, but by the standards of 18th-century Europe, Geneva was "free," a place of "liberty." If we compare Geneva with the absolute despotism of Frederick the Great, which we looked at in the previous lecture, we understand why Europeans thought so. Rousseau was always proud to call himself *citoyen du Genève*, a citizen of Geneva, and frequently signed his books that way. His title on his works, plain "citizen" was good enough for him. In other words, that's what he sort of regarded himself as.

90   ©2003 The Teaching Company Limited Partnership

Now, citizenship in Geneva, of course was a complicated thing; only a fraction of the population, probably less than a quarter, were actually citizens with full rights. Citizen meant full membership of an exclusive kind of club. The rest were either *habitants* (inhabitants), or *natifs* (native-born without rights). Yet, the image of the Roman Republic, which I discussed in Lecture Two, gave this system prestige as a system of civic virtue.

The republic, in theory, rejected the society of title and rank and hierarchy. For Rousseau, to use the simple title *citoyen* in Old Regime Europe was a form of rebellion itself.

Rousseau was involved in a movement called the Enlightenment, which we shall be meeting in several of the biographies that we're looking at in this course. Enlightenment is really hard to define. It's a kind of movement of ideas, and it doesn't easily fall into one category. Dictionaries normally start with the image of light. You see the mental or spiritual light. We say "an enlightened person," or "to see the light," but where does the light come from? The traditional answer was God, and revelation that gave us the divine light.

The Enlightenment, because it was a revolution in thought, put the "light" in the 18th century no longer as the light of revealed truth, but as the light of human reason. The story is one of a very complex evolution unique to Europe, and an essential element in the evolution of modern society. The implications of the "light of reason" are that: 1) if all are endowed with natural reason, the world should be better because people should act that way; 2) the fact that it does not, shows that reason must be impeded by ignorance and superstition, and by "superstition," men of the 18th century meant "belief in God"; 3) education, therefore and the elimination or reduction of religion was thus an essential part of the freedom of the human mind.

The new basis of authority was the authority of individual reason. In Immanuel Kant's famous essay "What Is Enlightenment?" he said, "Enlightenment is man's emergence from his self-incurred immaturity. Immaturity is the inability to use one's own understanding without the guidance of another. This immaturity is self-incurred if its cause is not lack of understanding, but lack of resolution and courage to use it without the guidance of another. The motto of enlightenment is therefore: *Sapere aude!* Have courage to use your own understanding!"

To some extent, Enlightenment, especially in Protestant countries was an extension of Protestant conscience. Martin Luther, in his *Address to the Christian Nobility of the German Nation,* in 1520, put it this way, and I quote:

> If our faith is right, 'I believe in the holy Christian church,' the Pope cannot alone be right; else we must say, 'I believe in the Pope of Rome,' and reduce the Christian Church to one man, which is a devilish and damnable heresy. Beside that, we are all priests, as I have said, and have all one faith, one Gospel, one Sacrament; how then should we not have the power of discerning and judging what is right or wrong in matters of faith?

In other words, the independence of the Christian conscience at some level is the root of the Enlightenment. What the Enlightenment did, however, was to replace Martin Luther's faith with reason, but the results were equally powerful. In one view, since God is reason, hence the world is a reasonable machine, as in Joseph Addison's great hymn:

> The spacious firmament on high,
>
> With all the blue ethereal sky,
>
> And spangled heav'n's, a shining frame,
>
> The great Original proclaim.
>
> Th'unwearied sun, from day to day,
>
> Does his Creator's pow'r display.

You could imagine this kind of gigantic planetarium in Addison's mind, reflecting God's reason.

The other view, which was not uncommon in the Enlightenment, is that there is no God. The universe is simply a great machine governed by the laws of nature. Rousseau's friend, Baron d'Holbach, who was born in 1723, was a leading atheist. D'Holbach's estate was a meeting place for the most important French radical thinkers, the so-called *philosophes,* of the late 18th century. He was an atheist, a determinist, and a materialist. D'Holbach was also, of course, protected in his extreme views by his high aristocratic rank and wealth. It was a paradox of the Old Regime that in spite of its repressiveness, it had little islands of liberty, which existed because of the thicket of rights and privileges, which I described in previous lectures.

Thus, the Enlightenment was a kind of spectrum of views on the role of reason, of God, the nature of man, the just society, the causes of inequality, the problem of luxury, which was European in scope. There was a Scottish Enlightenment, and two of our European lives, Hume and Smith, are products of it, as we shall see in Lectures Eight and Thirteen. There was an English Enlightenment, a German Enlightenment, or *Aufklärung*, an Italian Enlightenment, and indeed a Spanish Enlightenment, which we shall see in Lecture 21 on Goya.

Now, the Enlightenment took place in the new public sphere. Economic growth and economic ideas played a part in the spread of the Enlightenment because money and mobility transformed social structures. Dr. Samuel Johnson, whom we shall be talking about in the next lecture, said, "Gold and silver destroy feudal subordination." That is to say, wealth ignores social hierarchies in ancient distinctions. Money circulates. It flows and it brings society into movement. The idea that money corrodes social stability will recur in the reaction to the French Revolution, which we shall see in Burke, and also in the anti-Semitism which greets the rise of Nathan Mayer Rothschild, whom we shall look at in Lecture 20.

Now, Jürgen Habermas developed the idea of the bourgeois public sphere. Habermas, who was born in 1929, is a German philosopher and emeritus professor at the University of Frankfurt. Habermas had a very smart idea, which was first published in 1962, and nobody noticed it at the time, but now it's an industry. There are public sphere websites and the word is in everybody's mouth. Habermas thought that the 18th century was one in which a new space emerged, beyond, alongside, outside the court of the closed corporation and of family. This public sphere was both real, that is there were places where it actually happened, as we shall see, in coffeehouses, but it was also imaginary in places that didn't yet have a society that could afford coffeehouses.

The public sphere was a function of the growth of towns, of printing presses, of literacy, and the number of books and journals goes up very sharply after 1700. The market for goods and services develops, and coffee is an example. The coffeehouse was the perfect institution of the public sphere. It was open to all, irrespective of rank in society. It provided newspapers and conversations open to all. The English, who were the first to develop a middle class, were the first to develop them in any numbers. An anonymous critic in 1673 wrote about these places:

> A coffeehouse is a lay conventicle, good-fellowship turned puritan, ill-husbandry in masquerade, whither people come, after toping all day, to purchase at the expense of their last penny, the repute of sober companions: A Rota [a club room], that, like Noah's ark, receives animals of every sort, from the precise diminutive band, to the hectoring cravat and cuffs in folio; a nursery for training up the smaller fry of virtuosi in confident tattling, or a cabal of kittling [that is carping] critics that have only learned to spit and mew.

Now, note how the critic rejects that fact that "animals of every sort" are present (i.e., it is open to the public and there is no class distinction). There is no respect for rank. It is literally a new public sphere. Now, in the French version, there was the salon, an open house in the apartments of the prince or wealthy aristocrat, and that was the place where careers were made and broken. It was also a place frequently run by women, and they too enter the public sphere. Baron de Grimm writes of the salon of Madame Julie de Lespinasse:

> Her circle met daily from five o'clock until nine in the evening. There we were sure to find choice men of all orders in the State, the Church, the Court, military men, foreigners and the most distinguished men of letters. Everyone agrees that though the name of M. d'Alembert may have drawn them thither, it was she alone who kept them there. Devoted wholly to the care of preserving that society, of which she was the soul and the charm, she subordinated to this purpose all her tastes and all her personal intimacies. She seldom went to the theatre or into the country, and when she did make an exception to this rule it was the event of which all Paris was notified in advance...Politics, religion, philosophy, anecdotes, news, nothing was excluded from the conversation, and, thanks to her care, the most trivial little narrative gained, as naturally as possible, the place and notice it deserved. News of all kind was gathered there in its first freshness."

Now, the salon competed for the stars of the French literary scene. The presence of M. d'Alembert was a great coup for Madame de Lespinasse. Jean-Le-Rond d'Alembert, born in 1717 was a French mathematician and philosopher. Diderot made him co-editor of the *Encyclopédie*, the encyclopedia, for which he wrote the preliminary discourse and the mathematical, philosophical and literary articles.

The encyclopedia was the most important physical expression of the Enlightenment. In Trinity Hall we had a copy of the first edition in Cambridge, and I used to use it. It's a great big thing, about 20 volumes, and then there are 12 volumes of plates with the most fantastic detail of every single profession. What are the tools of a jeweler? What are the tools of a watchmaker? It was an attempt to systematize and democratize knowledge so that everybody had access now to the new knowledge. It was also of course completely areligious. The Jews, for example are described not as the Christ killers cursed by God, but simply as a group of people who live according to certain rather peculiar laws, rather the way a social scientist would look at them.

Here you have a second generation of philosophers who are now able to live by their wits, whose careers are open to the talents, great or humble in social standing. And here are some of the names. You could make it if you were very smart; Rousseau, born in 1712, Diderot born in 1713, Condillac born in 1715, Helvétius born in 1715, d'Alembert born in 1717, Grimm born in 1723, and d'Holbach born in 1723. They're all a generation of people, some aristocrats, some very humble, like Jean-Jacques Rousseau.

Now let's turn to the specific life of Rousseau. Women played a crucial role in Rousseau's life and in the story he told the world about that life. He was born in 1712 in Geneva. His father was a watchmaker. His mother died soon after his birth, and his father left Geneva when Jean-Jacques was only ten. Rousseau was apprenticed at the age of 13, first to a notary and then to a coppersmith, but after three years he ran away.

After several days of wandering, he was directed to the household of a wealthy and charitable lady, Madame Louise de Warens, at Annecy in Savoy, who subsequently sent him to a hospice institution offering accommodation in Turin. Now this is the first important theme in Rousseau's life, which was a function of his relationship to women.

And without being too Freudian, one could ask: Was he looking for his lost mother? Madame de Warens, who was 13 years older, was the first and most important influence in his life. She was his first lover, and introduced him to arts and letters.

From that point on, Rousseau's life involved a succession of mistresses, patronesses, lovers, and one wife. They all appear in his *Confessions* and are very literally described. His sexual appetites were apparently very strong, but rather specialized. His idea is what we now call the "dominatrix," and I won't go into the kind of kinky images with which such persons are portrayed in some of the porno magazines. Rousseau's attitudes towards women were that, however, as he describes in his *Confessions*. He writes, quote, "To lie at the feet of an imperious mistress, to obey her command, to be obliged to beg her forgiveness, these were sweet pleasures."

He describes the way he came to write his novel, *Julie ou la Nouvelle Héloïse*, (*Julie or the New Heloise*), which was a bestseller and made him famous all over Europe, when published in 1761. I quote:

> I pictured to myself love and friendship, the two idols of my heart, in the most ravishing of guises. I delighted in embellishing them with all the charms of the sex I had always adored. I invented two friends, women rather than men, because if examples of this are rare, they are also more appealing…Bewitched by my two charming models, I identified as closely as I could with the lover and friend, but I made him young and amiable, while giving him for the rest the virtues and defects I felt I myself possessed.

Now the relationship between the hero and heroine in this novel, St. Preux and Julie, is entirely autobiographical. The hero is a middle class tutor and the heroine is a noble lady. And once again we get the theme of sexual dominance. St. Preux says to Julie, "My Julie, you were made to rule. Your empire is the most absolute I know. It extends to my very will. You impose your will on mine. You overwhelm me. Your spirit crushes me. I am nothing in your presence." When one thinks of the use of absolutism in the previous lecture, what could be further from Frederick the Great's world than this kind of stuff?

It's worth pausing for a minute to reflect on the significance of Rousseau's masochism, though. It's defined in the dictionary as a form of sexual perversion in which a person finds pleasure in abuse and cruelty from his or her associate. And the word was first used at the end of the 19th century in 1893. The point here: it's not so much Rousseau's predilections as the fact that he's talking about them that matters. Rousseau is the first person in modern history to make his private life public. He let it all hang out. In 1771, he began public readings of his *Confessions*, and they are really pretty explicit. Thus, the new self, the new human being, somebody who in some ways is recognizably like our own becomes a literary artifact.

The next important element in Rousseau's success is Paris itself. Paris and the salon were the keys to his career. In 1742, he settled in Paris to begin his career ironically as a musician and composer because he was a person of astonishing talents. His opera, *Les muses galantes*, made his reputation. It involved him in a very important public controversy about the French versus the Italian style. Rousseau was a protagonist of the Italian style. Because he suddenly was famous, he met Diderot, he met Condillac and he entered the salon world.

His first philosophical breakthrough was a curious 18th century exercise, a prize essay competition, which the Academy of Dijon had proposed. These were public competitions and you simply sent in your essay and if you won you got very famous indeed. The essay's question was: "if the reestablishment of the sciences and the arts has contributed to the purification of customs." That is to say, has the Enlightenment made people better? They invited answers. Rousseau's central argument was this: "It is thus that the dissolution of morals, a necessary consequence of luxury, brings with it in its turn the corruption of tastes." Now, this was signed, not "Rousseau," but "A Citizen."

The discourse was a sensation because it was an attack on the Enlightenment's view of progress in urban life. Rousseau argued that luxury and the city destroy morals. Rousseau declared that man is essentially good, a "noble savage." By the way, that's where the phrase "noble savage" comes from, when in the "state of nature."

Society, on the other hand, is artificial and corrupts human nature. There's a paradox here. Rousseau's career depends on the city, but here he is rejecting it. He leaves to become a kind of hermit. In his *Confessions* he writes, "It was on the 9th of April, 1756, that I left

Paris, never to live in a city again, or in another place; Paris, city of noise, smoke and mud, where women no longer believe in honour or men in virtue." Thus, the new Rousseau was a citizen and a hermit, and a prophet of the natural and of the savage.

In his *Dissertation on the Origin and Foundations of the Inequality of Mankind*, which he published in 1755, he made an attack on society as such. "Such was," I quote, "or may well have been, the origin of society and law, which bound new fetters on the poor, and gave new power to the rich; which irretrievably destroyed natural liberty, eternally fixed the law of property and inequality, converted clever usurpation into unalterable right, and, for the advantage of the few ambitious individuals, subjected all mankind to perpetual labour, slavery and wretchedness."

Now, Jean-Jacques Rousseau is the godfather of all greens, of all green movements. From Rousseau through Thoreau to the anti-globalization demonstrators of today, Rousseau's spirit lives on. He was the first to use the word "romantic," to publicize his tears, and to uncover his vices and virtues to the public. This alone would make Jean-Jacques Rousseau permanently famous. He was also one of the most important philosophers of all time, though. Between 1750 and 1762 he published: "The First Discourse" (which I've discussed) *Whether the Restoration of the Arts and Sciences has assisted the purification of morals*, and as we saw, Rousseau gave the answer "no"; then, in 1754, *A Discourse upon the Origin and Foundations of the Inequality among Mankind*, the so-called "Second Discourse"; *Julie ou la Nouvelle Héloïse*, his blockbuster novel in 1761; *The Social Contract* in 1762; and *Émile ou l'education* in 1762, in the same year.

Now, this is an astonishing achievement. Any one of these works would have been enough to make Rousseau immortal. *Émile ou l'education*, is the least known of his great works. The philosopher Kant compared its publication to the outbreak of the French Revolution. Allan Bloom, the American philosopher who wrote *The Closing of the American Mind*, edited a fine edition of *Émile* and wrote about it, and I quote, "*Émile* is one of those rare total or synoptic books, a book with which one can live and which becomes deeper as one becomes deeper, a book comparable to Plato's *Republic*, which it is meant to rival or supercede."

Then, of course there's *The Social Contract*. *The Social Contract* is an exploration of the dilemma of pure democracy. How can the citizen be free if his or her will is subjected to the will of the majority? The first chapter begins with one of the most famous phrases ever written. I quote: "Man is born free, and everywhere he is in chains. One thinks himself the master of others and still remains the greater slave than they. How did this change come about? I do not know. What can make it legitimate? That question I think I can answer." The answer was the establishment of the social contract. Each citizen surrenders all rights to the community. I quote, "Each of us puts his person and all his power in common under the supreme direction of the general will, and, in our corporate capacity, we receive each member as an indivisible part of the whole."

The *Volonté générale* or the General Will, remains deeply controversial. The problems in it are: 1) What protects us against the tyranny of the majority? 2) What if the General Will is wrong? 3) Then there's the assumption that citizens are alike and equal; it's not realistic—are they? 4) How can we set limits to the power of the sovereign? Rousseau dismissed these. He said:

> Again, the Sovereign, being formed wholly of the individuals who compose it, neither has nor can have any interest contrary to theirs; and consequently the sovereign power need give no guarantee to its subjects, because it is impossible for the body to wish to hurt all its members. We shall also see later on that it cannot hurt any in particular. The Sovereign, merely by virtue of what it is, is always what it should be.

Well, this was an extremely dangerous assumption, one which his critics have used to call Rousseau the father of totalitarian democracy, the inspirer of Jacobins and communists, because the ideal of *The Social Contract* is precisely what the Founding Fathers rejected. The people who wrote the constitution were not democrats. That's the last thing they wanted. That's why, for example, we have the Electoral College. The Constitution of 1787 was in a sense an attempt to prevent the general will, to prevent the democracy, not to encourage it.

Isaac Kramnick, who edited a fine edition of *The Federalist Papers*, writes, "The spirit of Rousseau hovered over these Anti-Federalists [that is those who opposed the constitution] as they identified with simple, small, face-to-face, uniform societies."

Now, it's been for me a really great discovery to try to assess Rousseau's true greatness. I am terribly grateful to The Teaching Company and to you, the students, for making me come to terms with Rousseau. Rousseau was the first to plot the evolution of a modern self. He was the first to be that self and write the theory of that self-philosophical basis. He thought about how that individual self could be incorporated into the community and how the community had to operate. What was the meaning of democracy and what was the will of the people?

However, he was also, I think, the first seriously to glorify the role of women in society, to see romantic love as the source of the self-identity and the importance of women in this relationship. It is, I suppose, his greatest contribution to have foreseen, in more detail than almost anybody I can imagine, the outlines of the world in which we now live.

Since it is the object of this course to place, as it were, markers on the road from the Old Regime to the modern world, we have to place a very large one before the life of Jean-Jacques Rousseau. Jean-Jacques Rousseau taught us for the first time what it was like to be us, the way we now see ourselves, to have the kind of interior world that he himself represented. As I say, for me, and I hope for you, one of the greatest benefits of this particular course of lectures might be to encourage students to go back and read some of the great works of Jean-Jacques Rousseau.

Lecture Six
Samuel Johnson—The "Harmless Drudge"

Scope:

Samuel Johnson (1709–1784) became the most famous literary figure in England during the 18th century. In 1755, he published his two-volume dictionary, the biggest commercial publication of its time. Johnson's witty definitions made it an immediate success:

1. **Lexicographer:** a writer of dictionaries, a harmless drudge.

2. **Oats:** a grain which in England is generally given to horses, but in Scotland supports the people.

3. **Patron:** One who countenances, supports or protects. Commonly a wretch who supports with indolence and is paid with flattery.

"Dictionary Johnson," a huge and irascible figure, became the center of a circle of wits. Equally important was James Boswell, a Scot who attached himself to Johnson in 1763 and wrote his biography. Boswell's *Life of Johnson* stands as the greatest biography in the English language and has a double connection in this course. Johnson, the professional author, became the subject of biography, but both subject and biographer represent a new stage in the evolution of modern communications: the emergence of publishing as an industry. Writing, publishing, bookselling, together with the new public ready to "consume" literary products, created the new market for ideas and entertainment. Johnson and Boswell's *Life of Johnson* mark a further stage in the transformation of the premodern world into something we begin to recognize as our own.

Outline

I. The growth of the book trade was a feature of the English economy in the 18th century.

    A. The author's rights underwent a legal transformation.

        1. Copyright is an exclusive right given by law for a certain term of years to an author, composer, or designer to print, publish, and sell copies of his or her original work. We tend to take this right for granted now, but until the 18th century, it was not necessary.

2. The sovereign had previously held the right to control publication, which presented no problem when books had to be copied by hand. Printing "democratized the word," and the government issued exclusive licenses to certain printers and maintained strict censorship.

3. In 1709, the English copyright act, the first such act in history, changed the rules. Its full title was *An Act for the encouragement of Learning by Vesting the Copies of Printed Books in the authors or Purchasers of Such Copies*. No other European state followed the English model until much later.

4. The break was fundamental. Previously, the right to print granted by the Crown limited the business of books, and the market was under control. Now, the market became the arbiter of bookselling and publishing.

B. The professional author was a consequence of the change.

1. A new profession became conceivable: that of professional author. A writer might make a living selling books, just as he or she might by selling any other commodity.

2. Samuel Johnson's career illustrates this new possibility. He was one of the first and, perhaps, the greatest of professional authors.

II. The magazine emerged as a new vehicle for professional authors.

A. In 1731, Edward Cave founded the *Gentleman's Magazine*. Its purpose was to summarize the news of the month.

1. Cave's success was a consequence of the copyright act of 1709 and the ferocity of partisan politics under the Hanoverian kings (see Lecture Three on Walpole).

2. The *Gentleman's Magazine* was an instant success, and its offices became a meeting place for writers and publishers.

3. The social implications of this change can be seen in two ways:

a. First, the erosion of aristocratic exclusiveness was accelerated, and barriers between classes were weakened. The magazine was like the coffeehouse, an institution of the public sphere. (See Lectures Three on Walpole and Five on Rousseau.)

b. Further, the sheer volume of journalistic activity created significant openings for poor, clever lads (and lasses) able to "write to order." Most journalism was anonymous or signed "The Spectator" or "The Gentleman"; the writer could be a woman, a lower-class person, anybody. The journalistic hack, people with "pens for hire," were now a recognizable type.

B. The *Gentleman's Magazine* used a subterfuge to publish parliamentary reports.

1. In 1732, the House of Commons would not allow speeches of members to be printed even after the end of the session. The House of Lords followed the same practice even more stringently.

2. Cave invented an imaginary country, which he called *Magna Lilliputia* (from Swift's *Gulliver's Travels*, published a few years earlier in 1726), gave it a parliament, and proceeded to report that country's parliamentary debates.

3. Samuel Johnson was hired to write these imaginary debates. Sometimes he used notes of those present; sometimes, "the mere coinage of his imagination," as Boswell elegantly put it; in other words, he made them up.

4. Johnson could write three columns of the magazine in an hour. He was the perfect lobby correspondent, establishing a new career path with the mix of publishing, politics, and the public.

III. Who was Samuel Johnson?

A. Johnson was from Lichfield near Birmingham and was born in 1709. Like Ned Cave, he was a poor boy who made it in the new publishing and journalistic industries. His father was a bookseller.

B. Samuel was a huge, lumbering, ill-coordinated boy who suffered as a young man from scrofula, a form of tuberculosis of the lymph glands. The disease left him disfigured and nearly blind in one eye.

C. Johnson's habits were very odd. He was said to suffer "queer convulsions" and make "strange gesticulations" on entering a room.

D. Johnson's poverty was another important element in his career:

    1. A scholarship took him to Pembroke College, Oxford, but he had to quit because he could not afford it. He faced an uncertain life, with a bankrupt father and no prospects, when he met "Betty," an older woman whom he loved dearly and who had a little money. With her cash, Johnson tried to found a school, but it failed.

    2. London was the last hope for a career. In 1737, he and his friend, David Garrick, later the most famous actor of the era, walked from Lichfield to London to seek their fortunes. They chose an ideal time to go: The new journalism and the commercial theater were looking for bright young men who did not cost much.

IV. Johnson, the subject of Boswell's biography, always had a strong attraction to the genre.

    A. Johnson wrote lives of famous statesmen for Cave's magazine, in addition to his poems and parliamentary reports.

    B. In 1744, Johnson wrote *The Life of Richard Savage*, a kind of self-portrait, given that Savage, though higher born, was also a "pen for hire." Johnson's portrait of a literary hack marked a further stage in the modernization of literature.

    C. Johnson wrote other lives, including the three volumes of *The Lives of the Poets* (1777) and *The Life of Pope* (1781).

V. James Boswell (1740–1795) is the alter ego in Johnson's life.

    A. Boswell, a Scottish gentleman of terrible character, arrived in London in 1762. He was a toady, a name-dropper, a sexually irrepressible rake. His *London Journal, 1762-1763*, reveals that he was an anxious depressive who suffered from mood swings, hypochondria, and fears of venereal disease.

B. Boswell's genius was the perfect foil to Johnson's. Boswell had several rare gifts, including an insatiable curiosity about other people and the ability to make them talk about themselves.

C. Boswell had a superb prose style, along with great wit and charm, and was a fascinating diarist.

D. His relationship to Johnson was complicated. His attachment to Samuel Johnson, who was 30 years older than he, was special; in some mysterious way, Johnson made him feel better about himself. Early in their relationship, on June 14, 1763, Boswell wrote: "I never am with this great man without feeling myself bettered and rendered happier."

E. A few weeks later, Boswell decided to record Johnson's conversation word for word. Later that night, at a tavern in Fleet Street, Boswell confessed his religious doubts and struggles to Johnson, a deeply pious, if eccentric, Christian. As Boswell recorded in his *Journal*: "He was much pleased with my ingenuous open way, and he cried, 'Give me your hand. I have taken a liking to you.'"

VI. Boswell's *Life of Johnson* rests on one of the greatest literary collaborations in history.

   A. Johnson acts as the master of conversation and opinion; Boswell, the faithful scribe, writes it down. The book is often pure dialogue.

   B. Yet the reality is actually more complicated. Boswell's need for Johnson's approval was limitless. Johnson remarked: "Of the exaltations and depressions of your mind, you delight to speak, and I hate to hear. Drive all such fancies from you."

   C. For 25 years, Boswell refashioned his notes and created a portrait of the living Johnson. Both the subject and the biographer were literary geniuses, great stylists, both preoccupied with the art of biography. The book evolves almost like a novel.

   D. Both Johnson and Boswell agreed on the method of biography: to look for the small, telltale particulars of character.

1. Boswell observed that minute particulars are frequently characteristic and always amusing when they relate to a distinguished man.

2. Johnson agreed: "More knowledge may be gained of a man's real character by a short conversation with one of his servants than from a formal and studied narrative, begun with his pedigree and ended with his funeral."

3. Both writers used English in its classical period. Johnson and Boswell wanted to achieve balance and pithiness of phrase, as shown in Johnson's beautiful letter of condolence to a friend, describing the reality of grief:

   > The continuity of being is lacerated; the settled course of sentiment and action is stopped; and life stands suspended and motionless, till it is driven by external causes into a new channel. But the time of suspense is dreadful.

4. Both writers also strove for what Boswell called "the perfection of language," the idea that there is some choice of words that perfectly expresses an idea.

VII. The careers of both Johnson and Boswell depended on the functions of the new publishing industry: Johnson, the poor scholar from the provinces, and Boswell, the Scottish lord, met in the new market for literary products. Both became "celebrities" in the modern sense of the word. The media of the day made them famous and they, in turn, exploited the media. Thus, the "modern" media star is a function of the industrialization of literary communication, the spread of the mass press, and the creation of the "author" as a new type.

Essential Reading:

James Boswell, *Life of Johnson* (Oxford World's Classics), R. W. Chapman and J. D. Fleeman, eds.

Frederick A. Pottle, ed., *Boswell's London Journal: 1762–1763*.
Supplementary Reading:

Allen Reddick, *The Making of Johnson's Dictionary, 1746–1773*.

Questions to Consider:

1. Why are readers interested in the lives of authors, and does it help the reader to understand the books if he or she knows about the author's life?

2. Were Johnson and Boswell right that human character reveals itself in certain small but specific ways of behaving?

Lecture Six—Transcript
Samuel Johnson—The "Harmless Drudge"

In the previous two lectures we looked at Frederick the Great and Jean-Jacques Rousseau, who were both born in 1712. In this lecture, we look at Samuel Johnson, who was born in 1709. He became the most famous literary figure in England during the 18th century, and in 1755 he published his two-volume dictionary, which was the biggest commercial publication of its time.

It became an immediate success, because Johnson's definitions were so funny. A lexicographer he defined as "a writer of dictionaries, a harmless drudge." Oats were "a grain which in England is generally given to horses, but in Scotland supports the people." A patron is "one who countenances, supports or protects. Commonly a wretch, who supports with indolence and is paid with flattery."

"Dictionary Johnson," a huge, awkward and irascible figure, became the center of a circle of wits, but most importantly, a Scottish lord, James Boswell, who attached himself to Johnson in 1763, wrote his biography. Boswell's *Life Of Johnson* stands as the greatest biography in the English language, and thus forms a double connection in this course. Johnson, the professional author, becomes the subject of biography, but both subject and biographer represent a new stage in the evolution of modern communications: the emergence of publishing as an industry. Writing, publishing, bookselling, together with a new public ready to "consume" literary products creates the new public market for ideas and entertainment. In terms of this course, Johnson and Boswell's *Life Of Johnson* mark a further stage in the transformation of the pre-modern world into something we can begin to recognize as our own. I suppose Johnson is a kind of 18th-century megastar.

Now, the growth of the book trade was a feature of England in the 18th century, and it depended on an important legal transformation, which was the introduction of copyright. Copyright is an exclusive right given by law for a certain term of years to an author, composer, designer, or whomever to print, publish and sell copies of his or her original works and to keep the rights. It seems obvious to us now, but in the 18th century it was, in most European countries, not necessary, because the sovereign had the control of publication and the right to say what was or was not published. So there wasn't any need for copyright; when books had to be copied by hand there wasn't any problem.

Printing, which in effect "democratized the word," posed a problem for the government, because now they had lots of books, and so the government issued licenses to certain printers and maintained strict censorship. When, therefore, in 1709, the English copyright went into effect, it just changed the rules completely, because this was the first such act in history, and no other European state followed the English model until much later.

Its full title was *An Act for the encouragement of Learning by Vesting the Copies of Printed Books in the Authors or Purchasers of Such Copies.* Now, this break was fundamental, since previously the right to print was granted by the Crown, and that limited the business of books; the market was under control. Now, the market became the arbiter of bookselling and publishing, and for example, the U.S.A. only adopted its first copyright statute in 1790, much, much later.

This in turn meant that the professional author became a new feature in the market for books. A new profession became conceivable; a writer might make a living by selling books, like any other commodity, and Samuel Johnson's career illustrates this new possibility. He was one of the first and perhaps the greatest of professional authors. Because he was now free, you got new forms, and there was the invention of the magazine. Now, the word "magazine" is a metaphor. The original meaning of the word is a place where goods are stored, and that's exactly how, in 1731, Edward Cave, who founded the *Gentleman's Magazine* explained its purpose, and I quote:

> To give a monthly view of all the newspapers which of late are so multiplied as to render impossible, unless a man makes it his business to consult them all...No less than 200 half-sheets are thrown from the press only in London...This consideration has induced several gentlemen to promote a monthly collection to treasure up, as in a magazine, the most remarkable pieces on the subjects above mentioned.

Now, Edward Cave was himself a new kind of professional, and he's a perfect example of the type of human being I'm talking about. He was a cobbler's son. Born in 1692, he was a scholarship boy at the Rugby School, a fancy English public school, and was kicked out for robbing the headmaster's chicken coop. Even as a boy he had a reputation for insolence and unwillingness to accept authority.

In 1712, he was apprenticed to Mr. Freeman Collins, a printer, and took the opportunity to break out and set up his own office at St. John's Gate in Clerkenwell. The reason for Cave's success was a function, I think of two changes. The first we've mentioned, which is the Copyright Act. The second is the ferocity of partisan politics under the Hanoverian kings which we discussed in Lecture Three on Robert Walpole.

Now, Joseph Addison, who was himself no mean publicist and the founder of *The Spectator*, wrote in *The Freeholder* on June 22, 1716, "Our children are initiated into faction before they know their right hand from their left. They no sooner begin to speak but 'Whig' and 'Tory' are the first words that they learn. They are taught in their infancy to hate one half of the nation and contract all the violence and passion of a party before they come to use their reason."

Now, the *Gentleman's Magazine* was an instant success, and its offices became a meeting place, another one of those places of the public sphere. As an observer wrote, "Here hack writers and members of Parliament, scholars and scientists, nobles and statesmen were to jostle one another in going to what became the most famous editorial offices of the 18th century, to smoke a pipe with Ned Cave."

Now, consider the social implications of the magazine. Two important points need to be noted here. First, the erosion of aristocratic exclusiveness. Anybody could go to their magazine, anybody could publish in the magazine. The barriers between the classes were weakened; it was like the coffee shop, an institution of the public sphere.

Second, the sheer volume of journalistic activity, 200 sheets being dumped on the market in London every day, created a huge opening for poor clever lads able "to write to order," and as we shall see in the lives of Mary Wollstonecraft and the life of George Eliot, Lectures 17 and 23, for lasses as well. Since most journalism in those days was anonymous, or signed "The Spectator" or "The Gentleman" the writer could be a woman, a lower-class person, anybody.

In effect, the new journalistic hack was a person with a "pen for hire," and this was now a recognizable type. The *Gentleman's*

Magazine created a new market. By 1746, Cave was selling 3,000 copies per week at sixpence.

Now, for comparison a newspaper cost tuppence a day (two pennies), and Johnson reckoned that he could live in a garret for 18 pennies a week. That meant that the magazine actually cost a third of your weekly rent; it wasn't cheap, but it was a good buy because it actually summarized all the newspapers, so instead of spending 18 pence on all these newspapers you could spend six and get them summarized.

A second factor was the beginning of parliamentary reporting. In 1732, the House of Commons forbad the speeches of members to be printed even after the end of the session. On April 13, 1738, the House of Commons adopted the following resolution: "It is a high indignity to and a notorious breach of the privilege of this House to give any account of the debates as well during the recess as the sitting of a Parliament."

Now, the House of Lords, which was both a noble senate, equivalent of a senate, but also the highest court in the land, refused even more firmly to allow its debates to be published. Mr. Cave had a really bright idea. He invented an imaginary country, which he called *Magna Lilliputia* (after *Gulliver's Travels*), with a parliament, and he began to report its debates.

Boswell explained in his *Life Of Johnson* 40 years later, "Parliament then kept the press in a kind of mysterious awe, which made it necessary to have a recourse to such devices." Samuel Johnson was hired to write these imaginary debates. Sometimes he used notes of those people who had listened to them, and sometimes as Boswell put it, "The mere coinage of his imagination." In other words, he made them up, but then after all nobody could complain because it was an imaginary country.

Johnson was incredibly quick. He could write three columns of the magazine in an hour, so he was the perfect lobby correspondent (before the lobby or White House correspondent was invented). In this way, a new career path was established by the mix of publishing, politics and the public sphere.

Now who was Sam Johnson? His early life was that of a poor but worthy lad. He was born in Lichfield, near Birmingham, in 1709, and like Ned Cave he was a poor boy who made it in the new publishing and journalistic industries. His father was a bookseller. Sam, the son, was a large, lumbering, ill-coordinated boy who suffered as a young man from scrofula, which I had to look up; it's a form of tuberculosis of the lymph glands.

Leslie Stephen, the founder of *The Dictionary Of National Biography,* and the father of Virginia Woolf by the way, of *The Hours*, described him as follows: "The disease had scarred and disfigured his features otherwise regular and always impressive. It had seriously injured his eyes, entirely destroying it seems the sight of one. He could not, it is said, distinguish a friend's face half a yard off, and pictures were to him meaningless patches in which he could never see the resemblance to their objects."

The statement is perhaps exaggerated, for he could see enough to condemn a portrait of himself. He expressed some annoyance when Reynolds painted him with a pen held close to his eye, and protested that he would not be handed down to posterity as "Blinkin' Sam."

Johnson's habits were extremely odd, Leslie Stephen describes them:

> The queer convulsions by which he amazed all beholders were probably connected with his disease, though he and Reynolds ascribed them simply to habit. When entering a doorway with his blind companion, Miss Williams, he would suddenly desert her on the step in order to 'whirl and twist about' in strange gesticulations. The performance partook of the nature of a superstitious ceremonial. He would stop in the street or the middle of a room to go through it correctly. Once he collected a laughing mob in Twickenham meadows by his antics; his hands imitating the motions of a jockey riding at full speed, and his feet twisting in and out to make his heels and toes touch alternately.

It strikes me as extremely difficult to do.

He was poor; a scholarship took him to Pembroke College, Oxford, but he had to quit because he couldn't afford it. He faced a very uncertain life with a bankrupt father, and no prospects when he met his "Betty," a married older woman whom he loved dearly and who had a little money. With her cash, Johnson tried to found a school, because he was a good Latin scholar, but it failed. London was his last hope. In 1737, he and his friend David Garrick, later the most famous actor of the era, the Garrick Club of London is named after him, walked from Lichfield to London to seek their fortunes. They chose a perfect time to go. The period was ideal for both; the new journalism and the new commercial theatre were looking for bright young lads.

Now I'm going to talk about Johnson, Boswell, and the problem of biography. Johnson himself was interested in biography from the beginning, and he was preoccupied with lives all his life. He wrote lives of famous statesman for Cave's magazine, in addition to his poems and parliamentary reports. In 1744, Johnson wrote *The Life of Richard Savage*, which was a kind of self-portrait, since Savage, the nobly born, was also a "pen for hire." Boswell disapproved of Savage, and I quote, "His character was marked by profligacy, insolence and ingratitude."

Yet, he shared with Johnson the experience of extreme poverty in London. Boswell wrote, "Johnson and Savage were sometimes in such extreme indigence that they couldn't pay for a lodging, so they have wandered together whole nights in the streets." By associating with Savage, who was habituated to dissipation and licentiousness of the town, Johnson was imperceptibly led into some indulgencies.

Now, *The Life of Richard Savage* was a new kind of biography. It was the first portrait of an entirely new type of person, a literary hack, or hired pen, an inhabitant of what Johnson came to call "Grub Street," and it marked a further stage in the modernization of literature. Johnson wrote other biographies, he wrote other lives; one of my favorites are the three volumes *The Lives of the Poets*, which he published in 1777, and this was again a typical commercial venture. Dodsworth the publisher went to Johnson and said, "I'm going to make a huge edition of all the great English poets, and I want you to write the introductions."

Well, the edition never came out but *The Lives Of The Poets*, these wonderful essays, some long, some short, which Johnson intended as introductions to the poetry, have come out, and is one of the books I would save from a burning house if that's all I had left. His *The Life of Pope* was equally enchanting.

Now, Boswell and Johnson got involved into a very complicated biographical relationship, and I have got to say a word about James Boswell. Boswell was born in 1740, so he was young enough to be

Johnson's son, and I think there's a lot in that comparison. Boswell was not poor; Boswell was a Scottish gentleman who arrived in London looking to find out what the new metropolitan scene was like in 1762.

Boswell had a truly terrible character. He was a toady, he was a namedropper, he was sexually irrepressible, and he was a rake. In his *London Journal*, which were published only a few years ago, of 1762–63, he reveals that he was an anxious depressive who suffered from mood swings, hypochondria and was perpetually afraid of venereal disease, and when you read about what Boswell used to get up to in Vauxhall Gardens you can hardly be surprised. I quote one little passage, "I this day began to feel an uncomfortable alarm of unexpected evil, a little heat in the members of my body sacred to cupid," and those of you who are interested, by the way, in 18th century contraceptive practices will find all the how to do that you need in Boswell's journals.

Although Boswell had a terrible character, he was also a genius and was the perfect foil to Johnson. Boswell had several rare gifts; the novelist Oliver Goldsmith said that Boswell "had a method of making people speak." He had an insatiable curiosity about other people, as he wrote: "My desire of being acquainted with celebrated men of every description had made me obtain an introduction to Dr. Samuel Johnson." Boswell had a superb prose style, great wit and charm and was a phenomenal diarist; the diaries are just wonderful.

Now, his relationship to Johnson was always extremely complicated. Samuel Johnson, who was 30 years older than he, came from a very different social class and had a very different set of values. In some mysterious way, though, being next to Johnson made Boswell feel better about himself, and very early in their relationship, in June of 1763, he recorded in his diary, "I never am with this great man without feeling myself bettered and rendered happier." Clearly, then, Johnson performed some sort of psychological function for Boswell. One can speculate that Boswell got along very, very badly with his father, Lord Auchinleck, and maybe in some curious way Johnson supplied that need for paternal authority.

A few weeks later, Boswell decided to record Johnson's conversation word for word. This is what he wrote in his diaries, "I shall mark Johnson's conversations without any order or without mocking my questions, only now and then I shall take up the form of a dialogue." Later that night, at the Mitre Tavern in Fleet Street, and, by the way, a tremendous amount of the biography and Johnson's life and Boswell's life takes place in the public sphere, in taverns, in inns, in hotels, in restaurants, in precisely those places which we now take for granted, but which in the 18th century are actually developing a new kind of function in society, anyway, they were sitting in the Mitre Tavern in Fleet Street, and Boswell confessed his religious doubts and his struggles to Johnson.

Now, Johnson was a deeply pious, self-mortifying, if rather eccentric Christian. I have a close friend who was a great historian called Eamon Duffy who actually says that Dr. Johnson is the English version of a saint. Anyway, so Johnson was listening to all this stuff, and Boswell recorded in his journal, "He was much pleased with my ingenuous open way and he cried, 'Give me your hand Sir, I have taken a liking to you,'" and that was the beginning of this extraordinary double biographical relationship.

I want to say a word about Boswell's *Life of Johnson*, which, if you don't know it, I recommend it to you, and if you end up getting nothing else from this course but buying a copy and reading Boswell's *Life of Johnson,* the course will have been a success. It is one of the most enchanting books ever written, and it rests on one of the oddest and greatest literary collaborations in history. Johnson acts as the master of conversation and opinion, and Boswell is the faithful scribe who writes it down. Sometimes the book is, in spite of Boswell's intention, pure dialogue. It says Johnson, Boswell, Johnson, Boswell. And one of my favorites, which is not in my notes, but I can't forebear, is that they were talking one day about entertaining, and Boswell says, "Sir Alexander Dick tells me that he entertained three thousand people last year," (counting each person who dined as one, and each time that they dined). And Johnson said, "Oh, that's about a thousand people, that's about three a day." To which Boswell says, "How your idea lessens the thing." To which Johnson says, "That Sir, is the good of counting. It brings everything to a certainty which before floated in the mind indefinitely." How can you resist that stuff?

Anyway, the reality is that the book is often pure dialogue, but it's also much more complicated. Boswell's need for Johnson's approval comes out in the book, and it apparently had no limits. Johnson wrote in exasperation to Boswell, "Of the exultations and depressions of your mind you delight to speak and I hate to hear. Drive all such fancies from you."

Now, for 25 years, Boswell refashioned his notes, and created a portrait of the living Johnson, while the living Johnson was living. Both the subject and the biographer were literary geniuses and great stylists, and preoccupied with the art of biography. The book evolves almost like a novel, of a father-son relationship.

Now, the principles of biography, which they both observed were these: Both Johnson and Boswell, both subject and biographer agreed on the method, to look for the small telltale particulars of character. Boswell observed that "minute particulars are frequently characteristic and always amusing when they relate to a distinguished man." Johnson agreed: "more knowledge may be gained of a man's real character by a short conversation with one of his servants than from a formal and studied narrative, which begins with his pedigree, and ends with his funeral."

Now, both wrote English in its most classical period. Johnson and Boswell wanted to achieve balance and pithiness of phrase. If you look, actually, at some of Dr. Johnson's sentences, and I've done this, you can see that there's a central clause, and then there's a sub-clause, and then there's another sub-clause, and then there are sub-clauses, and there are sub-clauses, and they build out almost exactly the way certain kinds of 18th-century buildings do.

The plan for Trinity Hall in 1743 is exactly like one of Dr. Johnson's sentences. There's a clause, and then you've got two wings and they're balanced, and then you have two wings and they're balanced, and so on. Somerset House in London is another one of these 18th-century buildings which actually looks like this particular kind of balanced prose, it's very much the physical embodiment of the spirit of the Enlightenment. They both tried to say things with extreme precision, and I think one of the things that fascinates me about the book is its remarkable wisdom.

Now, try to say this better or in fewer words: "Kindness is in our power, but fondness is not," you could be nice to people but nothing will make you love them if you don't. "Kindness is in our power, but fondness is not." We can't control our emotions, we can control our behavior. Or, and this is of course another pet subject of the book, anybody who is interested in the art of writing can find absolutely everything here she needs in Boswell's *Life of Johnson*, because among the things they talked about all the time, since both were in a sense professional authors, making their living this way, was how you write about things, and people wrote to Johnson asking him how to write sermons and so on. There's a wonderful letter in which Dr. Johnson gives advice to a young clergyman on how to write sermons, and it begins with the following lapidary advice, "Invent first, and then embellish."

Now, how can you say that better? "Invent first, and then embellish." In other words, get yourself a text and then you can fix it up, and years of writing scripts and texts and lectures has taught me the wisdom of that, once you actually have a text you feel a great sigh of relief. Goethe once described the anxiety of the blank page, when you sit there and you've got nothing in front of you, and Johnson understood all that. Invent first and then embellish.

There is a beautiful letter of condolence to a friend describing the reality of grief, which I think describes what it is like after you've lost somebody dear to you, better than anything I think I've ever read. I quote: "The continuity of being is lacerated; the settled course of sentiment and action is stopped; and life stands suspended and motionless, till it is driven by external causes into a new channel. But the time of suspense is dreadful." That, I think, is just perfect. There is that period after the death of somebody you love which is a time of suspense, it's as if life had suddenly stopped, and for that awful period, until something moves you on, you live in this dreadful, dreadful suspense.

Both Johnson and Boswell strove for what Boswell called "the perfection of language," and they both had the idea that there is some choice of words which perfectly expresses an idea, and when you've hit it you think, "Ah, that's it, I've done it."

Now, what is all this about, then? The careers of both Johnson and Boswell depended on the function of the new publishing industry, the fact that it was now possible to make a living without a patron, without the kind of help and support which even Rousseau, or Diderot, or d'Alembert, their French equivalents, had to have.

It was impossible to make a living by going to a salon. Somebody had to pay you in the French system, and when we come to look at the life of Goethe, we will discover, for example, that nobody in the

German intellectual community could live without a job. There was no market, so somebody like Schiller, or when we come to Lecture Nine, somebody like C.P. Bach was actually a servant; he was the servant of Frederick the Great. You might also be a house tutor to some nobleman, or you were a librarian at court, or in fact, for most of the continent, a lot of these people were clergymen. That was the way in which the intellectual life was possible, you had a small parish, you neglected your parishioners and that was the way in which you could make a living.

In the London of the mid-18th century, Dr. Johnson, along with several other figures, Daniel Defoe, Tom Jones, Henry Fielding, these were people who for the first time in human history were actually able to sell books. Now, *Clarissa* and *Pamela*, by Samuel Richardson, were the products of the man who was himself a bookseller publisher, so he wrote the novels, printed them himself, and sold them.

In the entire time of Dr. Johnson's career until his 50s he never had any kind of patronage or support from anybody. There's a fantastic story. When the dictionary came out in 1755, and in the Trinity Hall Library we had copies of these, a great big thing like that, very, very expensive, this was done as an entirely commercial venture, and when the Earl of Chesterfield, the great lord, a lord among wits and wit among lords, suddenly heard this he thought, "Oh, this is nice, I'll ask Dr. Johnson to dedicate this great work to me," because if you look at most 18th-century works there's usually a fulsome dedication to some patron who, of course, paid for it. Johnson wrote the most famous putdown letter, I think, in the history of literature in which he said, "No, thank you, I have done this alone, and I'm not asking anybody to be a patron of something which I've done by my own devices."

We're now looking at the beginning of a new kind of market for ideas. Boswell, the Scottish lord, and Sam Johnson, the son of a poverty-stricken bookseller from Lichfield, now meet in this new public sphere, irrespective of the difference of their social class in the new market for literary products. Both became "celebrities" in the modern sense of the word, compared to Rousseau who became a celebrity too, or perhaps more accurately, compared to Diderot and d'Alembert, until they published the encyclopedia, they were private stars, they starred in the salon.

118

Here, Johnson and Boswell star in the market. The media of the day made them famous, and they in turn exploited the media. Thus, the new modern media star is a function, I think, of the industrialization of literary communication, the spread of the mass press, and the creation of the "author" as a new type. The author as a new type, a person in whom we are interested, in his or her capacity as author. If you think about how this particular genre has spread, just think of the fact that there is on television a Biography Channel, which does nothing else, now, but bring prominent media stars onto the screen so the rest of us can participate in their lives.

Now, why we should want to do that is another question, but that genre, in some sense the godfather of the Biography Channel, is none other than James Boswell, who, in his idea of writing down, interviewing day by day, this great living figure, turned a living person, Dr. Samuel Johnson, into the kind of media star for whom the Biography Channel now takes much lesser people. Thus, we're dealing with yet another of these extraordinary milestones on the transformation of the world, from the Old Regime in which everything was private, and the property of the prince, and not available to the public sphere, into one which, for the first time, the very personality of the author becomes itself the subject of interest.

Lecture Seven
Maria Theresa—Mother of the Empire

Scope:

Maria Theresa (1717–1780) ruled over a complex of states and territories that had no overall name. She was archduchess of Austria above the Enns and archduchess of Austria below the Enns; queen of Bohemia, Hungary, Dalmatia, and Slavonia; and Duchess of Burgundy. The most important title, Holy Roman Empress, could not be hers, because Salic law forbade female succession; her husband, Francis Stephen, duke of Lorraine, became Emperor Francis I in her place. This fact raises the first of several gender issues for our exploration: How did it matter that Maria Theresa was a queen, not a king? Was there anything "feminine" in her success? In addition, the long reign of this remarkable queen/archduchess raises, for the first time in this course, "the Austrian problem," a set of issues that dominated European politics from 1740 to 1914. It was, after all, an Austrian crisis, the assassination of the Archduke Franz Ferdinand on June 28, 1914, that destroyed Europe in the First World War and ushered in the catastrophes of the 20th century. Maria Theresa began her reign by fighting to defend her inheritance in the War of the Austrian Succession (1740–1748) and, in a sense, the First World War marked the last War of the Austrian Succession. What was the Austrian problem, and why could Europe never solve it?

Outline

I. Part of the Austrian inheritance was the question of Austria's statehood.

    A. Maria Theresa's problem was how to be queen in her territories. The absence of a unified kingdom meant that she had different titles and powers in different places. The map of Europe in 1700 shows the different authorities.

        1. We saw in Lecture Two, in the case of the Grand Duchy of Baden, that authority in Old Regime Europe suffered from extreme fragmentation. At the local level, this was even more marked.

2. Baden's map shows that the essence of *l'ancien régime* was the minute fragmentation of authority. One small region of southwestern Germany contained dozens of semi-independent archbishoprics, bishoprics, free abbeys, free cities, principalities, duchies, margravates, landgravates, lordships, and so on.

3. This was the legacy of the feudal history of Europe. The disintegration of central authority in the Middle Ages and the splitting and dying out of ruling families produced chaos.

B. The lost world of the Old Regime had certain distinguishing features.

1. It was an age of particularism. Rights were specific, not general. Certain territories, groups, trades, guilds, orders of monks, towns, barons, and so on had certain historic rights and privileges.

2. Some common features were also important. The societies were overwhelmingly agricultural. Only Britain and Holland depended at all on commercial or trading activity.

II. The Holy Roman Empire of the German nation was the central framework of Maria Theresa's life.

A. The Holy Roman Empire was literally impossible to understand, even by its greatest experts.

B. Its structure was intricate.

1. There was an elected emperor and a kind of parliament: the Imperial Assembly, or Diet (the *Reichstag*).

2. The Imperial Assembly consisted of three councils: those of the electors, the princes, and the free cities or imperial cities.

3. The electors were called prince-electors. According to law, the Council of Electors consisted of seven members: the king of Bohemia (Maria Theresa, queen of Bohemia from 1740, was, hence, an elector); the archbishop of Mainz; the archbishop of Trier; the archbishop of Cologne (Köln); the duke of Saxony-Wittenberg (electoral Saxony); the margrave of Brandenburg (the King of Prussia after 1713); and the count palatine of the Rhine.

4. The *Reichsfreiherren* ("imperial knights"), free cities, sovereign abbeys, and prince-bishops were represented in the lowest house.

C. The Habsburg dynasty depended on the Holy Roman Empire: Its history was tied to it.

1. Albert V of Austria married the daughter of Holy Roman Emperor Sigismund, succeeded him as king of Bohemia and Hungary, and in 1438, was chosen German king as Albert II. With one exception, the head of the House of Habsburg was elected German king and Holy Roman Emperor from 1438 to 1806, when Napoleon abolished the empire.

2. The "exception," Charles VII (elector of Bavaria, a member of the Wittelsbach family, 1742–1745), occurred because Maria Theresa was a woman and was, in Charles's view, not the legitimate heir of Charles VI.

3. Hence, the essential Habsburg dilemma: Their highest title, their greatest prestige, rested in their elections as emperors. Yet the empire was a huge anachronism, an unwieldy medieval mess. It was incomprehensible, unreformable, indispensable, and in no way, a state.

4. Still, the Habsburgs depended on it for prestige and taxes. Their best soldiers were drawn from the empire. Their other crowns and kingdoms were not enough. "Austria" was not an entity on its own.

5. The essential Austrian problem from 1715 to 1914 was the same: Its rulers were doomed to be enemies of progress. They were condemned to cling to antiquated structures, but without improving those structures and increasing the control of their territories in the 18th and 19th centuries, the Habsburgs were certain to be destroyed by more "modern" states.

III. "Austria" was a family enterprise.

A. Maria Theresa inherited territories by marriage, death, and complex legal battles.

B. The problem of female succession led to the Pragmatic Sanction of 1713. It was issued by Holy Roman Emperor Charles VI to alter the law of succession of the Habsburg family. We must examine the situation step by step to grasp it.

1. In 1705, Emperor Leopold I died and was succeeded by his son Joseph as emperor.

2. In 1711, Joseph I died, leaving two unmarried daughters: Maria Josepha (1699–1757), who married (1719) the future Elector Augustus II of Saxony, king of Poland, and Maria Amalia (1701–1756), who married (1722) Charles Albert (1697–1745), elector of Bavaria.

3. Charles VI, brother of Joseph I, was elected emperor and inherited the Habsburg lands according to the succession pact of the family issued by Leopold in 1703.

4. On September 26, 1711, Charles VI made a will in which he gave his daughters precedence over those of Joseph in case of extinction of his male line (in violation of the family pact of 1703). This led to fierce precedence disputes between the archduchesses at court. A "private conference" (composed of Prince Eugene of Savoy, Count Seilern, and two privy councilors) recommended the publication of a succession law.

5. The Pragmatic Sanction of 1713 was collectively termed "the laws of the House of Austria" and passed the succession to Charles's eldest female child if there were no living males.

C. The problem was how to get the Pragmatic Sanction of 1713 accepted, first by the family, then by the Austrian lands and other European states.

1. In 1719, Maria Josepha married Augustus the Strong.

2. Because Augustus wanted to be king of Poland, he traded his wife's rights for support from Charles VI.

3. The family was dissatisfied with the arrangement, which resulted in immediate international consequences: Most states guaranteed the Pragmatic Sanction in 1732, but an important exception was that of Elector Charles Albert of Bavaria, who married the other daughter, Maria Amalia, in 1722. Bavaria was an important dukedom, and Charles Albert had ambitions to be elected Holy Roman Emperor. He succeeded in doing so but ruled only from 1742 to 1745.

4. When Maria Theresa acceded to the Habsburg throne in 1740, she had to defend her rights in a long and bitter struggle, the War of the Austrian Succession (1740–1748), in spite of all the guarantees her father had obtained.

5. The Treaty of Aix-la-Chapelle of 1748 confirmed the Pragmatic Sanction.

IV. Maria Theresa's personality was a powerful element in her success as a ruler.

A. Her early life shows that Maria Theresa was truly remarkable. She was born May 13, 1717, into the foremost royal family in Europe.

1. She had little proper education and spoke German with a broad Viennese accent, which made her extremely popular. Her nickname was *Reserl* ("little Tess") in Viennese dialect.

2. When her first male grandson was born to her son Leopold in 1768, she announced the news by rushing onto the stage at the Royal Theater, stopping the show, and exclaiming in Viennese: "Our Leopold has had a lad!"

3. Her naturalness was unusual in the stiff world of royal protocol, which in the Habsburg case, had come from the stiffest protocol in Europe, that of the Spanish court.

B. Maria Theresa's physical strength was important in her success, as well. She had no need for much sleep, bore 16 children in 19 years, and survived smallpox. Even while queen of Europe's biggest state, she attended to every detail of the children's upbringing.

C. She encouraged close advisors to tell her the truth at all times.

1. One advisor, Emanuel Count Sylva-Tarouca (1696–1771), was employed as her official critic. His job was to tell her all her mistakes.

2. Another was her former governess, Countess Maria Carolina Fuchs ("Fox" in English), whom she called *Foxy* and *Mami* ("mommy").

3. Her relationship with these advisors stands in marked contrast to those of other rulers. Think of telling Frederick the Great the truth! (See Lecture Four.)

D. Maria Theresa's marriage was another important element in her reign.

    1. Her husband, Francis Stephen, duke of Lorraine (1708–1765), was the love of her life. When she was 16 and Francis was 25, she fell in love with him, insisted on having him, and succeeded, despite political complications. The match was a passionate and successful marriage of two partners.

    2. Francis Stephen was a gifted businessman and administrator. He was given the position of grand duke of Tuscany in exchange for giving up his native Duchy of Lorraine. Cheerful, sensible, and good tempered, he settled down to govern Tuscany with his young wife. He earned a huge fortune in Italy and, after 1740, helped manage the finances of Maria Theresa's kingdoms and estates. Unfortunately, he was a dreadful soldier and field commander, and his failures in war made him unpopular with the Austrians.

    3. Yet Francis Stephen was ideal for Maria Theresa. His death in 1765 was a near fatal blow to her, from which she never fully recovered.

E. Maria Theresa practiced a ruthless form of marital politics.

    1. Though she married for love, her children were not granted any freedom at all. They were family assets to be used for diplomacy.

    2. All their marriages were arranged on purely political considerations. Her daughter Maria Carolina of Habsburg-Lorraine (1752–1814) was sent out to marry the ghastly king of Naples in 1768 when her sister Josepha died, a victim of the 1767 smallpox epidemic.

3. Maria Theresa knew how awful Carolina's life was but accepted that her daughter had become "a victim of policy." Service in Habsburg marital politics was a fact of life.

4. Another move in marital politics, which proved fatal but was an apparent triumph at the time, was to marry her youngest daughter, Marie Antoinette (1755–1793), to the future king of France, Louis XVI. As we shall see in Lecture 14, that marriage brought the young queen to the guillotine in 1793.

V. Maria Theresa was a state-builder.

   A. The preservation of the monarchy was her main concern.

     1. In 1740, she seemed to have all of Europe against her, yet she saved the monarchy against all her enemies. She won the loyalty of the Hungarian nobility: "I am only a woman but I have the heart of a king," she announced to the Magyar parliament. Her charm and sense of drama in 1741 saved the House of Habsburg.

     2. Her policies arose from a mixture of her prejudices and habits, her stubbornness and deep Catholic piety.

     3. Her greatest virtue was courage—she refused to be cowed by Frederick the Great and the sovereigns of Europe in the War of the Austrian Succession.

   B. Her other great virtue was much rarer in royalty: common sense. Maria Theresa had a kind of genius for politics. She was not theoretical, but exceptionally shrewd.

     1. Her hatred of the partition of Poland (1772) is an example. Russia and Prussia proposed to carve up Poland. Maria Theresa refused at first. Eventually, Austria took the eastern province of Galicia in order not to be left out.

     2. Frederick the Great scoffed: "She wept but she took." In fact, she allowed her foreign minister Kaunitz and her son Joseph to override her common sense.

VI. Maria Theresa's long reign, her reforms, and sensible changes in government made a great difference, but above all, her personality was the key to her impact. In 1740, the Habsburg lands were all completely separate, joined only by personal union to the queen. When she died in 1780, there was a feeling that all belonged to a single state of which Maria Theresa was the "mother." Her accent, her style, her humanity, her maternal qualities were essential elements in her success.

Essential Reading:

All the good biographies of Maria Theresa in English are out of print. For German readers, I recommend the excellent Edwin Dillman, *Maria Theresa* (Munich: Deutsche Taschenbuch Verlag, 2000).

As substitute for a biography, others might look into Charles W. Ingrao, *The Habsburg Monarchy, 1618–1815*.

Questions to Consider:

1. How did it matter that Maria Theresa was a queen, not a king?

2. What does it mean to say that a ruler has "common sense"?

Lecture Seven—Transcript
Maria Theresa—Mother of the Empire

In the last lecture, Lecture Six, we were in the smoky taverns and noisy printing houses on London's Fleet Street in the midst of its new publishing industry. In this lecture, we move for the first time to Vienna, the capital of the Habsburgs, and to the first woman in our series *European History and European Lives: 1715 to 1914*, and she is Maria Theresa, the mother of the empire.

Now, I need to set the problem. Maria, who was born in 1717, a little younger than Frederick the Great, ruled over a very complicated series of lands and territories, and it had no overall name. In each territory she had her own title. She was archduchess of Austria above the Enns and the archduchess of Austria below the Enns. She was queen of Bohemia, she was queen of Hungary, she was queen of Dalmatia, she was duchess here, countess there, and the list is very long, it runs to about 40 or 50 different titles. The most important title, the one which mattered most to the Habsburgs, she could not have, which was that of Holy Roman Emperor, because the Salic law forbade female succession.

So her husband, Francis Stephen, duke of Lorraine, became Emperor Francis I in her place. This is the first time we run into a series of gender issues: Did it matter that Maria Theresa was a queen and not a king? Was there anything "feminine" in her success? In addition, the long reign of this very remarkable queen/archduchess raises, for the first time in this course of lectures, the Austrian problem, a set of issues which dominated European politics from 1740 to 1914. It was, after all, an Austrian crisis, the assassination of Archduke Franz Ferdinand on June 28, 1914, which ushered in the catastrophe of the First World War, and which brings to an end this whole series.

It's also true, though, that in 1740, a war of Austria's succession began about Maria's own accession to the throne. You could call the First World War the last War of the Austrian Succession. It raises the whole problem of what was Austria, and why could Europe never solve the Austrian problem.

I'd like first to look at the Austrian inheritance. The basic problem was how to be a state, or to be or not to be a state. Maria Theresa's problem was how to be queen of all her territories, not simply the hereditary ruler of each one. The absence of a unified kingdom meant that she had all these different titles and powers in different places, and the map of Europe reflects this. If you look at a map in 1700, it looks like a jigsaw puzzle, and we've already seen that if you look at the map of a particular territory like Baden in the same period, it really does look like a jigsaw puzzle with lots of different colored pieces.

The Old Regime suffered from a kind of fragmentation. At the local level this was even more marked, and the essence of this Old Regime was a minute fragmentation of authority. One small region of southwestern Germany contained semi-independent archbishoprics, bishoprics, free abbeys, free cities and free knights, (and by free that meant free of any local prince—abbeys or cities or knights owed their allegiance only to the emperor, that's what it meant to be free) principalities, duchies, margravates, landgravates, lordships of different kinds, all with very overlapping boundaries and jurisdictions. This was a result, as I suggested in Lecture Two, of the disintegration of imperial authority, and the feudal history of Europe.

The disintegration of the central authority in the Middle Ages, and of course the continuous splitting and division of various dynasties, produced a kind of chaos, so even in a small territory like the Grand Duchy of Baden there were two Baden dynasties claiming the throne, Baden-Durlach, and Baden-Baden. In that territory there were lands which belonged to the Austrians, lands that belonged to the count Palatine, there were lands that belonged to Prince Fuerstenberg, and none of these were contiguous or integrated. The abbey of Sankt Blasien, or Saint Blaise, was independent, or what was it, this little abbey. Was it a property? Or a tiny state? An estate? It's simply impossible to define.

Now, this lost world which I'm calling the "Old Regime" lived in a world of particularism. Rights were specific and not general. Thus, certain territories, certain groups, certain trades, certain guilds, certain orders of monks, certain towns, certain barons, had specific and rather well-defined historic rights and privileges, but everybody's rights were different in different places.

Common features were of course important. They were all overwhelmingly agricultural societies. The whole of central and eastern Europe had very few towns by comparison to the west. Only

Britain and Holland in this period depended on commercial or trading activity.

Now we have already once looked at the Holy Roman Empire of the German nation in Lecture Two, but it's the central structure of Maria Theresa, and we're going to have to look at it again, much as I'm sure you'll regret this. I said in Lecture Two, the old empire was literally impossible to define. It cannot be comprehended, and even its greatest expert was unable in some sense to understand it, that is to say, to give it a uniform and specific definition.

The most detailed description of the Imperial constitution can be found in the books by Johann Jakob Moser, who lived from 1701 to 1785, and as we saw in Lecture Two, even he couldn't make sense of it. Because I love this quote, and it won't harm you, I'd like to read it to you again:

> We have various kinds of lands, various forms of government, with estates and without them, imperial towns, a nobility some of who are immediate [that is to say, those who can appeal directly to the emperor] subjects of all different sorts, and a thousand other such things. To think for oneself, what good is it? Not the slightest. What can the philosopher do about it? Not the slightest. These are the plain facts that I must accept as they are…unless I want to deform and ruin our German Empire.

There were something like 3,000 definable independent entities making up the Holy Roman Empire of the German nation, and that didn't include kingdoms like Hungary and the kingdom of Prussia, which were outside its boundaries. We saw in Lecture Two that there was an elected emperor and a kind of parliament, an Imperial Assembly, or *Reichstag*, or Diet, which met in Ratisbon, and this Imperial Assembly consisted of three councils, a council of the electors, that is those princes who elected the emperor and were the greatest princes of the empire; then there was a second tier of princes who were independent but not electors; and then you had all the rest, the free cities and the imperial cities and so on.

Now, the electors were called prince-electors, *Kurfürsten*, and according to the law of the empire the Council of the Electors consisted of seven members. There was first the king of Bohemia, (and in her capacity as queen of Bohemia, Maria Theresa was an elector, but could not herself be elected); there was the archbishop of Mainz; the archbishop of Trier; the archbishop of Cologne; the three great prince-archbishops: the duke of Saxony-Wittenberg, who we've already met in his capacity as the duke of Electoral Saxony, that's Augustus in Lecture Two; the margrave of Brandenburg, who after 1713 is the king of Prussia, we met him in Lecture Four, that was Frederick the Great; and we have the count palatine of the Rhine. Now, beneath them was a whole bunch of imperial knights, free cities, sovereign abbeys, prince-bishops who were not represented or were represented in the lower house.

Now the dilemma was this, the Habsburg dynasty depended for its prestige and its highest title on the existence of the Holy Roman Empire and its history was tied to it. Albert V of Austria had married the daughter of Holy Roman Emperor Sigismund in the Middle Ages, and succeeded him as king of Bohemia and Hungary, and was chosen in 1438 German king as Albert II.

Henceforth, with one exception which happens in our period, the head of the House of Habsburg was always elected German king and Holy Roman Emperor, from 1438 to 1806, when Napoleon abolished the empire.

Now, the exception was Charles VII, the elector of Bavaria, a member of the Wittelsbach family who was emperor from 1742 to 1745. He was Maria Theresa's cousin's husband, and that occurred because, he thought, since Maria Theresa was a woman and therefore, in any case, in his view, she was not the legitimate heir of Charles VI; we're going to come to that thicket in a minute.

Now, the essential Habsburg dilemma was this (they were involved with this *Reichsfreiherren*): Their highest title, their greatest prestige, rested on their election as emperors, yet the empire was a gigantic anachronism, an unwieldy medieval mess. It was incomprehensible, unreformable, indispensable to them, but in no way could it be called a state. Yet the Habsburgs depended on it both for prestige and taxes. They got their best soldiers from many of their territories in the Reich, and so on.

All the other crowns and kingdoms, even the title of king of Hungary, or king of Bohemia was not enough, and Austria didn't exist; it was just a general title to cover a whole lot of territories, none of which were unified. Here they are, the rulers of this medieval mess, and the essential Habsburg problem from 1715 to 1914 was thus revealed. Because of their dependence on this antique, they were in some ways doomed to be enemies of progress. They couldn't allow too much change. They were condemned to cling to antiquated structures.

On the other hand, without improving their control over this realm in the 18th and 19th centuries, making it more modern, getting better taxes out of it, making it more uniform, they would not survive as a dynasty. They were always in this position that the reform of this antiquated structure would undermine their own authority, however.

Now, in Lecture 11 when we come to Maria Theresa's son, Joseph II, we'll see what happened when somebody really tried to turn this great medieval mess into a modern state and what the consequences were. The dilemma was real, though, and was never entirely soluble, and that's why, in a sense, they went to war in 1914, because they wanted to show that these congeries of 11 nationalities spreading over the map of Europe, organized in this fairly chaotic way still had the strength to be a great power. The issue we're talking about today really is the issue which brings about the first catastrophe of Europe in the First World War.

Now, royal families were of course also families, and Austria was a family enterprise. There was a famous description which went like this: *Bella gerant alii, tu felix Austria, nube*; "Let others wage war. You, happy Austria, marry." This meant that Maria Theresa inherited territories by marriage, by death and by complex legal provisions in princely wills.

Now, she was a woman, and that raised a whole series of complicated problems. The most important of these was: Could a woman succeed to the titles? The Pragmatic Sanction of 1713 was issued by the Holy Roman Emperor Charles, to alter the law of the succession of the Habsburg family.

Now, this is really complicated, but we need to go through it step by step. Let me see if I can take you all the way through it. First, in 1705, the Emperor Leopold I died, and was succeeded by his elder son Joseph as emperor. Joseph had only ruled for six years when he died in 1711, leaving two unmarried daughters: Maria Josepha, who married, in 1719, the future Emperor Augustus, the future Elector Augustus of Saxony, we met him in Lecture Two, later king of

Poland. There was also the younger daughter Maria Amalia, who would marry in 1722 Charles Albert, the elector of Bavaria. We've just met him, because he later on became Charles VII, Holy Roman Emperor. I hope you're still with me.

Now, these marriages are themselves indicative. The Habsburgs could only marry at the top level of society; they could only marry ruling princes of big states, they couldn't descend to marry small-timers, so they married electoral princes. Charles VI, the younger brother of Joseph I, was elected emperor and inherited the Habsburg lands according to the succession pact of the family, issued by Leopold in 1703.

The problem was that he had daughters also, so on the 26th of September 1711, Charles VI made a will in which he gave his daughters precedence over those of Joseph, in the case of extinction of his male line. In other words, his daughters would take precedence over his older brother's daughters who, in fact, ought to have had precedence if he didn't have a male heir. Now this was a violation of the family pact of 1703.

Now, those of you who live in families, and we all do, will know it doesn't take the succession to a great state to cause big family rows. I mean, there are no more bitter rows in my experience than those which arise in a family business, and here we have a row in a family business. The cousins were furious with each other, and it got so bad that a private conference was called of leaders of the state, the chair of which was Prince Eugene of Savoy, and it's a bit like making Norman Schwarzkopf the chair of some committee, some, you know, general who's above the battle to try and sort this thing out.

They recommended very courageously that the emperor issue a new succession law because they couldn't solve the problem. Thus, in 1713, the Pragmatic Sanction was issued, which was collectively termed "the laws of the House of Austria," and it formally passed the succession to Charles's eldest female child if there were no living males.

Now, this was controversial, and it was by no means clear that it would be accepted, because the problem was that yes, Charles could issue these laws, but what if foreigners did not accept it? First in the family, and then by the Austrian lands, and then by the other states.

Now, in 1719 the eldest daughter, Maria Josepha married Augustus the Strong, our friend from Lecture Two. Since Augustus wanted to be king of Poland, he was perfectly happy to trade away her rights which he then did, so we've now got rid of the eldest of the cousins. The younger cousin, though, had married the ambitious Charles, elector of Bavaria, and the rest of the family was exceedingly dissatisfied with this arrangement. That caused a variety of international consequences, because these family politics are the politics of great powers. It's as if you could imagine the United States with its president married to the sister of Vladimir Putin when it really matters.

Thus, most of the powers, and Charles, put on tremendous diplomatic efforts to try to get them to accept it. Most of the powers had guaranteed the Pragmatic Sanction in 1732, but an important exception was that of the Elector Charles Albert of Bavaria, who had married the younger daughter of Joseph I, and he said "Nothing doing, I won't accept this."

Now, Bavaria was a very important dukedom, and Charles Albert had ambitions to be a king the way Augustus the Strong did, but with a little luck he could be more than a king. He could become emperor; he said "no" to being king, and the other person who had eyes on this, and we shall see in 1740, was the king of Prussia, the new king of Prussia, Frederick the Great, because he saw an opportunity to gain land; he wasn't the least interested in the legalities of this. The great powers, France, Britain and Russia were not uninterested in the possibility of a division in the family between Charles Albert and the heirs of Charles VI because that would weaken the Habsburgs who were the most powerful royal family in Europe. The result was that when Maria Theresa did indeed accede to the Habsburg throne under the terms of the Pragmatic Sanction, in 1740, she immediately had to defend her right in a long and bitter struggle known as the War of the Austrian Succession.

It began in December 1740 with a completely unannounced and entirely unjustified attack, although Frederick the Great found some scrap of paper to justify it, on Silesia, which Frederick very frankly and very cynically called "my new Peru." That is to say that it was full of riches, and he wanted it and he took it and kept it. Thus, in spite of the guarantees that her father had obtained, Maria was plunged into war from the beginning. The settlement which he hated left Frederick the Great in control of Silesia, which he never got back, but at least the powers now confirmed the Pragmatic Sanction, and her position was safe, at least in law.

That's how Maria Theresa became queen and head of the Habsburg Empire. Now I want to turn to her personality. This personality played a great part in her achievements. She was a truly remarkable human being. She was born on May 13, 1717, into the most important royal family in Europe. She had very little proper education, and all her life she spoke German with a broad Viennese accent, which in the end made her extremely popular. It's a bit like imagining Queen Elizabeth of England speaking with a cockney accent. The locals had a name for her, she was called *Reserl* "Little Tess" in the Viennese dialect. When her first male grandson was born to her son Leopold in 1768 and she heard the news, she rushed onto the stage at the Royal Theater, stopped the show and said in broadest Viennese, "Our Leopold has had a lad." The people loved her for this.

Her naturalness was very, very unusual in the stiff world of royal protocol, which in the Habsburg case had come from the Spanish court, which had the stiffest protocol in Europe. Her physical frame played an important part. Maria Theresa had an amazing physical strength, and she had a lot of need for it. She never needed much sleep. She bore 16 children in 19 years and survived the smallpox. And even while queen of Europe's biggest state (it was bigger then than Russia), she attended to every detail of the children's upbringing. Here's an account of her daily regime: 8 a.m., rise, dress, breakfast and Holy Mass (one hour); 9:00 a.m. what I've called "quality time with the kids;" 9:30 business of absolute rule, seeing ministers, signing decrees, receiving official visitors; 12:00 short nap; 12:15 lunch; 1:30 coffee, children, family visits; 4:00 business of government; 8:30 leisure pursuits; midnight, bed.

Her court was very unusual. One advisor, Emanuel Count Sylva-Tarouca was employed as her official critic. It's a great idea, I wish we had it in the White House, his job was to tell her all her mistakes, a great idea. Another was her governess, Countess Maria Carolina Fuchs, which is "Fox" in English, whom she called "her Foxy," and also her "mommy," or "Mother," and was a close advisor. Foxy is the only non-royal person buried in the Habsburg crypt.

The love of her life was her husband. Her husband was Francis Stephen, duke of Lorraine, who was born in 1708 and died in 1765, and this was a true marriage of love. She met him when she was 16 and he was 23, she fell instantly in love. Now, Lorraine, was not a big shot duchy, it wasn't like Bavaria, it wasn't like Saxony, it wasn't like any of the great states in the empire, so he wasn't actually a big enough prince for her, but Maria Theresa insisted on having him, and succeeded. Though there were very strong political complications, in this as in other things she showed a very strong and stubborn will as a girl. Sir Thomas Robison, the British ambassador wrote, and I quote, "She's a princess of the highest spirit. Her father's losses are her own, she reasons already, and is of a temper formed for rule and ambition."

This match was a passionate and successful marriage of two real partners. They were married in 1736. He was aged 26, and she was 18. Francis Stephen was a tremendously gifted businessman and administrator, and in exchange for surrendering Lorraine he was given Tuscany, which I must say is a very good deal; Florence, Arezzo, all those wonderful places where people now go for holidays. He was a wonderful ruler of Tuscany. He was cheerful, he was sensible and he was good-tempered, and he settled down to govern Tuscany with his young wife, and while doing so he earned a huge fortune in Italy; after 1740 he helped Maria manage the finances of her kingdoms and estates.

When Francis Stephen died in 1765, his estate amounted to 20 million gulden. For comparison, the whole revenues in 1736 of the whole state of Hapsburg were only 40 million. Unfortunately, he was a dreadful and very unsuccessful field commander, and in those days that was bad, so he was unpopular with the Viennese crowd because he was French.

Yet, Francis Stephen was ideal for her. He was a sort of royal Dennis Thatcher, content to be number two, and his death in 1765 was a near fatal blow; she never recovered from it. Though she married for love, her children were not granted any freedom at all; children were simply family assets to be used for diplomacy, and all their marriages were arranged on purely political considerations.

Her daughter Maria Carolina, born in 1752, was sent out to marry the truly awful king of Naples in 1768 when her sister Josepha died, a victim of the 1767 smallpox epidemic. When she got to Naples as the wife of Ferdinand IV, king of Naples and the two Sicilys she had a truly awful time. She wrote, "He's very ugly, but one gets used to that. His character is better than people said, but life here is a real martyrdom, all the worse because one has to show a contented face to the world. I would rather die than go through again what I have had to endure."

Now, Maria Theresa knew perfectly well how awful Caroline's life was, but she accepted that her daughter had become what she called a "victim of policy." Service and Habsburg marital politics was simply the way things were. The old Maria Theresa brooked no opposition in this kind of thing; she was absolutely in charge.

Now, let's think for a minute about Maria Theresa as empress and state builder, "empress" I'm using loosely, because she never was actually empress. Preservation of the monarchy was her number one objective, and she achieved that when she had all Europe against her. She saved the monarchy against her enemies because she won the loyalty of the Hungarian nobility. In a famous scene, carrying a baby in her arms, she went before them and said, "I am only a woman but I have the heart of a king." The Magyar parliament rose as one and supported her. Her charm and sense of drama in 1741 actually saved the House of Habsburg.

Her policies were a mixture of prejudices and habits, her stubbornness and her deep Catholic piety. Her greatest virtues were courage, in that she refused to be cowed by Frederick the Great and the sovereigns of Europe in the War of the Austrian Succession, or later on in the Seven Years' War, and again Austria was a principle actor. She declared, "Never, never, never, will the queen renounce an inch of hereditary land, though she perish with all that remains to her."

Her other virtue is much, much rarer in royalty, and I fear it's much rarer in leadership and politics in general. She had really great common sense. Maria Theresa had a kind of genius for politics which was not theoretical but exceptionally shrewd. Let me give you an example, the kingdom of Poland, which we've already looked at in Lecture Two, was a vast, sprawling, chaotic territory, a buffer state, which ran from the Baltic down to the Black Sea. As Russia, Prussia, and Austria grew stronger, they covered his eyes on this enormous territory, and gradually it came to the moment when it was clear that Poland would have to be cut up. There were three partitions of Poland between Prussia, Russia and Austria, and 1772 was the first.

Russia and Prussia proposed to carve up Poland. Maria Theresa refused at first, but eventually Austria took the eastern province of Galicia in order not to be left out, and Frederick the Great made this famous remark, "She wept but she took." In fact, this was not her idea. She allowed her foreign minister Kaunitz and her son Joseph to override her common sense. She wrote against the partition, I'd like to read this to you because I think it's a very interesting example of what I mean by shrewdness and common sense.

> I do not understand the policy which, when two use their superior strength to oppress an innocent victim, allows and enjoins a third to imitate them and commit the same injustice, as a simple precaution for the future, and not a present expediency: this seems to me untenable. A Prince has no more rights than other mortals; the greatness and support of his State will not avail him when the day comes when we must all give account of our actions.

In other words, her view was, "It's wrong; one shouldn't do it." Now her very long reign, 40 years, her reforms and sensible changes in government made a really great difference to the history of the Habsburgs, and it was the key to her impact. In 1740, as I said at the beginning of this lecture, her lands were disparate, she had different titles and different rights, and any one of 25 or 30 different territories. When she died in 1780, there was a feeling that everybody belonged to a single state of which Maria Theresa was the "mother." She was known in the army as *Mater Castorum*, the mother of the camps, because she attracted somehow this kind of personal loyalty from her soldiers and from the population at large. Her accent, her relaxed style, her humanity, her maternal qualities were essential elements in her success.

I want to pause to just to reflect on this. Here too, I think what we're looking at is the transformation of Old Regime Europe into something else. Of course, Maria Theresa was an absolutist, of course she exercised exactly the same kind of absolute and despotic powers that Frederick the Great did, but she was doing that across a range of peoples and languages and cultures which made it very important that her personality come through to them. The proud and independent Magyar nobility, very jealous of their rights, obeyed her, the great Bohemian and Moravian nobles obeyed her, the Polish counts in Galicia obeyed her.

In other words, what she was actually doing was something, I think, fundamentally modern, she was beginning to appeal through her personal charisma to a multinational, although of course in 1780 it wouldn't have been called that yet, a multinational empire composed of 11 different nationalities, 12 if you include the Jews of the empire as well. The way she did it was through her own personality, and I think this is also a milestone on the road to modernity.

She was a courageous woman and her last words on November 29, 1780 were to her son Joseph. Her illness had been going on for a long time, and the royal family had gathered at the bedside, much concerned about the condition of the elderly empress. Toward the end she was herself very fat and was breathing very heavily, and he was very worried; she had seemed to twist herself into an uncomfortable shape, and he said, "Your Majesty is lying uncomfortably," and Maria Theresa replied, "Yes, but well enough to die," and she closed her eyes and she died. I think those last words are very characteristic of this very great lady who was the queen empress of a large empire.

Lecture Eight
David Hume—The Cheerful Skeptic

Scope:

Anthony Quinton begins his book by calling David Hume (1711–1776) "the greatest of British philosophers: the most profound, penetrating and comprehensive" (*The Great Philosophers*, 1999), and the famous philosopher and mathematician Bertrand Russell reserved a particularly painful chamber in hell for philosophers who tried to refute Hume. It may seem odd to follow an empress and queen who ruled over millions with a retiring Scots gentleman who wrote books, but the publication in 1739 of *A Treatise of Human Nature: Being an Attempt to introduce the experimental Method of Reasoning in Moral Subjects* can justly be compared to Frederick the Great's attack on Silesia in 1740. Both the act of naked aggression, scarcely justified by even the flimsiest legal claim, and Hume's application of the experimental method to ideas broke the continuity of human affairs, the one in international relations and the other in the way we think about ourselves. Frederick broke the rules of diplomacy, but Hume demolished the existing rules of thought.

Outline

I. Hume's ambition was to be "the Newton of philosophy."

    A. He was a successful essayist and historian, but his greatest work, *A Treatise of Human Nature* (1739), was not appreciated or understood.

        1. Hume's wry comment in his autobiography has become famous: "Never literary attempt was more unfortunate than my *Treatise of Human Nature*. It fell dead-born from the press, without reaching such distinction as even to excite a murmur among the zealots."

        2. The 19th century was out of sympathy with 18th-century values. The Enlightenment was viewed as a movement of "shallow and pretentious intellectualism."

        3. Hume was known in his time and in the 19th century more as a skeptic and debunker of religion than a great technical philosopher. "The Essay upon Miracles" made him notorious.

B. In the 20th century, Hume came to be widely regarded as the greatest philosopher of knowledge and the godfather of the analytic school of philosophy.

II. To begin, we must set the general context and note the peculiar character of the Enlightenment in Britain.

A. The Enlightenment involved both ideas and a set of people who propagated them; it differed in different countries (see Lecture Five).

1. The core of the Enlightenment is found in Immanuel Kant's famous essay: "What Is Enlightenment?" (1784): "Have courage to use your own understanding."

2. All enlightened thinkers shared certain underlying assumptions:

a. Human beings are naturally good.

b. There exists in each of us an innate *natural reason*.

c. Progress is inevitable, because it is a function of enlightened thinking.

d. Human nature is fundamentally uniform.

B. The British version of the Enlightenment was a product of its history.

1. The English Civil War (1640–1660) was a religious war; its protagonists were the representatives of three types of religion:

a. Religion is sacramental (Roman Catholic or Anglican): The priest, church, sacraments, and liturgy are necessary for salvation because the church is God's manifestation on earth.

b. Religion is Bible-based: In the Congregationalist, Baptist, and other biblically directed churches, individual conscience and Bible study allow direct access between the worshipper and God.

c. Religion is personal conversion: These were the various millenarian and sectarian movements, including the churches of the Holy Spirit, where frequently, neither pastor nor parishioner exists as a separate function. Some operate either without or beyond the Bible. Personal conversion is the test, but in the quietist sects, as in Quakerism, only the movement of the Spirit can be discerned.

2. Thomas Hobbes (1588–1679) was the philosopher of the English Civil War. Hobbes saw the religious wars as chaotic and dangerous to orderly rule. His *Leviathan* (1651) is a reflection of the chaos of civil war. It rested on three principles:

   a. A mechanistic view that life is simply the motions of the organism and that man is, by nature, a selfishly individualistic animal at constant war with all other men. In a state of nature, men are equal in their self-seeking and live out lives that are "nasty, brutish, and short."

   b. Fear of violent death is the principal motive that causes men to create a state by contracting to surrender their natural rights and to submit to the absolute authority of a sovereign.

   c. The sovereign's power is absolute and not subject to the law. Temporal power is always superior to ecclesiastical power.

3. Hobbes's philosophy was gloomy and authoritarian, but it was the first mechanical and realistic philosophy. Like Hume, Hobbes wanted to found a scientific study of man.

C. The period from 1660 to 1713 in England was one of instability. The failure of the restored Stuart dynasty to reestablish itself after 1660, partly because of its Catholic leanings, produced unrest and anxiety. The year 1688 and the Glorious Revolution put a liberal Protestant prince, William of Orange, on the throne, and after 1713, the Hanoverians, a German collateral line, became kings of England.

   1. The establishment of George I marked a further stage in the progress of parliamentary power and a victory for the Protestant parties. Religion in the new Hanoverian settlement was now divided in two camps:

      a. The deists believed that God and nature were essentially the same. They rejected revelation and the supernatural doctrines of Christianity in the name of *natural religion*.

      b. The religion of traditional Christianity rested on the Bible as a source but also on the Anglican Church as a "Catholic and Apostolic Church." The Church of England was established as the official religion of England but not in Hume's Scotland, where the Scottish kirk rested on Presbyterian principles.

2. In Scotland, religion was divided between the *moderates* and the *evangelicals*. The Act of Union of 1707 united Scotland and England and threatened to reintroduce bishops to Scotland. The Scottish kirk divided into strict Calvinists, who rejected all compromise, and moderates, who were prepared to live with elements of Anglicanism in Scotland. Hume's life and career took place under the ascendancy of the moderates.

D. Science, often called *natural philosophy*, had great prestige.

1. The effect of Dutch improvements in microscopes, lenses, and telescopes; the experiments of Robert Boyle (1627–1691); and the theories and experiments of Isaac Newton (1642–1727) created a new relationship between man and nature.

2. Science bequeathed an important legacy to philosophy: There was now the possibility that scientific, moral, and religious reasoning could be compatible. If the universe was a logical structure and there was a rational God, why could there not be a science of morals or of human understanding?

3. Bishop Joseph Butler (1692–1752) was an example of that attempt. Butler's sermons and his *The Analogy of Religion* (1726) were attempts to avoid "inquiring into abstract relations of things" but instead to begin "from a matter of fact, namely, what the particular nature of man is…"

E. Hume was impressed by Butler's work. In the introduction to *A Treatise of Human Nature*, Hume speaks of "some late philosophers in England, who have begun to put the science of man on a new footing, and have engaged the attention and excited the curiosity of the public."

F. Both the Old and New Testaments use miracles as testimony to God's power, which presented a problem for the new scientific philosophy.

1. Can a belief in miracles be compatible with a rational, law-based universe? In particular, revealed religion exhibited a degree of dependence on the miraculous in Christ's life.

2. The dilemma for Butler was resolved by his understanding of God as the human conscience—as Leslie Stephen wrote in his *English Thought in the Eighteenth Century*, "that great standing miracle—the oracle implanted in every man's breast."

3. Hume's place in these debates was to cut the ground from under them by making it impossible to know things in themselves and to introduce a wide-ranging skepticism about the truth of anything. It was a revolution in thought.

III. Hume was the son of Scottish gentry, an exceptionally studious and scholarly boy but unfit for law or business.

A. His great inspiration apparently came to him as early as 1729: to apply Newton to philosophy. He was only 18 when he got the idea and just 28 when he published his masterpiece.

1. He began feverish, furious work for four years but had a nervous collapse in 1733. He took a break from philosophy for a short period in business, which was unsatisfactory.

2. Because his modest family income went further on the Continent, Hume lived in France from 1734 to 1737, where he settled down to write his great work. He was always certain that he was producing "a total alteration of philosophy."

B. The prose of *A Treatise* is beautiful and clear and not by chance. Hume was always preoccupied with his written style.

C. Hume's revolutionary idea was that it was impossible to know more than the mental sensations in our heads. The "thing in itself" cannot be known, only the impression it makes on the brain. The category *existence* is, thus, impossible to separate from the idea of the thing. We believe in causation only as a result of *custom*, that is, because we have seen a certain chain of events happen. Hume's example is of billiard balls striking each other.

D. Hume shows that we cannot know causation as such, only the experience that the billiard balls have behaved this way in the past and we saw them do so. The following passage in the *Treatise* was so important that Hume put it in italics: *"There is nothing in any object consider'd in itself, which can afford us a reason for drawing any conclusion beyond it and that even after the frequent or constant conjunction of objects, we have no reason to draw any inference concerning any object beyond those of which we have had experience."*

E. One consequence of Hume's philosophy was that it argued for radical skepticism.

    1. We know nothing for certain. Human beings know only their mental processes and, therefore, we have no assurance that reason and thought are necessarily connected to reality.

    2. Hence, all essences or substances cannot be certainly said to exist. All we have to offer in their support are simply impressions of the mind, in other words, ideas in our heads. We cannot even prove that our selves exist, and the idea that there is a God must be completely unproven and impossible to verify in any way.

    3. Hume came as close to total skepticism as any philosopher ever has. He goes out of his way to show that he has exceeded the ancient Greek skeptics. Hume's case is impossible to refute. Mind and matter are apparently radically separated.

F. Hume's responses to his philosophy are much like the man himself.

    1. Hume was disappointed by the public's failure to understand his masterpiece. He later wrote more philosophy but decided to seek fame (and money) as a writer of essays and his *History of England.*

2. Hume was a person of extraordinary good cheer and was unusual in drawing no personal consequences from his philosophy. He believed that philosophers should know the limits of philosophy.

IV. At the age of 28, David Hume had completed one of the most important books ever written and set new limits to philosophy, even his own. He went on to write in grand fashion on economics, history, and religion. Although he never married, he was a cheerful, kindly, and good friend, without malice or rancor. His contemporaries regarded him as a kind of secular saint, and his French colleagues called him *le bon David.*

Essential Reading:

Anthony Quinton, *Hume: The Great Philosophers*, Great Philosophers Series.

Supplementary Reading:

David Fate Norton, ed., *The Cambridge Companion to Hume.*

Questions to Consider:

1. How can radical skepticism be combined with religious faith?
2. Is it reasonable to compare *A Treatise of Human Nature*, published in 1739 and 1740, with Frederick the Great's invasion of Silesia in 1740?

Lecture Eight—Transcript
David Hume—The Cheerful Skeptic

In the last lecture, we looked at the life of Europe's greatest queen, Maria Theresa, and now we move to the quiet study of the Scottish philosopher David Hume. The British philosopher Anthony Quinton begins his book on Hume by calling him "the greatest of British philosophers, the most profound, penetrating, and comprehensive," and the famous philosopher and mathematician Bertram Russell reserved a particularly painful chamber in hell for philosophers who tried to refute Hume. I quote: "Those philosophers, though in hell, have not learned wisdom." It may seem odd in this series of lives to follow an empress and queen who ruled over millions with a retiring Scottish gentleman who wrote books, but the publication in 1739 of *A Treatise of Human Nature*, being an attempt to introduce the experimental method of reasoning in moral subjects, can justly be compared to Frederick the Great's attack on Silesia in 1740. Both the act of naked aggression, scarcely justified by even the flimsiest of claims, and Hume's application of the experimental method to ideas broke the continuity of human affairs, the one in international relations and the other in the way we think about ourselves. Frederick the Great broke the rules of diplomacy, but Hume demolished all the existing rules of thought.

Now we're at about why Hume is so important. His ambition was, as he said, to be the Isaac Newton of philosophy, and he actually achieved that. In his lifetime, he had great success as an essayist, as an historian, but his greatest work of 1739, the *Treatise of Human Nature*, was not appreciated nor really understood, and in his autobiography Hume describes what happened to it: "Never a literary attempt was more unfortunate than my *Treatise of Human Nature*. It fell dead-born from the press without reaching such distinction as even to excite a murmur among zealots."

Hume had tried to annoy the Christians, and they hadn't even noticed it. The 19th century was absolutely out of sympathy with 18th-century values, and there's a famous, or infamous, definition of the Enlightenment in the *Oxford English Dictionary* from 1865, which sums it up. Under the heading "Enlightenment," it reads, "Sometimes used to designate the spirit names of the French philosophers of the 18th century, or of others whom it is intended to associate with them in the implied charge of shallow and pretentious intellectualism, unreasonable contempt for tradition and authority." So much for the dispassionate *Oxford English Dictionary*.

Now, Hume was known in his time, in the 19th century, more as a skeptic and a debunker of religion than as a great technical philosopher. "The Essay Upon Miracles" made him notorious. As Leslie Stephen wrote in 1876, his popular reputation indeed is almost exclusively based upon it. All else that he wrote is ignored.

Now, interestingly, in the 20th century, Hume has had a tremendous revival. He's now widely regarded as the greatest philosopher of knowledge, and the godfather of the analytic school of philosophy. Even John Maynard Keynes and Piero Sraffa, two of the leading economists of the 20th century, took time to write a commentary on one of his works. I looked it up in the University of Pennsylvania library catalog, which shows that there are 41 books on Hume's philosophy listed as having been published since 1990 alone, and in various languages. There really is, today, a Hume industry, and I'm giving a seminar on historiography in which the students automatically start with Hume and his theory of history. We're dealing with a philosopher who's had a very long shelf life.

Now, I want to begin by setting the general context for this particular life and have a look at the peculiar character of Enlightenment in Britain. Now, as we saw in the lecture on Rousseau, the Enlightenment is very hard to define. It involved both ideas and a set of people who propagated them although they differed from country to country. The core of the Enlightenment is in Immanuel Kant's famous essay, "What is Enlightenment?" which I have quoted before, but it's always worth reading again:

> Enlightenment is man's emergence from his self-incurred immaturity. Immaturity is the inability to use one's own understanding without the guidance of another. This immaturity is self-incurred if its cause is not lack of understanding, but lack of resolution and courage to use it without the guidance of another. The motto of the Enlightenment is therefore: *Sapere aude!* Have the courage to use your own understanding.

Now, to sum up some of the things that we've looked at in terms of the Enlightenment, the underlying assumptions which I think all enlightenment thinkers shared, is: 1) that human beings are naturally good; 2) that there exists in each of us a God-given or innate natural reason; 3) that progress is inevitable because it's a function of enlightened thinking; and 4) that human nature is fundamentally uniform and was more or less historically always the same, which is one of the reasons why we can't understand it.

Now, there is a British version of Enlightenment, which is a product of its own special history, and here we have to go back to the 17th century to the English Civil War from 1640 to 1660, which was a religious war, and its protagonists were the representatives of three types of religious faith. The first is sacramental religion.

Religion is sacramental in the Roman Catholic or Anglican churches; that is to say the priest, the church, the sacraments, the liturgy are necessary for salvation because the church is God's manifestation on earth. The church is the mystic body of Christ incarnate, as set forth in Paul, in some various passages, and more especially in Ephesians 4:4-13; the sacraments are effective because they function as part of that mystical body.

The second group of religious faiths were those based on the Bible: Congregationalists, Baptists, and other biblically-directed churches, where individual conscience and Bible study allow the individual direct access to God. There is a direct access between worshipper and God.

The third are those religions which involve personal conversion. They were and, of course, still are various millenarian and sectarian movements and other churches which are churches of the Holy Spirit, where frequently neither pastor nor parishioner exists as separate functions. Some operate either without or beyond the Bible. Personal conversion is the test, but in the quietest sects, such as in Quakerism, only the movement of the spirit can be discerned.

Now, in the English Civil War, all this came out. All these groups were present across the range of the political spectrum, religious spectrum. Thomas Hobbes, who lived from 1588 to 1679, a very long life, was the philosopher of the Civil War. Hobbes saw the religious wars as chaotic and dangerous to orderly rule and thus, in his *Leviathan* of 1651, he reflects on the chaos of civil war. It rested, this book, on three basic principles. Firstly, there is a mechanistic view that life is simply the motions of organisms and that man is by nature a selfish, individualistic animal at constant war with all other men. They are the kind of lessons you would get from a civil war. Men live in a state of nature, and when they do, they are equal and self-seeking and live out their lives which are, in a famous phrase, nasty, brutish, and short.

Secondly, fear of violent death is the principle motive which causes men to create this state, by contracting to surrender their natural rights and to submit to the absolute authority of a sovereign. In other words, it's better to live under a dictator and not get killed than to go through the civil war again.

Thirdly, the sovereign's power is absolute and not subject to the law. Temporal power is also always superior to ecclesiastical power.

Now, Hobbes's philosophy was very gloomy and authoritarian, but it was the first mechanical and realistic philosophy. Like Hume, Hobbes wanted to found a scientific study of man. The civil war was followed by a complicated period in English history between 1660 and 1713. The Stuarts were restored, the Stuarts fell from power in 1688, the so-called Glorious Revolution, and a new dynasty came in, and in the 18th century, of course, you get the Hanovarians.

Now, the failure of the restored Stuart dynasty, partly because of its Catholic leanings, to reestablish itself after 1660 produced a lot of unrest and anxiety, and in 1688, when a Protestant liberal prince, William of Orange, came to the English throne and again after 1713, when the Hanovarians, a German dynasty, collateral line, became kings of England, all of these things were very unsettling. Hume lived in the Hanovarian period. The establishment of the reign of George I marked a further stage in the progress of parliamentary power and a victory for the Protestant parties.

Religion in the new Hanovarian settlement was now divided into two great camps. There were, first, deists who believed that God and nature were essentially the same. They rejected revelation and all supernatural doctrines of Christianity in the name of natural religion. Leslie Stephen, writing his great *History of English Thought*, defined deism in the following way. I quote: "The deist postulates a God whose attributes are discernible by reason and whose law is the embodiment of reason." In other words, the universe is fundamentally reasonable, and God and reason are more or less the same.

On the other side were the advocates of revealed religion, the religion of traditional Christianity, which rested on the Bible as a source, but also on the Anglican Church as the "Catholic and Apostolic Church." The Church of England was established as the official religion of England, but not in Hume's Scotland where the Scottish kirk rested on Presbyterian principles. Now, in Scotland, there had been a tremendous battle after the Act of Union of 1707, when Scotland and England became a fused kingdom. There was the threat that bishops would be reintroduced to Scotland, something the traditional Presbyterians regarded as the end of the world, and the Scottish church divided into strict Calvanists, who rejected all compromise in anything to do with bishops, and moderates, who were prepared to live with certain elements of Anglicanism which came in with the Act of Union.

Now, Hume's life and career took place under the ascendancy of the moderates, and that's important, because the moderates were less doctrinaire, less authoritarian, and more prone to listen to a wider spectrum of ideas. So that's one bit of context, the religious bit. The other bit, I think, is the prestige of science, which was then called "natural philosophy."

Now, at the end of the 17th century, there had been enormous improvements in the technology of science, in microscopes, in lens grinding, in telescopes, and this had produced a whole series of really major breakthroughs in the history of modern science. There were the experiments of Robert Boyle and the theories and experiments of the great Sir Isaac Newton.

Both of these created new relationships between man and nature. Sir Robert Boyle invented the vacuum pump, and he used it in the discovery in 1662 of what is now known as Boyle's Law. Newton discovered the law of universal gravitation, developed calculus, and discovered that white light is composed of all the colors of the spectrum, and Newton's prestige is impossible to reduce. It was tremendous and is still tremendous. Science bequeathed an important legacy to philosophy. At the close of his *Treatise on Optics*, Newton wrote: "If natural philosophy in all its parts, by pursuing this method, shall at length be perfected, the bounds of moral philosophy will also be enlarged."

Let me translate that into our terms: If science goes on being perfected in the way that it has been, why shouldn't human affairs also be perfected in the same way and by using the same principles?

There was therefore, now the possibility that scientific, moral, and religious reasoning could actually be compatible, so to speak. One experimental method could be used across the whole range of human activities as well as across the range of the natural world. If the universe was a logical structure, and Newton believed that it was, and if there was a rational God, and Newton believed that also, why could there not be a science of morals or a science of human understanding?

Attempts were made in the first half of the 18th century to do just that. Bishop Joseph Butler, who was born in 1692 and died in 1752, was an example of that attempt. Butler published some famous sermons, six famous sermons, in a book called *The Analogy of Religion* in 1726, and in it he attempted to avoid "inquiring into abstract relations of things," but instead to begin "from a matter of fact, namely what the particular nature of man is, its several parts, their economy or constitution." Here we see an Anglican bishop attempting basically to construct a science of human nature. If you could construct a science of human nature, you could then understand what people were like. Now, this peculiar religious period between 1713 and 1763 is very hard to recover because none of these kinds of issues are really real to us anymore. The science of human nature has been long since abandoned, the prestige of a certain kind of view like this is just gone, deism doesn't exist anymore, so we need a bit of imagination. The issues seem musty, and they're kind of hard to recover, but the experiment is the background to understanding Hume.

Hume was very impressed with Bishop Butler's work, and in the introduction to *A Treatise of Human Nature*, Hume doesn't name him, but it's perfectly clear whom he's talking of when he says, "some late philosophers in England, who have begun to put the science of man on a new footing, and have engaged the attention and excited the curiosity of the public." That's clearly a reference to the work of Bishop Butler in the 1720s to construct a science of man.

Now, for this period, the key issue was the problem of miracles. Both Old and New Testament record miracles and see miracles as testimony to God's power, but can a belief in miracles be compatible with a rational, law-based universe? A miracle is, by definition, something which breaks the laws of the universe. In particular, what was the relationship of belief in either Jewish or Christian accounts of God's relationship with man, which rested on miracles? Did the Red Sea split? Were people raised from the dead? Indeed, was Christ raised from the dead? If you denied that, could you still be a Christian? What was the relation in effect between miraculous testimony and the law-based universe in which increasingly, in the 18th century, people were beginning to believe?

Now, Butler solved this problem by using the concept of conscience. As Leslie Stephen wrote in his *English Thoughts in the Eighteenth Century*: "The God whom Butler worships is in fact the human conscience deified. The evidence of his existence and interest in the world rests not on certain miracles wrought some centuries ago, but on the great standing miracle, the oracle implanted in every man's breast."

Well, this was a move of finesse, a way of getting around the problem that Christianity nevertheless has at the core of its belief and indeed in the creed which is recited daily by every Anglican, that "He rose from the dead on the third day." I mean, you have to deal with those kinds of things. The nature of the incarnation is itself miraculous.

Now, what Hume did in these debates was to cut the ground from under them by making it impossible to know things in themselves, and Hume introduced a wide-ranging skepticism about the truth of anything. It was, quite literally, a revolution in thought, because once you cannot know anything beyond the sense impression of them, you can't know causation, you can't know anything except what your senses reveal to you, there is a disconnect between the self which is perceiving and the world outside, and all of these questions of the essence of God and the nature of miracles then simply fall beside the way. You can't testify to them, and you don't know whether they're true or false.

Now, let me move now to Hume's life. His early life was relatively uneventful, and we know quite a lot about it because just before his death in 1776, he wrote a short and absolutely wonderful autobiography, which he described in a letter to Adam Smith. I quote:

You will find among my Papers a very inoffensive Piece called *My Own Life*, which I composed a few days before I left Edinburgh, which I thought, as did all my Friends, that my Life was despaired of. There can be no Objection, that this small piece should be sent to Messrs. Strahan and Cadell [publishers] and the Proprietors of my other Works to be prefixed to any future Edition of them.

Now, the outlines that Hume gives of his own life are very simple. Hume was the son of Scottish gentlefolk, gentry. As he writes: "I was of a good family, both by father and mother: my father's family is a branch of the Earl of Home's, or Hume's." The family actually spells it in two ways, and there was an English prime minister in the 1960s, the 14th or 13th Earl of Hume, who was a distant, distant relative of the philosopher.

Lady Anne Lindsay, who knew him as a child, wrote: "As a boy, he was a fat, stupid, lumbering clown, but full of sensibility and justice." David Hume was an exceptionally studious and scholarly boy, apparently unfitted for law and business, both of which he tried. He had a modest private income as the younger son of a good family, 50 pounds a year, and I draw your attention to this. A young gentleman could actually live on 50 pounds a year, and we remember in the lecture on Walpole how much money Walpole made, one hundred and some thousand. Fifty pounds a year gives you an idea of what it was possible to live on and keep a servant, by the way, on your own. It was never quite enough, but it was perfectly adequate to keep Hume going.

Hume had a great idea, and he had it very early, at the age of 18, which was to apply Newton to philosophy. Now, he was only 18 when he got the idea and just 28 when he published his masterpiece. He began a feverish work for four years, but he had a nervous collapse in 1733. It was too much for him, so he took a break from philosophy for a short period in business in Bristol, which was a fiasco. He wasn't very good at it, and he decided that he had 50 pounds a year and it would go further on the Continent, which was cheaper, which it was, so he decided to go live in France, and from 1734 to 1737, he lived in France where he settled down to write his great work.

Hume was always certain that it was a great work, that it would produce what he called a "total alteration of philosophy" and this, by the way, I think is a characteristic of many of the lives that we shall discuss in this series. The really great ones, like Marx or Hume, always knew that they were called upon to do something really great and that everything else must be sacrificed to the fulfillment of this idea. Where they got it from is again an interesting question. Why these great people suddenly know: I am called upon to write *Das Kapital* or *A Treatise of Human Understanding* is hard to understand. Now, *A Treatise of Human Nature*, being an attempt to understand the experimental method of reasoning in moral subjects, has a peculiar and very agreeable style.

Hume's writing is exceptionally fine. The prose is beautiful and clear, and that's not chance. Hume was always preoccupied with his written style. As he wrote in *My Life*: "I was seized very early with a passion for literature, which has been the ruling passion of my life and the great source of my enjoyments." So, unlike certain modern philosophers, let alone sociologists, Hume was always concerned to write beautiful English, and I suppose there is a special Scottish relationship to the English language anyway, because underlying Scottish English there is actually a different language, Scots, which is a Germanic language like English is but has certain different words and different usages.

The object of the work was also clear. In the introduction, Hume describes the fact that:

> There is nothing which is not the subject of debate…Amidst all this bustle 'tis not reason that, which carries the prize but eloquence; and no man needs ever despair of gaining proselytes to the most extravagant hypothesis, who has art enough to represent it in any favourable colours. The victory is not gained by the men at arms, who manage the pike and sword; but by the trumpeters, drummers, and musicians of the army.

It's a nice way to describe your fellow philosophers. Hume's own summary is this:

> The philosophy contain'd in this book is very skeptical…Almost all reasoning is there reduced to experience; and the belief, which attends experience, and is explained to be nothing but a peculiar sentiment of lively conception produced by habit. Nor is this all, when we

believe in anything of *external* existence, or suppose an object to exist a moment after it is no longer perceived, the belief is nothing but a sentiment of the same kind.

This was Hume's revolutionary idea. The revolutionary idea was simply that it is impossible to know more than the mental sensations in our brains. A thing in itself is not known, only the impression it makes on the brain. There is no way that I can do other than say I feel this lectern, I see it, I experience it, but I don't know what it is in itself. I cannot reach it. I am trapped, so to speak, inside my own mind, and this had profound consequences.

Existence is thus impossible to separate from the idea of the thing. Hence, we believe in causation only as a result of custom. That is because we see a certain chain of events happen. Hume's example of this is wonderfully graphic: Billiard balls striking each other. I quote: "Here is a billiard ball lying on the table and another ball moving towards it with rapidity. They strike, and the ball which was formerly at rest now acquires a motion." This is as perfect an instance of the relation of cause and effect as any which we know, and it is also beautifully described, yet Hume shows that we can't know causation as such, only the experience that the balls behaved this way in the past and we saw them doing so. This follows a passage in the *Treatise of Human Nature* which was so important that Hume put it in italics:

> *There is nothing in any object consider'd in itself, which can afford us a reason for drawing any conclusion beyond it and that even after the frequent or constant conjunction of objects, we have no reason to draw any inference concerning any object beyond those of which we have had experience.*

Now, there are a variety of consequences of Hume's philosophy. It argued for radical skepticism. We know nothing for certain. Human beings only know their mental processes, and therefore we have no assurance that reason and thought are necessarily connected to reality. Hence, all essences and substances cannot be certainly said to exist. All we have to offer in their support are simply impressions of the mind. In other words, ideas in our head. We cannot even prove that our selves exist, and the idea that there is a God must be completely unproven and impossible to verify in any way whatsoever.

Hume arrives at as a near a total skepticism as any philosopher ever has. He goes out of his way to show that he has exceeded the ancient Greek skeptics and that there is no philosophical answer, and in a certain sense Hume's case is impossible to refute. Mind and matter are radically separated. There is, by the way, a complicated philosophical argument which Kant raised that Hume gets the whole conception wrong, he needs a priori categories, but I won't go into this.

Now, Hume's own response to what happened was, of course, of disappointment. He was surprised that the public failed to understand his masterpiece, so while he wrote more philosophy, he decided to seek fame and money as a writer of essays and his *History of England*. Hume was a person of extraordinary good cheer. He was also unusual in drawing no personal consequences from his philosophy. He believed that philosophers should know the limits of philosophy. I quote:

> The *intense* view of these manifold contradictions and imperfections in human reason has so wrought upon me, and heated my brain, that I am ready to reject all belief...Most fortunately, it happens, that, since reason is incapable of dispelling these clouds, nature herself suffices to that purpose...I dine, I play a game of backgammon, I converse and am merry with friends; when, after three or four hour's amusement, I would return to these speculations, they appear so cold and strain'd and ridiculous, that I cannot find it in my heart to enter them any further.

It's a wonderfully human way which Hume ends Book I of *A Treatise on Human Nature*.

Now, a few final thoughts on David Hume. At the age of 28, Hume had completed one of the most important books ever written, and set new limits to philosophy, even his own. He went on to write in grand fashion on everything else. On economics he made an important contribution to the theory of international trade, history, and religion. He never married. His contemporaries regarded him as a kind of secular saint, without malice or rancor. He was cheerful, kindly, and a good friend. There was a natural goodness in his nature that led his French colleagues to call him *le bon David*, "the good David," and nothing more exemplifies his nobility of character than his reaction to his own death.

I'm going to read that in a second, but before I do, the fact that Hume was so manifestly good and so saintly and so friendly was a real problem, because here was this skeptic who had shattered everybody's belief, and yet he was so clearly everything which a believing Christian ought to be, and so rarely is. It is, in fact, the case that Adam Smith got in trouble only once in his life with the authorities, and that was because he wrote a very moving tribute to David Hume when he died, and that caused him a lot of trouble, because Hume was so extraordinary and a controversial character.

Let me close these reflections by reading Hume's last words:

> In spring 1775, I was struck with a disorder in my bowels, which at first gave me no alarm, but has since, as I apprehended it, become mortal and incurable. I now reckon upon a speedy dissolution. I have suffered very little pain from my disorder; and what is more strange, have, notwithstanding the great decline of my person, never suffered a moment's abatement of my spirits; insomuch, that were I to name the period of my life, which I should most choose to pass over again, I might be tempted to point to this later period. I possess the same ardour as ever in study, the same gaiety in company. I consider, besides, that a man of sixty-five, by dying, cuts off only a few years of infirmities; and though I see many symptoms of my literary reputation's breaking out at last with additional lustre, I knew that I could have but a few years to enjoy it. It is difficult to be more detached from life than I am at present.

Lecture Nine
C.P.E. Bach—Selling the Arts

Scope:

Carl Philipp Emanuel Bach (1714–1788) was the most distinguished son of the great Johann Sebastian Bach (1685–1750) and a great composer in his own right. As he said, "I never had a teacher other than my father." Yet their styles could not have been more different. The younger Bach's expressive style seems to reflect a change in the social reality and in the listening public. C.P.E. Bach lived through the transition from art as a form of glorification of God or the exaltation of a great king (see Lecture Two) to art as a commodity and the emergence of the public. He played the keyboard in the orchestra of Frederick the Great, serving to proclaim the magnificence of the king. At the same time, in 1753, he published a style manual, *Essay on the True Art of Playing Keyboard Instruments*, with exercises in the back for budding players, a commercial enterprise designed for a new middle-class public. The traditional arts *represented* the glory of God or the ruler; the new art *expressed* the soul of the artist. That transformation, in turn, marked the emergence of the market for works of art and a new distinction between public and private.

Outline

I. This lecture compares two of the world's greatest composers, Johann Sebastian Bach (1685–1750) and Carl Philipp Emanuel Bach (1714–1788), to show the ways in which the composition of German music changed during our period of study and draw parallels with the change from the European Old Regime to the society of the modern world.

II. Dozens of Bachs were musicians in the era from 1500 to 1800. Johann Sebastian Bach made his own list in his family history and counted fifty-three.

    A. The idea that musicians are "artists" has a short history, beginning in the life of C.P.E. Bach himself. Before that, they were servants or, if independent, were premodern guild members who practiced as craftsmen, similar to shoemakers or sadlers.

B. The immediate Bach family was amazingly gifted. Of Johann Sebastian's 20 children, several were well known as musicians. The eldest son, Wilhelm Friedemann (1710–1784), was a brilliant organist and well-known composer. Two younger sons, Carl Philipp Emanuel and Johann Christian, the "English Bach," were even more famous.

III. Johann Sebastian Bach really had no other activity but music. He was taught by his father and, later, by his brother Johann Christoph and was a boy soprano in Lüneberg.

A. In 1703, he became a violinist in the private orchestra of the prince at Weimar but left within a year to become organist at Arnstadt. Bach went to Mühlhausen as organist in 1707. There, he married his cousin Maria Barbara Bach, who was to bear him seven children.

B. In 1708, he was made court organist and chamber musician at Weimar and, in 1714, became concert master. Prince Leopold of Anhalt engaged him as musical director at Köthen in 1717. Three years later, his wife died, and in 1721, he married Anna Magdalena Wilcke, who eventually bore him 13 children.

C. In 1723, he became music director at the Church of St. Thomas, Leipzig, and its choir school; he remained in Leipzig until his death.

D. Bach had had only two types of employers: the princes and the Church. His art was used to *represent* the power and glory of God or the prince. He did not sell his music but served his part in a grander purpose.

IV. Emanuel was the second son of J.S. Bach, who was his only teacher.

A. For a time, Emanuel studied at the University of Leipzig and thought of becoming a lawyer but, at 24, took the post of harpsichordist at the court of Frederick the Great. His chief duty there from 1738 to 1767 was to accompany the monarch's performances on the flute. The king hated Emanuel's music and refused to play it himself or hear it played.

B. In 1768, Emanuel succeeded his godfather, Georg Philipp Telemann, another great Baroque composer, as musical director at Hamburg.

C. Note that C.P.E. Bach, like his father, also had only types of two employers: the king—Frederick the Great—and, instead of the Church, the city of Hamburg.

D. A change in the social situation opened new possibilities. Even while he was playing the harpsichord for Frederick the Great, Emanuel Bach had begun to market his wares. The number of amateur musicians suddenly increased, spawning a demand for "how-to" books. For the first time, there was a middle class, wealthy enough and with enough leisure to make music at home.

E. By 1770, Emanuel Bach had a mail-order business for his compositions, and his catalogue was an important financial asset. It listed works by date, groups of instruments, and places of composition. It also served as the basis for his posthumous *Nachlass-Verzeichnis*, or "estate catalogue," which he bequeathed as a kind of capital stock to his wife.

F. Bach was a canny businessman and only printed works he thought he could sell. His conception of his art was thoroughly modern. He used his works as articles for sale and as transferable asset to his heirs.

V. A comparison of certain features of the music of father and son highlights the transformation that took place in art at this time.

A. C.P.E. Bach's favorite instrument was a clavichord; his father played similar keyboard instruments. Both also used the same forms. For example, both of the following pieces are themes and variations for keyboard: Theme and variation No. 1 of the *Goldberg Variations*, composed in 1741 by J. S. Bach, and the first of 12 variations on *La folia d'Espagne*, composed in 1778 by C.P.E. Bach.

B. J.S. Bach was a deeply pious Lutheran and, for him, music was a way to God's truth. Music and mathematics were the thoughts of God, and composing was a form of worship. For his son, Emanuel, the musician must be able to place himself in the same emotional state as he wishes to arouse in his hearers. Music is about expressing emotions.

1. The generation of C.P.E. Bach developed a theory of emotions called *Die Affektenlehre* ("Doctrine of the Emotions"). It came from classical ideas of rhetoric and oratory and was based on the theory that certain devices used in speech would influence audiences. In the same way, certain musical figures could move audiences. Baroque treatises discussed this idea.

2. Music was composed in terms of ruling affections. Each composition must express only one "affection." The doctrine expressed the demand for a new emotional content in music.

3. J.S. Bach was attacked by the critic Johann Mattheson (1681–1764) for "wishing to be moved rather than to move; that is to say, they aim more at the touch of the fingers than to touch the heart."

C. In the father and son, we also see the father's music of form and the son's music of feeling.

1. J.S. Bach's music was too complicated for the new age; it had "too many notes." Critics and public demanded "feeling," music to "touch the heart."

2. The son Bach was a composer of feeling. One extraordinary example is C.P.E. Bach's *Trio* (*Sangineus und Melancholicus*) of 1749. Violin and flute "play" the cheerful and melancholy personalities in a tiny musical drama.

VI. The theoretical explanation for these differences can be found in Jürgen Habermas's *Structural Transformation of the Public Sphere*.

A. As noted earlier, Jürgen Habermas set forth the theoretical explanation of the emergence of the "private" and "public" and the new art. Habermas ignored music; yet C.P.E. Bach is the perfect test case. Habermas's theory explains the transformation of art and culture in the 18th century.

B. Habermas's book first appeared in 1961 as *Strukturwandel der Öffentlichkeit*; an English edition was not brought out until 1989 as *Structural Transformation of the Public Sphere: An Inquiry into a Category of Bourgeois Society*.

C. The emergence of a public sphere, as we have seen, began in England in the late 17th century and reached France and Germany in the mid-18th century.

1. The spread of the money economy and goods for sale (see Lecture Three) created a new market situation of specialized sale and distribution of commodities, such as coffee and others. The public purchased art, knowledge, goods, or services with the same cash.

2. There was a new public "space" made up of newspapers, coffeehouses, and publishers (see Lecture Six), along with commercial taverns, theaters, museums, and pleasure gardens.

3. Public opinion emerged through the new press for the first time.

4. The new market for art and culture developed quickly, spawning a need for critics to write reviews and tell consumers what to buy.

5. Artists now "created" for the public and were no longer forced to be servants of their lords or the Church. The poet and playwright Friedrich Schiller wrote: "I write as a citizen of the world who serves no prince…The public is now everything to me…"

6. Artists may have been free of the lord, but they became slaves of the market. They were also free to starve if their works did not sell.

7. The artist expresses his or her soul. Because the public buys art to enjoy in private, the private emotions of the artist are important. The private self is the opposite of the public sphere; the private self expresses emotions, as Mattheson argued in 1749.

8. The new doctrine of the emotions is the art of the new public, because the private sphere is the other half of the public sphere.

VII. As I hope our comparison has shown, C.P.E. Bach is a transitional figure, simultaneously a servant of the king and a musical entrepreneur; a devoted disciple of his father, yet a composer of the emotions capable of touching the feelings of the new public.

Essential Reading:

T.C.W. Blanning, *The Culture of Power and the Power of Culture: Old Regime Europe, 1660–1789*, pp. 108–109.

Jürgen Habermas, *Structural Transformation of the Public Sphere: An Inquiry into a Category of Bourgeois Society*.

Questions to Consider:

1. What happens when art becomes something to be bought and sold?

2. Do you agree that the music of J.S. Bach and that of his son C.P.E. Bach express different musical philosophies?

Lecture Nine—Transcript
C.P.E. Bach—Selling the Arts

In the last lecture we considered the philosophical revolution brought about by David Hume's *A Treatise of Human Understanding* of 1739. In this lecture, we move to central Germany to consider what I think of as a musical revolution. A change in the meaning and purpose of music, what it was for and what it meant. Actually, as I've been reflecting in these lectures, it dawns on me that it's about this period—the middle of the 18th century—that there is a fundamental change across a wide range of activities. Frederick the Great, who becomes king in 1740, introduces a new conception of the ruler's role. We've seen in Dr. Johnson's London, a transformation of the relationship between the writer and the public. In Rousseau, in the middle of the 18th century, we see the emergence of a new kind of human being, a new self. Here in music in the 18th century, I think we see a very similar kind of deep fundamental change, and it's one that's much less noticed, and much more often overlooked.

Now, I need to give you some background to what I'm going to try to do in this lecture, because it is frankly an experiment. The great Alfred North Whitehead, whom I love dearly as both a Cambridge and Harvard man, once said, "A lecturer should give his audience the impression that the process of thought is going on." I can assure you in this particular lecture, which is, I think, the hardest one in the whole series, I will be thinking and also sweating.

Now, the lecture forms part of the large design of this whole series, the way in which the Old Regime gradually turns into a world we recognize as modern by 1914. But it also moves in real breaks. There are moments when you can actually see a clear break. We've moved into a different phase, and I think this one is one. I want to construct in this lecture a kind of case study. I think we can observe a fundamental change in the way German music is composed, a difference in style, and real change in the meaning and purpose of music in society, and I think I can show you why. I think I know why.

Now, the lecture may not work; experiments at the lecture podium are always tricky, and in history, they're particularly tricky. We can't rerun the past with the variables altered, but what we can do is compare, and I wan, in this lecture to make a really precise comparison. This precise comparison is between two of the greatest composers who ever lived, who happen to have been father and son. I want to look at Johann Sebastian Bach, the father, who was born in 1685, and died in 1750, right in the middle of our 18th century, and his son, Carl Philipp Emanuel Bach, who was born in 1714, and died in 1788.

C.P.E. Bach is a direct contemporary of the people we've been looking at. He's the same age as Rousseau, he's the same age as Frederick the Great. Indeed, he was a servant of Frederick the Great. And he belongs to the generation of Dr. Johnson, the generation of the *philosophe*.

Now, what makes this particularly exciting is that C.P.E. Bach only had one teacher, his father. Never had another teacher. More interesting, he used exactly the same instruments. What I'm going to be able to demonstrate with a little musical clip later on, is the same sound, father and son, teacher and pupil, making music in a completely different spirit, and in a completely different way. I hope that experiment will then illuminate what I think this great break actually involves.

First, though, we have to take a look at the Bach family as a family. There were several dozen Bachs who were musicians in the era from 1500 to 1800. Johann Sebastian Bach made his own list in his family history which he did in 1735, *Ursprung der musicalisch-Bachischen Familie*, "The Origins of the Musical Bach Family." By that stage, he counted 53 members of the Bach family who had been professional musicians. I'm told, I've never seen these, that the Bach family is a wonderful case study for geneticists who are looking for the examples of inherited characteristics.

Now, what did it mean to come from a family in which there had been 53 musicians? I think the first thing we have to do is put our head back into a world in which the musician was not as he or she is today, a great maestro or maestra, but a craftsperson. The idea that musicians are artists, let alone geniuses, has a very short history, and it begins in and during the life of C.P.E. Bach himself. Before that, they were essentially servants.

For example, the great Franz Joseph Haydn, one of the greatest composers who ever lived, 1732 to 1804 [sic 1809], was most of his life, not only a servant, but he had to wear livery. He was a servant of Prince Esterhazy who employed him as a musician. It was only in the 1790s, after the period we're talking about, when Haydn came back from his triumphal tour in London, where the London symphonies were composed, that Prince Esterhazy actually invited Haydn to sit at his table. Up to that point, Haydn had been a kind of glorified footman.

If they weren't servants, they were craftspeople, and they were members of guilds. Pre-modern guilds who practiced a craft like shoemakers, or saddlers, or wigmakers. And when Tomaso Albinoni, the wonderful Venetian composer, signed his compositions *amatore della musica* (An amateur in music), he did not mean what we mean, that he wasn't a professional, he just meant he was not a member of the guild of professional musicians in the City of Venice. He was actually a member of the cardmakers' guild, people who make playing cards. He wrote music and operas on the side, but he was "amature," that is to say he was not a member of the guild.

Now another reason why there were 53 Bachs who were musicians was something which I've come back to several times, which is the structure of the Old Regime. There were something like 3,000 entities in the old Holy Roman Empire, and many of these were modest sized principalities, or archbishoprics or abbeys. Because of the need for glory, which we saw in Lecture Two, Augustus the Strong wished to glorify the state, one of the ways in which most of these princes competed was, in fact, having the best musician. It was a great market for a musician, because there was a lot going for you. There was a tremendous need for orchestras and conductors, and it was a coup to get yourself a star like one of the Bachs. The political structure of Germany provided a really good market.

The immediate Bach family were just stunningly gifted. Johann Sebastian's eldest brother, Johann Christoph Bach, 1671 to 1721, was an organist at Ohrdruf. By the way, by this stage, the great North German organ tradition had established itself. It's said that Bach walked a 200 mile roundtrip to hear the great Buxtehude play. That, of course, tells you something. In our world, you just go down to the local Borders or Barnes & Noble and you pick up Buxtehude on a CD. You could not hear these people. You had to go and hear them physically. You might only hear them once. When Johann Sebastian's parents died, he moved in with his brother, and his brother was his teacher. Of the 20 children of Johann Sebastian, several were well-known as musicians. Probably the most gifted was Wilhelm Friedemann Bach, the eldest, who was born in 1710. He was a very unstable, temperamental man, and rather unhappy. Two younger sons, Carl Philipp Emanuel Bach, and Johann Christian Bach, who moved to London and came to be known as the "English Bach," were themselves very serious composers.

Of these, though, I think there's no doubt that C.P.E. Bach was by far the most important composer of the transition period between Johann Sebastian Bach and the world of Mozart and Haydn. Mozart said of C.P.E. Bach that he was the person from whom they all learned.

Now, I want to say a word about the lives of father and son actually led. Johann Sebastian Bach really had no other activity but music. He was taught, first by his father, and later by his brother. He was a boy soprano at Lüneburg in 1703. He became a violinist in the private orchestra of the prince at Weimar, but left within a year to become organist at Arnstadt. He then went to Mühlhausen as an organist in 1707, and there he married his cousin, Maria Barbara Bach, with whom he had seven children. In 1708, he was made court organist and chamber musician at Weimar, and in 1714, he became concert master there. Prince Leopold of Anhalt engaged him as musical director at his palace at Köthen. Three years later his wife died.

In 1721, he married Anna Magdelena, who many of you know from the little book of exercises which he designed for Anna Magdalena, and he had another 13 children. In 1723, he took the important post of music director of the Church of St. Thomas in Leipzig and of its choir school, and he was there until his death. Now, that's really all there is to say about the movements.

Let's notice the social structure of J.S. Bach's career. It's important to notice that Johann Sebastian Bach had only two types of employers. Either he worked for princes: the prince of Weimar, the grand duke of Weimar or Anhalt-Dessau, (and both Weimar and Anhalt-Dessau were sovereign princes, but medium-sized states, perhaps half the size of an American county, but with a palace and with a court, and with enough revenue to support a substantial orchestra) or alternatively, he worked for churches. Neue Kirche in Arnstadt, St. Blasius Church in Mühlhausen, and the St. Thomas Church in Leipzig. His art was employed to represent something. To represent the power and glory of God, or of the prince. He did not sell his music. You could not buy it. He served as a part of a grander purpose. Now, if you compare Johann Sebastian Bach with what we saw of Samuel Johnson in Lecture Six, Samuel Johnson came to London and sold his art right from the beginning. There was already a market for what Johnson was doing. Now if you think of what Bach actually did in Leipzig, it's a wonderful grand church, the Thomas Church, he was a local church organist.

He also had to put up with people who came with colds, with unruly children in the choir school, with complaints from the parish council. He was always in trouble with the town council of Leipzig who were involved in the Thomas Church, because he didn't do this, and did do that. He actually spent a couple of days in jail for losing his temper. In other words, he lived not the life of the grand artist flying around the world in a private jet that we take for granted today. He lived in the world of an ordinary church organist, and he was expected to turn out cantatas at the rate of one a week. They were to be rehearsed and performed. There are, I think, over 150 surviving, but at least as many did not. That's Father Bach. The son, Carl Philipp Emanuel Bach, was the second son of Johann Sebastian, who was in fact, his only teacher.

Interestingly, there was an alternative kind of career available to C.P.E. He could, in fact, have become a lawyer, and he went to Leipzig University with that in mind, but he was so gifted that it was clear in the end that he would become a musician. At the age of 24, he took the post as harpsichordist at the court of Frederick the Great.

Our characters, our lives, are overlapping here. His chief duty for 28 years was, so to speak, as keyboard player in the orchestra for the king. What we have to imagine is a full symphony orchestra which was only there for the king's pleasure. Not to give concerts. You couldn't hear it. When Frederick the Great came in and felt like playing a flute concerto, he snapped his fingers and the orchestra assembled, and all these wonderful musicians were there to play background music so the king could play his flute. He also, by the way, Frederick the Great, wrote some really nice music. Very conventional, but really nice. He liked to hear it played on his house orchestra.

Now, I said in the previous lecture, the Hohenzollerns were very frugal, and indeed they were, compared to Augustus the Strong of Saxony, whom we looked at in Lecture Two. But this was the king's one real luxury, to maintain a fulltime symphony orchestra just for his own pleasure. C.P.E. Bach was writing music while he was playing the keyboard, but the king hated it. Didn't like it, he thought it was too modern, too new-fangled, didn't want it played. And so during the entire 28 years, poor old C.P.E. Bach never heard one of his pieces played on this marvelous orchestra. If you look at the social structure of C.P.E. Bach's life, it's exactly the same.

He, too, only had two types of employer like his father. He worked for the king, Frederick the Great, and he worked for the City of Hamburg. Now, instead of a church, Emanuel Bach worked for the city. And by the way, in 18th century German practice, it's your third name which is your real name. So it's Carl Philipp, but he was called Emanuel. Emanuel Bach worked for a city. Hamburg was already an important commercial port, had a flourishing opera. But it was a traditional job. You were there holding a post which was like the one that his godfather, Telemann had held. Now, the difference is that something happens in the middle of the 18th century, in Germany, which has happened earlier in England, and I think changes the whole structure of the way art is produced and received.

Beginning in the 1720s and 1730s, a new middle class begins to emerge in Germany. And one sign of this is J.S. Bach (Father Bach's) wonderful "Coffee Cantata," which is one of the few comic pieces Johann Sebastian ever wrote. It's about Lieschen, a spoiled young woman who is the idol of her rich father, who gets a coffee addiction. All she wants to do is drink coffee. She won't go out. She won't receive suitors, and she won't do anything. The father threatens her that she won't have a husband unless she gives up the coffee, and so on. It's very funny. But it also tells you that coffee, which we've seen in London already well-established in the coffeehouses in the 1670s, 50 to 60 years later, has now reached places like Leipzig. It's now possible to have coffee. To have coffee circles. Not quite yet to go to coffeehouses, because Germany wasn't that developed, but it's spreading.

Now, this change in the social situation opened up new possibilities, because even while he was playing the harpsichord for Frederick the Great, Emanuel Bach had begun to market his music. The number of amateur musicians suddenly went up, and the demand arose for "how-to" books. How to do things became part of the accomplishments of a genteel young lady, to be able to play the keyboard. And it is absolutely amazing! I looked these things up. Between 1750 and 1757, a whole range of "how-to-do" books were published independently, but with the same purpose. In 1750, the famous critic and musician, Friedrich Wilhelm Marpurg published his *Die Kunst das Clavier zu spielen*, "*The Art of Playing the Clavichord*" which was reprinted in 1751. In 1752, Johann Joachim Quantz, who was Frederick the Great's flute teacher and the greatest virtuoso of his day wrote his *Versuch einer Anweisung, die Flüte traversiere zu spielen*, "*An Attempt at Instruction on How to Play the Traverse Flute*." That is the modern "cross" flute as opposed to a recorder, or what the Germans called a *Blockflöte*, which is, of course, straight up and down.

In 1753, our own C.P.E. Bach produced his very famous *Über die wabre Art, das Klavier zu spielen*, "*Essay on the True Art of Playing Keyboard Instruments*." And when you look at this book, it comes with 19 or 20 little examples in the back. Tells you how to make a trill the way Emanuel Bach did it. It tells you how to imitate the style. And of course, in modern marketing terms it would certainly come with a cassette, with Emanuel Bach playing these things himself. I mean, this is a real commercial venture. Leopold Mozart, the father of the great Wolfgang, in 1756 produced an attempt at a basic violin training. The very famous critic, Johann Johann Friedrich Agricola published in 1757, *Anleitung zur Singekunst*, (*An Introduction to the Art of Singing*). Now this cannot be a coincidence that out of nowhere all these prominent musicians in the same generation suddenly discover that there's a market out there, and there is.

With the exception of Quantz, who was older, every one of these authors were born within a few years of each other, and they are all tapping a new market for manuals and guides. For the first time, there is a middle class. A class wealthy enough with enough leisure to want to make music at home. Now, C.P.E. Bach was, in fact, a high-powered musical entrepreneur. He made a catalog of his own works. As far as I know he was the first musician ever to do it, and it's still used. By 1770, he had a mail order business for his compositions all over Germany. And his catalog was modern. It listed works by dates, by groups of instruments, by places of composition, and he also saw it as a posthumous estate; the index to his catalog, he bequeathed to his wife, so she could go on selling his music to people as well.

He was a very canny businessman. He printed only on demand. When there were orders, he printed the stuff. Very modern. Lasting kind of ordering. His conception of his art was thoroughly, thoroughly modern. Used his work as articles for sale, as transferable assets to his heirs. Now, I'd like to play my musical experiment. Now an experiment in history is always a complicated thing. I think all you can do is try to design conditions so similar that, and so exactly as possible, that you can see the differences. The function of comparative history is to reveal differences otherwise not obvious. It is a difficult thing to do, but I think this one may work. Now what are the conditions? The two little pieces we're going to be playing for you are played on the same kind of instrument. Emanuel Bach's favorite instrument was a clavichord built by Gottfried Silverman.

His father also played instruments absolutely similar in kind, hence a real comparison is possible. I have chosen to two excerpts, which come from exactly the same kind of form—both are variations. I will play for you the variation No. 1 from the *Goldberg Variations* of Johann Sebastian Bach composed in 1741, and then I will play you the first of 12 variations on *La folia d'Espagne*, which was famous and well-known at the time, which is composed by Emanuel Bach in 1778. I hope that you will actually be able to hear that these are two completely different types of music.

<Professor plays variation No. 1 by Johann Sebastian Bach>

<Professor plays Emanuel Bach's variation>

They sound different. And they are different, because they embody completely different conceptions of what music is about. Father Bach was a deeply pious Lutheran, a mystical person. For him, music was a way to God's truth. For the father, who was the only non-mathematical member of the Leipzig Mathematicians Club, music and mathematics were the thoughts of God, and it was a kind of form of worship. The Tübingen musicologist, Ulrich Siegele, discovered that quite a lot of Bach's later pieces were based on the Fibonacci series. You know, that 1+1=2, 1+2=3, 2+3=5. Bach converted these into letters, musical letters, and then composed around them. He did a lot of that kind of thing. And in one or two of the pieces, for example, in the *Saint Anne Prelude and Fugue,* Ulrich Siegele found that the first letters of the creed are built into the music. I said to him, "Why did Bach do this?" He said, "We don't know," but it's likely that Bach found musical composing so easy, that it seemed sinful to him.

He set himself higher and harder tasks all the time. We know, for example, that in *The Well-Tempered Clavier*, the two books of preludes and fugues which he wrote in 1722 and 1744 going round all the tones, he got this from a book in 1691 by Andreas Werckmeiser, *The Musical Temperature.* That is, tempering a keyboard instrument, or the clear and true mathematical instruction for music. So from the way in which we now tune a keyboard instrument actually comes out of this world of mathematics, of mysticism, of music as being, in some sense, God's thoughts. When you listen to the *Goldberg Variations* you can see that something of that kind is going on. There are principles there which are quite different.

Now, for Son Bach, there's a very different doctrine here at stake. The generation of C.P.E. Bach developed a theory of emotions called "The Doctrine of the Emotions." It came from the classical ideas of rhetoric and oratory, no longer from Lutheran mysticism. It was based on the idea that certain kinds of musical devices would automatically evoke certain sorts of emotions. Just as speech moves audiences. There was a big literature discussion in the 18th century about which musical figures could provoke which emotions. Thus, composers were required now to compose their music in terms of the ruling affect, the ruling emotion, rather than the principles which the father had done.

As a result, J.S. Bach's music began to seem old-fashioned even while he was alive. The famous critic Johann Mattheson complained in 1739, "For some years now composers have been writing sonatas for keyboard to great acclaim, but they do not yet have the right form, wishing to be moved rather than to move; that is to say, they aim more at the touch of the fingers than to touch the heart." That's a direct attack on the way in which Johann Sebastian Bach made music.

We have now the music of feeling versus the music of the mind of God. Johann Sebastian Bach's music was too complicated. It had too many notes. The public wanted more feeling. They wanted music to touch the heart.

The Son Bach was a composer of feeling. When he died, in one of his obituaries the critic Triest wrote of him that he was "a Klopstock using notes instead of words." Klopstock was the most popular romantic poet of the period. There's an extraordinary example, which I don't have here to play for you, of C.P.E. Bach's *Trio* sonata, called the *Sangineus* and the *Melancholicus,* in which the violin plays the melancholy man, and the flute plays the cheerful man. It's a trio sonata in which they talk to each other. Eventually, the cheerful man convinces the melancholy man that it's better to be cheerful, they end up playing the cheerful man's theme. It's unthinkable that the old man could've written music like that.

Now, how did this happen? Why did this happen? Well, I haven't got much time to go into it, but we have already mentioned the structural transformation of the public sphere. Here I can just very briefly draw your attention to the work of Jürgan Habermas, the German philosopher, who created this idea that in the 18th century a public sphere comes to being. Now, Habermas didn't know this particular musical example. This is my own contribution to the debate, but I think C.P.E. Bach is a perfect test case. Habermas's theory that the spread of the money, economy, and the transformation of art into a commodity also brings with it a different approach to what art means.

For J.S. Bach, it's very clear what art represents. It represents the glory of God, the meaning of life. Or for Haydn, art represents the glory of the prince, but for C.P.E. Bach, art expresses. It expresses the emotion of the individual. Thus, we're actually looking here at the musical equivalent of Rousseau's *Confessions*. The soul is expressing itself through the music.

Habermas goes on to argue that the public sphere makes this possible. You are now selling music to people you don't know, and what you do is you sell your soul. You sell your genius. You sell your art. You express yourself. After all, Rousseau did public readings of his *Confessions* in exactly the same way. That means you have to have critics who tell you whose soul is better than who else's soul. You need to have a whole apparatus of buying and selling of this art. And also, Habermas goes on to argue, that as soon as you have the public, you also have the private in a way that you didn't have before because now you've got a public world where you go out and buy things, you take it home, and you listen to it in the privacy of your own world.

We're dealing then with a change in the structure of music. There is a new "space" made up of newspapers, coffeehouses, publishers, as we've seen in the London of Dr. Johnson. There are commercial taverns. There is also now in Germany for the first time the possibility of actually making a living not as a servant of the prince. Artists who express themselves now create for a new public who can buy their works. They don't have to be servants of some despotic prince or some ill-tempered archbishop like poor old Mozart was. The great German poet and playwright Friedrich Schiller expressed it in 1784 like this, "I write as a citizen of the world who serves no prince…The public is now everything to me, my preoccupation, my sovereign, and my friend. Henceforth, I belong to it alone."

Well, that's fine as long as you're employed, and your stuff sells, but now you also have the possibility the genius is starving in the garret because the stuff doesn't sell. The genius expresses his or her soul, her private self, and the public buys that private self as art to enjoy in private.

Well, our little experiment is over. It convinces me. I hope it convinced you. You, I think, must agree that in some fundamental sense, C.P.E. Bach is a transitional figure. He simultaneously was the servant of the king, and he was also a musical entrepreneur, he was a capitalist. He's a devoted disciple of his father, and yet, he's a composer of the emotions. C.P.E. Bach is now serving a public which wants their feelings touched, and they still do want that. The music of emotion, the music which this new generation begins to create, which then ends in romanticism, is what the public actually wants. That's what these new composers give them.

Lecture Ten
Catherine the Great—Russian Reformer

Scope:

Catherine the Great (1729–1796), empress of Russia, belongs in that long line of Russian reformers, from Peter the Great to Valdimir Putin today, who would like to Westernize Russia. To make Russia like the West, however, means an erosion of its historic identity. Opponents of change fear that it will cease to be Russian. This dilemma, expressed in the battle between Slavophiles and Westernizers, has bedeviled every attempt to force Russia to change its nature. Catherine's astonishing successes and her equally clamorous failures suggest that elements in Russian society and history simply will not give up their "Russian-ness" without a fight, even though Russian-ness has often been synonymous with backwardness. The dilemma of all Russian reform has been the possibility that backwardness may make up an essential element in the Russian national character. Yet without reform, Russia cannot survive as a great European and, now, world power. Must Russia, in gaining the world, lose its soul?

Outline

I.   Several key factors help explain why Russian history has been different from that of Western Europe.

    A. First, medieval Russia was an Asian principality.

        1. A basic date in Russian history is 988, the baptism of Vladimir and the conversion of Russia to Christianity (but pagan beliefs continued among ordinary folk and still do).

        2. In 1147, Moscow was founded by Yuri Dolgoruki and, in 1156, the first Kremlin was built in Moscow.

        3. In 1227, Genghis Khan died, and in the years 1237–1242, his sons spread out in all directions and set up four *khanates*. They were the Great Khanate, which comprised all of China and most of East Asia; the Jagatai khanate in Turkistan; the Kipchack khanate, or the Empire of the Golden Horde, founded by Batu Khan in Russia; and a khanate in Persia.

4. The grand duke of Moscow became just a local prince who paid tribute to "the Golden Horde." The Mongols set up a loosely governed state comprising most of Russia. The name *Golden Horde* was derived from the Russian *Zolotaya Orda*, used to designate the Mongol host that had set up a magnificent tent camp along the Volga River.

5. In the years between 1430 and 1466, the Golden Horde disintegrated. The parallel with tribal warlords in Afghanistan today gives us an idea of how easily that can happen.

6. Russia was part of Asia while Europe went through the High Middle Ages and the Renaissance.

B. Second, the Russian Orthodox Church is part of the identity of Russia.

1. In July 1054, both the Roman Catholic and Greek Orthodox Churches excommunicated each other and split Christianity into two hostile camps. The ancient and invisible line between Latin and Greek Christianity persists to this day. The line marks the eastern boundaries of Lithuania, Poland, and Hungary.

2. In 1448, the Church of Russia was declared *autocephalous*, that is, the Russian Orthodox patriarch no longer recognized Constantinople.

3. The Holy Church in Russia began to see itself as the custodian of true Christianity and think of itself as the "Third Rome."

4. To be Russian was (and is, for some) to be an Orthodox Christian.

C. A third key factor in the explanation of Russia's development is that the grand duke of Muscovy was the heir of the Byzantine emperor.

1. In 1453, the Ottoman Turks captured Constantinople and put an end to the Byzantine Empire, the last direct successor of the Roman Empire.

2. In 1472, Ivan III, known as "the Great" (1462–1505), married Zoe (Sophia), a niece of the last Byzantine emperor, and claimed the imperial title.

3. That is how the Russian royal title of *tsar* or *czar* came about. It comes from the Latin *Cæsar*, "emperor." Ivan the Great was the first to call himself tsar, or caesar.

D. Further, the nobility in Russia were seen as servants of the tsar.

1. The *boyars*, the upper nobility, occupied the highest state offices and, through a council, advised the prince. They were great landlords. Ivan IV, "the Terrible," broke their power and influence.

2. This is the first time in this course that we encounter the Eastern European pattern of nobility, which was the rule in Poland, Hungary, and Russia. There were a few great magnates and many, mostly untitled, usually poor nobles of the lower aristocracy.

3. The word for all the Russian nobility was *dvoriantsvo* from *dvor* ("house" or "court"), that is, the tsar's court. As one Russian reformer in the early 19th century said, "In Russia, there are only two classes: the servants of the Tsar and the servants of the servants of the Tsar."

4. Nobility could be acquired by taking a post in the civil service or in the military services. The large class of rural gentry was rather impoverished.

E. The absence of the Roman law also played a role in Russia's history.

1. In Lecture One, I suggested that Western Europe was an amalgam of Roman, Judaeo-Christian, and feudal features. Medieval and early-modern Russia lacked the first and third element.

2. The Roman Empire was a unique city-state that became a world empire. Its procedures were based on *citizens*, that is, inhabitants of a city or town and, in its other meaning, someone who possessed civic rights or privileges, a burgess or freeman of a city (see Lecture Two).

3. Because the Russian Empire had few towns and no tradition of Roman civil codes, it had unspecific categories for important Western terms, such as *property*, *individual*, or c*ontract*, all of which have origins in the inheritance of Roman law.

F. Russia had no bourgeoisie, as most Western European countries did.

   1. The word *bourgeois* (German: *burger*) was originally the name for the inhabitants of walled towns in medieval France and Germany. The growth of towns was an essential feature of the European West. The towns and the bourgeoisie had certain rights.

   2. Towns emerged late in Russian history. In 1564, the first book was printed in Moscow. By that time, the book trade had been flourishing in Western Europe for more than 100 years.

G. Serfdom flourished in Russia.

   1. Serfdom is a system in which the agricultural worker is a kind of slave. It is the exact opposite of the citizen. During Catherine's reign, serfdom was at its height; 34 out of 36 million peasant families were either landlord serfs or state peasants. Peasants were prohibited from moving from their estates without the permission of their landlord and owed him service.

   2. The *mir*, or "commune," was another uniquely Russian feature. The lord's land, or *demesne*, was divided by the peasant commune (*obshchina* or *mir*) into three large fields, worked on a rotation crop system. Each field was divided into strips, and each family was given so many strips in each field according to the number of male workers in the family or the number of mouths to feed. The system was a form of peasant communism.

H. Russia has a strong tradition of Slavophiles (versus Westernizers).

   1. Though the terms were invented in the 19th century, they are useful in our discussion. The Slavophiles preached the unique Russian way, prizing the communal principle over the principle of personality (another of those fundamental Latin words).

   2. The great Russian writer Alexander Herzen once said, "Thank God that Russia has been spared the three great scourges of the West: Roman Catholicism, the bourgeoisie and the Roman law."

I.   In sum, Russia was both immensely backward, yet extremely complex. It had a harsh climate, a short growing season, bad roads, and few warm-water ports. The low productivity of Russian agriculture, combined with ignorance, illiteracy, drunkenness, superstition, and the traditions of the "Holy Fool" all contributed to the poverty and backwardness of society. Yet the Russian Empire was a European great power and full of potential.

II. Modernization came to Russia through the influence of Westernizing tsars.

A. Peter the Great (1672–1725), tsar of Russia from 1682 to 1725, was a major figure in the development of imperial Russia. He built St. Petersburg as a "window on the West" and Westernized manners. He banned beards and Muscovite dress. He reformed the calendar and simplified the alphabet. He transferred the capital from "backward" Moscow to "modern" St. Petersburg.

B. Catherine the Great (1729–1796) reigned from 1762 to 1796.

1. She was a German princess, born April 21, 1729, in Stettin. Her father was Prince Christian August of Anhalt-Zerbst, and she was christened Sophia Augusta Frederica. Her family was a typical small royal family, subdivided into rulers of mini-states.

2. Little Sophie was a phenomenon, irrepressible, smart, and obstinate. German princesses were the breeding farms of European royalty because there were so many states and so many royal families. When the childless Empress Elizabeth of Russia sought a bride for her nephew, heir to the throne, the Grand Duke Peter, she found Sophie.

3. On February 9, 1744, Sophie, aged 15, came to Russia at the invitation of the empress and, on August 21, 1745, was married in St. Petersburg. She had to give up her German Lutheran faith and was christened into the Russian Orthodox Church as Ekaterina Alexeevna; hence, she became Catherine.

C. Catherine observed that her young husband lacked direction, and his sexual inadequacies were soon apparent, as well. Catherine looked elsewhere; found a handsome Guard officer, Sergei Saltykov; and had a baby. Everybody knew that the future Tsar Paul I was almost certainly not Peter's son, but he was a male heir.

1. Grand Duke Peter was obsessed by Frederick the Great and war. He played with human toy soldiers, his Holsteiners, and joined them in drinking and stupidity. He refused all things Russian and flaunted his "German" tastes. In 1762, Empress Elizabeth died, leaving Peter, her inadequate and disturbed nephew, tsar.

2. Because he refused to learn Russian and had seized Orthodox Church lands, he was unpopular from the start. Just as Russia and Austria were about to crush Frederick the Great, he ended the war with Prussia. Instead, he declared war on Denmark to regain his Holstein lands.

3. The army hated him. On June 28, 1762, there was a coup d'etat: Gregory Orlov, Saltykov's successor as Catherine's lover, and his four brothers mobilized the Guard regiments. They seized Tsar Peter; bundled the befuddled fool off to prison, where he died "in a drunken scuffle" (that is, murdered); and made Catherine tsarina.

III. Despite an uncertain hold on power and the difficulties presented by her gender, Catherine attempted to introduce reforms and a Westernizing influence in Russia.

A. Catherine's hold on power was always uncertain. There was no real Romanov succession, because the future tsar, Paul, was not the son of Tsar Peter III.

1. False Peters arose frequently in the peasantry and threatened Catherine's hold on power.

2. Catherine was foreign and known contemptuously as the "German" in spite of her devotion to Russia.

B. Catherine was the opposite of Maria Theresa, who in 1737, formed a chastity league to reduce promiscuity among the aristocracy. Catherine was openly libertine and made no secret of her powerful sexual drive.

1. Her list of known official lovers, or "favorites" (later, "pupils"), is long and distinguished, including Potemkin, and others.

2. A European pornographic literature sprang up to describe her unbridled lust. The reality was much more complicated. Orlov (lover from 1762–1772) and Grigori Aleksandrovich Potemkin (lover from 1774 on) played important roles in the unstable and primitive state. They provided essential links to power, to the army, and to the nobility.

3. Potemkin (1739–1791) and Catherine had what today would be called an "open relationship" after 1776, but they never quite separated. She took other lovers and he did, too, but they remained, in an odd way, like a married couple; his counsel and assistance in making policy were essential.

4. The problem of female rule in Russia raised peculiar difficulties. Because there was a total absence of rights for wives and women in general, Russian nobles and members of the royal family thought nothing of dismissing unwanted wives to convents.

C. Catherine was strongly influenced by the French Enlightenment and read widely in the latest French philosophy. She corresponded famously and openly with Voltaire and Diderot.

1. She was determined to open Russia to Western influences and, early in her reign, decided to open Russian society to foreigners.

2. She attempted to reform and Westernize Russian laws in 1776. The new law code spoke the reasonable language of the Enlightenment, but it had to be applied in the reality of a drunken, illiterate, savage society, full of superstition and religious to its core.

3. Catherine's travels were famous. Because communications were difficult and roads frequently impassable, Catherine's tours might take months. In such a vast territory, there was no effective way to enforce the laws, no sanctions nor any easy means of showing the monarch to her people.

4. She introduced reforms of government and society in famous decrees. The Charter of Nobility of April 21, 1785, is an interesting example: Catherine established feudal rights four years before the French Revolution abolished feudalism and nobility. Westernizing transformed social relations and the essential Russian character was eroded.

5. Her foreign policy was, on the whole, successful. Through the three partitions of Poland, she gained vast territories and pushed Russia's frontiers far to the west. Together with Potemkin, she pursued several successful wars against Turkey and pushed the empire's borders to the Black Sea and into the Caucasus. In 1795, the new city of Odessa on the Black Sea was founded.

IV. Catherine's choice of symbol for her reign was the bee, with the motto *l'utile*. The busy bee expressed her concept of work. She wanted to see order and hated Russian sloppiness. Ultimately, Catherine remained an orderly German at heart and never became a proper Russian.

Essential Reading:

Simon Dixon, *Catherine the Great*, Profiles in Power Series.

Questions to Consider:

1. Is it justifiable to consider certain societies as "backward"?

2. What do you think about the way Catherine the Great took her male lovers?

Lecture Ten—Transcript
Catherine the Great—Russian Reformer

In the last two lectures, we looked at David Hume's philosophy, and we looked at the break in the nature of musical composition by comparing father and son in the Bach family in the middle of the 18th century. In this lecture today, we move for the first time to the edges of European civilization. We move to the Russian Empire. In particular, we look at the remarkable career of Catherine the Great. I want to begin, as I have done in previous lectures, by setting some contextual framework for us.

The first part of this lecture is going to outline the ways in which Russia is not the West, or historically had a different development. I'm going to illustrate that by developing a set of what I think of as key factors in Russian development, with which I hope to explain why its history has been fundamentally different from that of the Western Europeans.

Key factor number one is that medieval Russia was an Asian principality. Basic dates in Russian history: In 988, Vladimir, king, becomes baptized and converts to Christianity, but pagan beliefs continue, as of course they still do. In 1147, Moscow was founded by Yuri Dolgoruki. In 1156, the first Kremlin was built in Moscow. Shortly thereafter, however, the independent kingdom of the Russe was overrun.

In 1227, Gengis Khan died, and in the years 1237 to 1242, the sons of Gengis Khan spread out in all directions and set up four independent kingdoms known as *khanates*. They were the Great Khanate, which comprised all of China and most of East Asia. The Jagatai khanate in Turkistan; the Kipchack khanate, or the Empire of the Golden Horde, founded by Batu Khan in Russia; and a khanate in Persia. Thus, the grand duke of Moscow became just a local prince who paid tribute to "the Golden Horde," as the Mongols were called. The Mongols were just a loosely governed state comprising most of Russia. The name "Golden Horde" was derived from the Russian designation *Zolotaya Orda*, used by the Russians to designate the glittering Mongol host who had set up a magnificent tent camp along the Volga River.

In the years that followed, the Golden Horde eventually disintegrated, in the middle of the 15th century. You can imagine, if you think about what is happening in Afghanistan today, the way warlords, who don't obey the sovereignty of the nominal ruler, break up into conflicting tribes. The important point here is that Russia was part of Asia while Europe went through the High Middle Ages and the Renaissance.

Russia was part of a particularly primitive Asia, because the Mongolian Horde was simply comprised of tribesmen on horseback, so that Russia missed that entire development. Think of Western history without the cathedrals, without the development of towns, without the saints and scholars, without the Crusades, without the contact with Islam, which brought them so much new science, and access to the ancient world. That is key element one.

Key element two, which is still important, is that the Russian Orthodox Church is the identity of Russia. In July of 1054, both the Roman Catholic and the Greek Orthodox churches excommunicated each other, and split Christianity into two hostile camps.

Now, that ancient invisible line between Latin and Greek Christianity persists to this very day. It is also not chance that of the 10 new states that are joining the European Union at the beginning of the 21st century, they're all on the Western side of the border between Latin and Greek Christianity. I can remember teaching in Lithuania, and asking my students, "What is Europe, and what is not Europe?" What was not Europe for them was everything beyond their Eastern border. That is to say, the whole of Russia they did not regard as Europe. The Russian Orthodox Church, then, became in a sense, the identity of the Russian kingdom.

In 1448, the Church of Russia declared itself independent, *autocephalous*, as the word is. That is to say, the Russian Orthodox patriarch no longer recognized Constantinople. The Holy Church in Russia began to see itself as the custodian of a true Christianity, and think of itself as the "Third Rome." First there was Rome, then there was Byzantium, and then there was Holy Moscow. To be Russian was, and is still today for some people, to be an Orthodox Christian. Somebody who is not an Orthodox Christian cannot be a Russian.

Key element three is that the grand dukes of Muscovy became the heirs of the Byzantine emperors. In 1453, the Ottoman Turks captured Constantinople and put an end to the Byzantine Empire, the last direct successor of the Roman Empire. In 1472, Ivan III, known as "the Great," married Zoe, a niece of the last Byzantine emperor, and thus claimed the imperial title. That's how the Russian royal title, "tsar," or "czar," came about. It's a Russianization of the word *Cæsar* or "emperor." Ivan the Great was the first to call himself "tsar" or "caesar."

Now we come to a special factor which we have not run into before, and that is the nobility. The Russian nobility were servants of the tsar. They were divided into two groups, the *boyars*, the upper nobility, who occupied the highest state offices and advised the prince, and they were the great landlords. Ivan IV (Ivan the Terrible), broke their power and influence. Then there was a lower nobility. This is the first time in this course that we have encountered the Eastern European pattern of nobility, which was the rule in Poland, Hungary, and Russia. There were a very few great magnates, and great lords, and a very, very numerous, mostly untitled, usually poor, lower aristocracy. The so-called "Seven Plum-Tree nobility" in Hungary, or the *szlachta* in Poland.

Interestingly, I asked my Slavicist friends for the title in Russian for this group of lower nobility, and there isn't one, which shows that it lacked even a sense of corporate identity. Now, the word for all the nobility, great and small, in Russian is *dvoriantsvo* from *dvor*, "house" or "court," that is, the tsar's court. As one great Russian reformer, Michael Speransky said early in the 19th century, "In Russia there are only two classes: the servants of the tsar, and the servants of the servants of the tsar."

Nobility in Russia was not what it was in the West, where it was regulated by feudal distinction, was inherited, and titles and rights and privileges, all the kinds of things we saw when we looked at the Holy Roman Empire. Nobility could be acquired by taking a post in civil service, or rising to a certain rank in the military service. There was also a large class of rural gentry, rather impoverished. Now I've designed a table, which shows the distribution of noble landholdings by the size of holding in 1892. The Russian measurement is one *dessyatin*, which equals 2.5 acres. What the table shows is that 49 percent of all Russian nobles had estates of less than 250 acres, meaning that half the Russian nobility lived on what were, in effect, very small farms.

Now think of the size of Russia, with its 12 time zones, and consider all these little estates, with their terrible roads, cut off in winter. You can immediately see this is not a Western European grand nobility. This is not the duke of Bedford. These are people who barely eke out a living in their remote small homesteadings.

Now, another key factor is the absence of the Roman law. In Lecture Two, I suggested that Western Europe was an amalgam of Roman, Judaeo-Christian, and feudal features. Medieval and early modern Russia lacked both the first and the third element. It did not inherit through the Greek tradition, the Roman law, the Roman code. We also saw that the Roman Empire was unique, a city-state, which became a world empire. Its procedures were based on citizens, that is, inhabitants of a city or often a town. In its other meaning, it meant someone who possessed the basic civic rights or privileges, a burgess or freeman of a city.

Since the Russian Empire had hardly any towns, and no tradition of Roman civil codes, it had very unspecific categories for extremely important Western terms, like "property," or "individual," or "contract," all of which had their origins in the inheritance of the Roman law.

Another key factor was that there was, in effect, no bourgeoisie, no middle class, and you see this. It's fantastic when you travel, when you walk around the streets of St. Petersburg, Leningrad. There are palaces as far as the eye can see, but there's no middle class housing, because there wasn't one. The word "bourgeois," in German, the *burger* was originally the name for somebody who lived in a walled town in medieval France or Germany.

As I argued in Lecture Two, the growth of these towns was an essential feature of the European West. The towns and the bourgeoisie in it had rights. There was a famous feudal dictum, "City air makes you free." The free cities of the Holy Roman Empire were directly under the empire, and not the local princes or kings. The corporation of the city of London is a surviving example.

Now, I'm sure you don't know it, but the queen has no rights to enter the City of London without the permission of the alderman and corporation. When you walk down the Strand, you come to the Temple Bar, which separates the city of Westminster from the city of London. The Temple Bar is a real bar. When the queen does go to the City of London, the alderman and corporation meet her at the bar and escort her in. It is a surviving relic of the time in which the City of London had rights against the Crown.

Now, towns emerged very late in Russian history. In 1564, the first book was printed in Moscow. By that time, the book trade had been flourishing in Western Europe for more than 100 years in Frankfurt, Leipzig, Holland, London, Basel, Wittenburg, Prague, Geneva, Paris, Amsterdam, Brussels, Ghent, this enormous number of flourishing Western European towns with their lively printing and book trade. Think, for example, of what printing and book trades meant in the 18th century in London.

Another key factor is serfdom. Now, serfdom is a system in which the agricultural worker is a kind of slave. It's the exact opposite of a citizen. During Catherine the Great's reign and the end of the 18th century, serfdom was at its height. Thirty-four out of 36 million peasant families were either landlord serfs or state peasants. That is to say, serfs who owed their allegiance directly to the crown. Peasants were completely prohibited from moving from their estates without the permission of their landlords. They also owed landlords compulsory service. One of the features of peasant agriculture which was very characteristic of Russia was the *mir*, just as the Soviet spacecraft is called the Mir, or the "commune."

Now, this was another uniquely Russian feature. The lord's land, or domain, was divided up by the peasant commune into large fields which were worked on a rotation crop system. Each field was divided into a series of strips, and each family got a series of strips roughly according to the number of male workers in the family, or the number of mouths to feed. It was a kind of peasant communism. From time to time, the land would have to be repartitioned. As you got older, and as your sons moved away, you were entitled to fewer strips. Every 10 years or so the commune would meet, and you'd lose strips, and somebody else would get them. It meant, actually, that agriculture was very limited, because these strips meant that you couldn't use large scale agricultural procedures and you had to walk a long way. It was estimated that the typical Russian peasant would walk hundreds of miles between the strips, because there were some that were very far from the village, and some were near. Communal property, then, and of course later on, communism, is not so alien in the Russian mentality as it is in the West.

The final key factor is what I call, what has been called, Slavophiles, and Westernerizers. Lovers of the Slav way, and modernizers. Though the terms were only invented in the 19th century, they are useful here. The Slavophiles preached a unique Russian way.

Sir Donald Mackenzie Wallace, who was an intrepid British Scottish explorer, walked around much of the Russian Empire in the 19th century, and in his wonderful book he quotes a conversation in St. Petersburg in 1877. A Slavophile told him, and this is really interesting; I quote, "In Europe the principle of personality is supreme; with us it is the communal principle. Europe is pagan, Russia—holy and Christian. In the West reigns apparent liberty, a liberty like that of a wild animal in the desert. The true liberty is found among us, in the East." In other words, not only is this particular Russian world different from the West, it should stay so. The great Russian writer Alexander Herzen once said, "Thank God that Russia has been spared the three great scourges of the West: Roman Catholicism, the bourgeoisie, and the Roman law."

Let me summarize these key features. Russia was both immensely backward, and yet, extremely complex. It had a harsh climate, a short growing season, bad roads, and few warm-water ports. The low productivity of Russian agriculture, ignorance, illiteracy, drunkenness, superstition, serfdom, the traditions of the "Holy Fool," that is, the fool is more Christian than the wise person, all contributed to the poverty and backwardness of society. Yet, the Russian Empire, in the period we're going to be looking at, became a European great power, and is full of potential.

This brings us to the other side of the equation, where Catherine the Great is to be found. The great Westernizing tsars. The Westernizing tsars are Peter the Great, Catherine the Great, Alexander II, Lenin and Stalin, and, I suppose, Vladimir Putin, people who realized that Russia cannot stay the way it has been. It has to become more like the West.

Peter the Great started this. He was tsar of Russia between 1682 and 1725. He was an astonishing man. Well over six feet tall. Immensely strong. He decided that Russia would become Western. In order to do this, he built a completely new capital from scratch, St. Petersburg, which was to be his "window on the West," and which was to have a Westernized manner. He banned beards and Muscovite dress. He reformed the calendar and simplified the alphabet, and he transferred the capital from "backward" Moscow to "modern" St. Petersburg. St. Petersburg is the most beautiful city I have ever seen. I always imagined this as kind of dark and dingy. In fact, it's a riot of color. One pink, blue, canary yellow, green, baroque palace after another. Now, it's a swamp, and when Peter wanted something, it had to happen. Forty thousand workers died creating this city in this swamp. They had to move gigantic slabs of granite from the Baltic coast up to this bay of the Neva in order to build the thing.

He abolished the onion dome on churches, and insisted on Western spires. What I love most, and I think it's so characteristic of Russian modernization, he said, "Churches should have spires like they have in the West." And the first one he built was the Cathedral of Peter and Paul in St. Petersburg, and they stuck a spire on it all right! It is 70 meters tall, 150 feet high! It's a gigantic needle. During the Second World War, they had to cover it up, because it was a perfect target for the Germans to aim at. I mean, the idea that you put a spire on, like in the West, in Peter the Great's mind, becomes this enormous transformation.

Now, Catherine the Great is the second great modernizing tsar. Her life is also the basic subject of today's lecture, so now I want to put her into this context. She was a German princess. And we know all about them now. She was born on April 24, 1729, in Stettin, now Szczecin, in Poland. Her father was Prince Christian Augustus of Anhalt-Zerbst, and she was christened Sophia Augusta Frederica. Her family was a typical small royal family, subdivided into rulers mini-states. Anhalt-Zerbst, which we've just run into, Anhalt-Dessau, Zerbst-Dornburg. That whole thicket, which the Russian historian V.O. Kliuchevsky, talking about her family background, called "an archaic feudal anthill." That's what it was like.

Now, her father was a ruling prince. He was the prince of Anhalt-Zerbst, but Anhalt-Zerbst wasn't big enough or rich enough to support him in grand style, and offered him no career, so like many of the medium size German princes, he had, so to speak, a "day job." That is, he was a general, and rather a good one in Frederick the Great's army.

Now, little Sophie was a phenomenon, irrepressible, smart, and obstinate. German princesses were the breeding farms of European royalty, because there were so many states and so many royal families. When the childless Empress Elizabeth of Russia was looking for a bride for her nephew, heir to the throne, the Grand Duke Peter, who was also a German prince, born Karl-Ulrich, son of Charles Frederick, the disposed Duke of Holstein-Gottorp, and the daughter of Peter the Great, she found Sophie.

On February 9, 1744, Sophie, age 15, came to Russia at the invitation of the empress. On August 24, 1745, she was married in St. Petersburg. She had to give up her German Lutheran faith, which I don't think she minded all that much, and was christened into the Russian Orthodox Church as Ekaterina Alexeevna, and hence became Catherine.

Now Peter, her husband, the grand duke, was not a very smart or a very stable young man. Catherine observed sarcastically about her young husband, "The grand duke had about as much direction as cannonball." His sexual inadequacies were soon apparent to her. They, as far as we can tell, never actually had any sexual intercourse at all, so Catherine looked elsewhere. She found a handsome guard officer, Sergei Saltykov, and had a baby by him.

Everybody knew that the future Tsar Paul I was almost certainly not Peter's son, but he was a male heir, so they overlooked it. The Grand Duke Peter was a very odd figure. He was obsessed by Frederick the Great and war, although he was actually a terrible field commander, and he played with human toy soldiers, his Holstein regiment. He joined them in drinking bouts and other acts of stupidity. He refused to learn Russian, and had contempt for all Russian things. He also flaunted his German tastes, which as you can easily imagine, made him unpopular.

In 1762, Elizabeth died, and now this inadequate and disturbed person was Tsar Peter III. Since he refused to learn Russian, and had seized some Orthodox Church lands, he was unpopular from the start. Just as Russia and Austria were about to crush Frederick the Great in the Seven Years' War, he ended the war with Prussia because he admired Frederick so much. By the way, that was called the "miracle of the House of Brandenburg." In April of 1945, when Hitler was sitting in his ruined Berlin and Roosevelt died, he and Goebbels said, "Aha! At long last, the miracle of the House of Bradenburg has occurred again." Well, it hadn't.

Anyway, he tried to declare war on Denmark to regain his lost Holstein lands, and the army was against him. On June 28, 1762, there was a coup d'etat: Gregory Orlov, Saltykov's successor as Catherine's lover, and his four brothers, who were Guard officers, mobilized the Guards regiments. They seized Peter, and they bundled the poor old fool off to prison, where he died, "in a drunken scuffle," i.e., he was murdered, and they made Catherine tsarina of all the Russians.

This inauspicious beginning was the way Catherine the Great began her reign, which lasted from 1762 to 1796. Now, her hold on power was utterly unlike Maria Theresa's, whom we've already looked at. There was no real Romanoff succession, because the future tsar, Paul, was not the son of Peter III. False Peters popped up all over the place in the peasantry and threatened Catherine's hold on power. In 1773, Emilian Pugachev, a very dramatic peasant rebel, claimed to be the *real* Peter III, and set off a huge and very dangerous peasant rebellion. If you think about the conditions of serfdom, you can see how that's always a possibility.

Catherine was foreign, and she was known contemptuously as the "German," in spite of her devotion to Russia. Then there was the question of her sexuality, which was a European phenomenon. Catherine was exactly the opposite of Maria Theresa, who in 1737 founded a chastity league to reduce promiscuity among the aristocracy. Catherine was openly libertine, and made no secret of her very powerful sexual drive. She had one lover after another, right to her very old age. They got younger and younger and younger, but they were still in her bed when she was old enough to be their grandmother. There was a huge European pornographic literature about her unbridled lust.

The reality is much more complicated. Orlov, who was her lover from 1762 to 1772, and Grigori Aleksandrovich Potemkin, of the Potemkin village who was her lover from 1774 on, played really important roles in an unstable and rather primitive state. They provided the essential masculine links to military power, to the army, and to the nobility. Potemkin and Catherine had a very unusual relationship. I guess, today, you'd call it an open marriage. They never quite separated; she took other lovers, and he did, too. Nonetheless, they remained, in an odd way, like a married couple. His counsel was always essential, and made policy.

There were problems with female rule in Russia which raised peculiar difficulties, because the society had no rights for women. Russian nobles, and members of the royal family thought nothing of dismissing unwanted wives without a divorce, just sending them to convents and getting rid of them.

Now, Catherine approached her job full of the ideas of the Enlightenment. And by this stage, by Lecture Ten, I think you now have a pretty good idea of what the ideas of the Enlightenment were: rationality, reason, the good of the state. She was influenced by the French. She read widely in French philosophy. She corresponded famously and openly with Voltaire and Diderot, and Diderot had a couple of rather uncomfortable years at her court. She was determined to open Russia to Western influences.

Hence, very early in her reign, she decided to open Russian society to foreigners. In the text of this decree, which was one of her first, gives something of the flavor of Russian autocracy. Let me just read you a bit:

> The manifesto of the Empress Catherine II, July 22, 1763. We, Catherine the second, Empress and Autocrat of all the Russians at Moscow, Kiev, Vladimir, Novgorod, Czarina of Kasan, Czarina of Astrachan, Czarina of Siberia, Lady of Pleskow and Grand Duchess of Smolensko, Duchess of Esthonia and Livland, Carelia, Twer, Yugoria, Permia, Viatka and Bulgaria and others; Lady and Grand Duchess of Novgorod in the Netherland of Chernigov, Resan, Rostov, Yaroslav, Beloosrial, Udoria, Obdoria, Condinia, and Ruler of the entire North region and Lady of the Yurish, of the Cartalinian and Grusinian czars and the Cabardinian land, of the Cherkessian and Gorsian princes, and the lady of the manor and sovereign of many others. We permit foreigners to come into Our Empire in order to settle in all the governments, just as each may desire.

Now foreigners without enough money would receive subsidies to travel to Russia. In 1776, she wanted to Westernize Russian laws. There are three clauses I picked out which are worth noticing. Chapter One, paragraph six, Russia is declared to be "a European state." Chapter Two, paragraph nine, "the sovereign is absolute, for there is no other authority but that which centers in his single person that can act with a vigor proportionate to the extent of such a vast domain." Then there's 13, the idea that the monarchy is there to establish the state good. Now the new law code spoke the reasonable language of the Enlightenment, but it had to be applied in the reality of a drunken, illiterate, savage, serf society, full of superstition and religious to its core.

Catherine made famous journeys. Since communications were very difficult, and roads frequently impassable, Catherine's tours might take months. The journey from Moscow to Kiev might take a month in good weather, and much longer in bad weather. In such a vast territory, there was no effective way to enforce the laws. No sanctions, nor any easy means of showing the monarch to her people, other than these journeys. She introduced reforms of government and society in famous decrees, such as "The Status of Local Administration and Provinces of the Empire," of 1775, or, "The Charter of Nobility," of April 21, 1785.

That's a really interesting case. Catherine established feudal rights for the nobility four years before the French revolution began to abolish them. In other words, she actually tried to create the very feudal nobility which the Russians didn't have, and which the West was just about to get rid of.

Consequently, Westernizing transformed social relations. The essential Russian character was eroded, and that's been a problem ever since. Her foreign policy was, on the whole, remarkably successful. Through the three partitions of Poland, which we looked at when we studied Maria Theresa, she gained vast territories, and pushed Russia's frontiers closer to the West. Together with Potemkin, she pursued several successful wars against Turkey, and pushed the Russian Empire's borders to the Black Sea and into the Caucuses. In 1795, the new city of Odessa on the Black Sea was founded, and Odessa was the frontier. It was where anybody with any energy could settle; all the rules were off. Jews could settle there, and become as rich as they liked, and it was a real window for Russian trade into the world.

Now how do we assess Catherine the Great's reign? Elisabeth Vigee-Lebrun, the Parisian portrait artist, recalled Catherine in her memoirs. She noted how, "she'd imagined her to be prodigiously tall, as high as her reputation." By 1789, though, the 60-year-old Catherine "was very fat (and toothless)...she still had a handsome face…Genius was stamped upon her brow, which was broad and very high…I have said that she was short, [yet] on days when she appeared in state, everything about her—the head held high, the eagle eyes, the assured bearing that comes with the habit of command—was so majestic that she seemed to rule the world."

Catherine's choice of symbol for her reign was the bee, with her motto, l'*utile,* (useful). The busy bee expressed her concept of work. She wanted to see order, and she hated Russian sloppiness. Moscow stood for everything she disliked. I quote from Catherine, "In Moscow, one quite often sees a lady covered with jewels and elegantly dressed, emerging from an immense yard filled with all possible refuse and mud adjoining a decrepit hut; in a magnificent carriage drawn by eight horrible hacks, shabbily harnessed, with unkempt grooms wearing handsome liveries, which they disgrace by their uncouth appearance."

Moscow was messy. She didn't like it, and she didn't like any of those kinds of Russian sloppiness and drunkenness which characterized Russian society. I suppose one could say that ultimately, Catherine remained an orderly German at heart, and never entirely became a proper Russian. Her reign, however, set the agenda with which we are still living. Is it possible for Russia to Westernize, to modernize, without ceasing to be what the Russians regard as its essential character?

Lecture Eleven
Joseph II—The Rational Emperor

Scope:

Joseph II (1741–1790), Holy Roman Emperor (1765–1790), king of Bohemia and Hungary (1780–1790), was the son of Maria Theresa and Holy Roman Emperor Francis I, whom he succeeded. Joseph attempted to rule his immense and quarrelsome territories by pure reason. He tried to rationalize the mess of royal possessions that Maria Theresa had ruled by common sense. The battle between mother and son over the lives of millions of subjects is dramatic enough on its own, but it reveals a process that rarely shows up so clearly: the law of unintended consequences in history. Joseph thought everybody should speak German, because it was the language of the court and the government. He forced it on Czechs, Croats, Poles, and Magyars, most of whom were peasants and could not read. Joseph, by creating schools to achieve a rational goal, unleashed the irrational force of nationalism.

Outline

I. As we saw in Lecture Seven, part of the Austrian inheritance was the question of its statehood. Maria Theresa's problem was how to be queen when each of her territories had its own constitutional arrangements.

   A. The crowns and lands were "real," with their own identities and histories. Consider, for example, the case of Hungary and its "Englishness."

      1. Liberalism grew up in Hungary on similar foundations as in England. The "Golden Bull" of Andrew II (1222) and the Magna Carta (1215) are similar, reflecting the demand for self-government by the Hungarian gentry and English barons.

      2. The official language of the kingdom of Hungary was Latin, a universal, non-national tongue, which all the various nationalities could use without offense.

      3. The Magyars, like the Angles and Saxons, invaded their territories in the early Middle Ages. The Magyars were conquerors, and in 895, under Arpad the Great, they occupied the great Danubian plain. Their alien identity

reflected the fact that the Magyars were a Mongol people who moved west from the Russian steppes.

    4. In the Habsburg lands, the basic identities were historical, not rational.

B. The Holy Roman Empire was the greatest dilemma for the Habsburgs.

    1. As we saw in Lecture Seven, another essential Habsburg dilemma arose from the fact that their highest title and greatest prestige was to be elected emperor.

    2. Yet the empire was an anachronism, an unwieldy medieval mess and, in no way, a state.

C. Emperor Francis I, consort of Maria Theresa, died unexpectedly on August 18, 1765, and Maria Theresa's son Joseph II was elected emperor. She, of course, could not hold the title because no female succession was permitted.

II. The consequence of this election was conflict between mother and son.

A. Joseph was the emperor, but his mother was the queen and was in charge. Inevitably, the 25-year-old Joseph would find the situation intolerable. He was exasperated by the lack of rational, enlightened thought and intellectual pursuits at court.

B. Maria Theresa lived easily with the historical principle, whereas Joseph II insisted on governing according to the rational principle.

    1. Joseph II was born in 1741, Maria Theresa's first child. Even as a boy, he showed that he was impatient by nature, wanting to "do good" according to the rules of reason, instead of following the traditional "rules, statutes and oaths."

    2. The generation of Joseph II was also the generation of the Founding Fathers of the American Republic. Joseph II shared similar views with John Hancock and Thomas Jefferson on the objects of government and the innate reasonableness of mankind.

3. The difference between Joseph II and Jefferson was not in the aim but the method. Who decides what are rational ends? For Joseph, it was the wise philosopher-king; for Jefferson, it was the people.

   a. Government for the generation of Jefferson was a rational activity. Joseph's way to achieve the rule of reason was through the benign rule of an *enlightened despot* (that is, himself). The "enlightened people" was Jefferson's alternative.

   b. What happens to our society if neither is right? In the era of "dumbing down," can we sustain our faith in our institutions and fellow citizens? Are "the people" really rational?

   c. There is a strong argument against reason as the basis of politics. In politics, belief in reason is the faith that we can improve things by thought. Burke argued for the importance of history: the belief that only that which evolves over time will work. He believed that political affairs are too complicated to plan. This is a major theme of this course, as we shall see in Lecture Fifteen.

III. How was the rule of reason applied in the Habsburg lands and the Holy Roman Empire?

   A. Historically, the Holy Roman Empire was a confusing mess, with myriad forms of governments and lands. The various estates and realms saw the need to protect their institutions against ambitious emperors, such as Joseph.

      1. For Joseph, the empire was maddeningly nonrational and a source of frustration.

      2. Yet the empire was also the source of his power. His election was an example of the odd rules by which electors chose the emperor. To attack these rules as irrational was contradictory. Joseph II was the man sawing off the branch on which he sat.

   B. Joseph II instituted a program of reforms, the object of which was the construction of the "enlightened state."

      1. He instructed his civil servants: "…national or religious differences must not make the slightest difference…and all must feel themselves to be brothers in a single

monarchy, all striving to be useful to each other" (Blanning, 1994, p. 59).

2. This was a completely utopian program. How were Hungarians and Croats, Croats and Serbs, Germans and Czechs to be "brothers in a single monarchy"? Was there to be no difference between Catholics and Protestants?

3. Joseph's complex and obsessive personality played a role in his attempt to institute reforms. He had huge energies and could give great dedication to a task, but he was terribly impatient. He believed in a set of axiomatic principles to be carried out over any opposition: All human beings were equal (except the emperor); reason was to be the only guide to action and the good of the state, the only end.

4. The combination of his impatience, his diligence and capacity for hard work, his intolerance, and his belief in certain axioms led to what his bureaucrats called *vielregieren* ("lots of governing"). He issued no less than 6,000 decrees between 1780 and 1790. Nobody could read them all, let alone carry them out.

C. Joseph's reforms fell into various categories.

1. Among his humane reforms was the abolition of torture and witchcraft trials. He imposed toleration of Protestants and Jews. He founded homes for the deaf and dumb, liberated peasants from servitude in parts of the empire, and tried to tax the peasants' lords. He founded hospitals and introduced street lighting.

2. Joseph also carried out religious reforms, including abolishing "useless" monastic orders and reorganizing the dioceses of bishops to correspond to the territorial borders of the empire. He reduced the pope's authority and clashed with ecclesiastical princes in the empire. He was determined to cleanse the church of "abuses."

3. In 1784, he decreed that German was to be the official language of the empire. It was to be introduced at once, and public employees were to be competent in it within a fixed time.

   a. Obviously, some nations objected to the standardization decree, but Joseph dismissed their complaints.

      b. Joseph's policies had a paradoxical outcome: The spread of schools to teach German to populations of mostly illiterate peasants required training schoolmasters. These young Poles, Magyars, Czechs, and Croats attended training colleges to learn German but used their native dialects when they taught. They were, in effect, teaching Czech, Polish, Croat, and Magyar as they taught German. Thus, rational standardization produced its opposite: nationalism. A rigorous application of reason yielded anti-reason in the cult of the nation.

   4. Joseph also attempted to suppress the ancient noble privileges and to humble and impoverish the grandees. The contrast with Frederick the Great of Prussia (see Lecture Four) was sharp. Frederick believed that a sovereign should regard it as his duty to protect the nobility.

D. The result of the reform program was that the whole monarchy increasingly rose in revolt against Joseph's tyranny, culminating in a revolution in the Austrian Netherlands in 1789.

E. Joseph grew tired and increasingly disappointed, even disillusioned. He fell ill and, on February 20, 1790, died. His brother Leopold, the new emperor, repealed most of the reforms.

IV. The contemporary assessment of Joseph and that of many historians claimed that Joseph was convinced of his failure "in all his endeavors."

A. Joseph had, however, gained deep affection among the poor, the peasants, the Jews, and the Protestants. He made real improvements in the laws, city government, and bureaucracy, but he had earned the hatred of the grand nobles and the privileged.

B. Joseph faced the dilemmas of enlightened despotism.

    1. His authority rested on non-rational structures. He was a king by birth, not by a competitive or reasonable system of selection.

    2. The nobility had a case against him, as perfectly stated by General Yorck von Wartenburg: "If your Royal Highness removes my rights and those of my children, who will defend yours?"

    3. Thus, the attempt to reduce and eliminate noble "privilege" ended in a paradox: The emperor was the most privileged of the privileged. His attempt to crush the rights of Belgian nobles was an attack on the Old Regime as a whole.

    4. Joseph was also caught in another paradox: the dilemma of all reform from above. How do you write a decree to make people citizens and brothers?

    5. The final paradox was that Joseph II did everything for the greater good of the state. The glorification of "the state" was his *palladium*, or "safeguard." But what was the state? It was either an abstraction or another name for the emperor's unlimited power.

C. Joseph's ultimate dilemma was that of all reformers who want to practice despotic reason by forcing human beings to be free. He ordered his subjects to behave reasonably and become uniform and identical citizens. He denied their collective identities and recognized no groups; there was the state and the individual.

D. Joseph II was the extreme example of the attempt to make us better by reason; his reign marks another step on the way to the rational, modern state.

Essential Reading:

T.C.W. Blanning, *Joseph II*, Profiles in Power Series.

Supplementary Reading:

Andrew Wheatcroft, *The Habsburgs: Embodying Empire.*

Questions to Consider:

1. To what extent is enlightened despotism a contradiction in itself?

2. Which side do you chose in the dispute between reason and history and why?

Lecture Eleven—Transcript
Joseph II—The Rational Emperor

One of the basic principles of this course, *European History and European Lives: 1715 to 1914*, is the principle of comparison, and one of its pleasures for me is the way in which we can compare these lives and begin to see some fundamental principles. We now have the third of the most famous enlightened despots to consider, Joseph II, and I think each one of these illustrates a kind of principle.

In Lecture Four, we looked at Frederick the Great, who showed us the limits of absolutism in our own human nature. In Lecture 10, we looked at Catherine the Great and saw the limits imposed by the backwardness of the realm. Today, in this lecture, I want to look at Joseph II, who I think shows the limits imposed by the very nature of reason itself.

Now, when we looked at the structure of the Habsburg Empire in Lecture Seven on Maria Theresa, we saw that there was a fundamental dilemma. The Austrian problem, the Austrian legacy or inheritance, was to be or not to be a state, and we saw that Maria Theresa's problem was how to be queen in her territories when each territory had its own constitutional arrangements. Now, these territories and these crowns and lands were real. They had their own identities and their own histories, and I just want to take a quick look at the case of Hungary and what I think of as its "Englishness."

Liberalism in Hungary grew up on very similar foundations to that in England. The "Golden Bull" of Andrew II of 1222, and the Magna Carta of 1215 are very similar both in their texts and in their import, and they reflected demand for self-government by the Hungarian gentry organized in their *comitati*, and by the English barons. The official language of the kingdom of Hungary was Latin, a universal, non-national tongue which all nationalities could use without offense. The Magyars, like the Angles and the Saxons, had invaded their territories in the early Middle Ages. The Magyars were conquerors, and in 895, under Arpad the Great, they occupied the great Danubian Plain.

Their alien identity was reflected in the fact that the Magyars were a Mongol people who moved west from the Russian steppes. Now, in the Habsburg lands, these basic identities were historical, not rational. The Holy Roman Empire, as we have seen, was the greatest of these dilemmas. As we saw in Lecture Seven, another essential Habsburg problem arose from the fact that their highest title and greatest prestige was to be elected emperor, yet the empire was a huge anachronism. I've called it an unwieldy, medieval mess, incomprehensible, unreformable, indispensable, and in no way a state.

When Emperor Francis I and consort of Maria Theresa died unexpectedly on August 18, 1765, Maria Theresa's son, Joseph, was elected Joseph II, emperor, in the famous crowning hall in Frankfurt am Main. She, of course, could not hold the title because no female succession was permitted. Now, you can imagine what the consequences were. Mother and son were in constant conflict. Joseph was emperor, but mom was the queen and in real charge. It was inevitable that the 25-year-old Joseph would find the situation intolerable, and here's an example of Joseph's exasperation with the old ladies of the court:

> An assemblage of a dozen old married ladies, three or four old maids, and twenty young girls who were known as Ladies of the Court, seven archduchesses, an empress, two princes and an emperor co-regent under the same roof—and yet no society at all, or at least none that is rational or agreeable, since they all keep themselves to themselves. The gossiping and squabbling between one old woman and another, lady and lady, archduchess and archduchess, kept everyone at home, and 'what will people say?' prevents the most innocent gatherings or parties…The intelligent, bored to death with the stupid women, eventually find an outlet for their intelligence, and then use it in most unsuitable ways, whereas if they had an opportunity to deploy it in good company they would never contemplate such follies.

Now, some of this was simply the inevitable friction of old and young, but the text provides some important clues to something deeper, and let's look quickly at Joseph's words: "Yet no society at all, or at least none that is rational or agreeable." Now, I think by now I have banged this point home often enough you will recognize in those phrases the language of the new public sphere of enlightened, rational conversation, of the meeting of minds.

Now, Joseph and Maria were divided on principle even more deeply. Maria represented and lived easily with the historical principle, whereas Joseph II insisted on governing according to the rational principle. Joseph was born in 1741, and was Maria Theresa's first child. Even as a boy, he showed that he was impatient by nature, and in his *Reveries* of 1763, he expressed the conflict very well:

> To be in the position to do all the good which one is prevented from doing by the rules, statutes, and oaths which the provinces believe to be their *palladium,* and, which, sanely considered, turn only to their disadvantage, it is not possible for a state to be happy, for a sovereign to be able to do great things…God, keep me from wanting to break oaths, but I believe that we must work to convert the provinces and make them see how useful the *despotisme lié* [limited despotism] would be to them.

Now, note the words again: "sanely considered." Joseph II means here according to the rules of reason. The greatest good of the greatest number involved more taxes rationally allocated according to the ability of each community to pay, and who after all could object to that?

Now, the generation of Joseph II was also the generation of the Founding Fathers of the American Republic. Joseph was born in 1741, and here are the dates of birth of some famous patriots: John Adams, born in 1735; John Hancock, born in 1737; Thomas Jefferson, born in 1743; John Jay, born in 1745; James Madison, born in 1751; and Alexander Hamilton, the baby of the group, born in 1755. Joseph II was born between John Hancock and Thomas Jefferson, and he shared very similar views on the objects of government. The words he used could have been theirs: Society, happy, sanely considered.

Now, there were shared values in that generation. They all believed in the innate reasonableness of mankind. Thomas Jefferson wrote to Count Diodati in 1789: "I have so much confidence in the good sense of man and his qualifications for self-government that I am never afraid of the issue where reason is left free to exert her force."

The difference between Joseph II and Jefferson was not in the aim, but in the method. Who decides what are rational ends? For Joseph II, it was the wise philosopher-king. For Jefferson, it was the people. I quote, and this is from a letter of Jefferson to the famous British scientist and radical Joseph Priestley from 1802: "Our people in a body are wise because they are under the unrestrained and unperverted operation of their own understandings."

Now, let us consider the rule of reason. Government, for the generation of Jefferson, was a rational activity. Joseph II's way to achieve the rule of reason was through the benign rule of an enlightened despot, i.e., himself, "despotism lie" he called it, limited despotism. The "enlightened people" were Thomas Jefferson's alternative.

Now, what happens to our society if neither of them is right? In the era of the dumbing down in America, can we really sustain our faith in the institutions and our fellow citizens? Are the people, in Jefferson's sense, really rational?

This is a really serious question and I don't propose to answer it here, but think about it, because if the people are not rational, if both Jefferson and Joseph II were wrong, what is the basis on which our institutions actually rest? In addition, the great struggle between reason and history in human affairs has never been resolved. There's a strong argument against both Jefferson and Joseph II, and against reason is the basis of politics. As we shall see, the belief in reason in politics is the faith that by thought we can improve things.

Edmund Burke, whom we shall look at in Lecture 15, argued exactly the opposite. He argued for history. The belief that only that which evolves over time, which is tested, will work. He believed that political affairs were much too complicated for even the smartest people to plan, and this is another major theme of this course, as we shall see in Lectures 15 and 16, when we contrast Edmund Burke and the new conservatism and Robespierre and the new radicalism.

Now, leaving aside the theoretical issues, which are complicated enough, let's take a look at the implications for the rule of reason in the Habsburg lands and in the Holy Roman Empire. Nobody can deny that you would not sit down to plan the Holy Roman Empire. It's like that old joke, where somebody's lost in Maine and asks a Maine farmer how to get to Bangor, and the farmer thinks for a minute and said, "I wouldn't start from here."

I mean, it's that kind of thing. I have used the definition given by Johann Jakob Moser twice before, but let me just do it again because we need to have it in mind. It sums up the historical messiness of the old Holy Roman Empire: "We have various kinds of lands, various

206

forms of government with the states and without them, imperial towns, a nobility, some of whom are immediate, subjects of all different sorts, and a thousand other such things. To think for oneself, what good is it here? Not the slightest. What can a philosopher do about it? Not the slightest. These are the plain facts that I must accept as they are, unless I want to deform and ruin our German Empire."

Now, the essence of Joseph's problem is in that passage. Joseph did want to reform, not ruin but improve, modernize, rationalize the empire, and that is the problem. How do you do it? The empire is maddeningly not rational, and Joseph's frustration is clear: "To be in a position to do all the good which one is prevented from doing by the rules, statutes, and oaths which the provinces believe to be their palladium." I looked "palladium" up in the dictionary, and the dictionary says a palladium is something on which the safety of a nation, institution, or privilege is believed to depend. It's a safeguard.

That is exactly how the various estates and realms saw their rights, as protecting their institutions, protecting them precisely against ambitious emperors like Joseph. Moreover, the empire is the greatest source of Joseph's power. It is also, whether he liked it or not, his palladium. His election and, after all, the whole system by which three archbishops and four princes elect the emperor of the Holy Roman Empire, is exactly the sort of various kinds of lands and various forms of governments and so on of which a philosopher despaired, which Moser talked about. Joseph is only emperor because of the non-rational character of the Holy Roman Empire.

To attack these rules as irrational is contradictory. Joseph II, by attempting to modernize these institutions, was like a man sawing off the branch on which he himself was sitting. Joseph introduced an amazing program of reforms. The object of these reforms was the construction of the enlightened state.

In 1785, Joseph gave instructions to his civil servants as follows: "As the good of the state is always indivisible, namely that which affects the population at large and the greatest number, and as, in a similar fashion, all the provinces of the monarchy make up a single whole with a common objective, national or religious differences must not make the slightest difference in all this, and all must feel themselves to be brothers in a single monarchy, all striving to be useful to each other."

There is actually an uncanny parallel here with the social contract of Jean-Jacques Rousseau, which we looked at in Lecture Five. You have a society composed of rational individuals whose will is expressed through the *Volonté générale* or the General Will. In some sense, Joseph was putting himself in the position of actually being the general will: "I express, through my rules, the will of all these people, and I do so because we share rationality. It's rational for all these people to behave in this way." This was, however, if you'll think about it, a completely utopian program. How were Hungarians and Croats, Croats and Serbs, Germans and Czechs "to be brothers in a single monarchy"? Was there to be no difference between Catholics and Protestants?

The style of the emperor contributed as well. Joseph had a complex and obsessive personality. He had energies and, like Frederick the Great, whom he greatly admired, could give great dedication to his task. He simplified court etiquette. He refused to live either in Schönbrunn, to raise his great powers outside Vienna, or the vast Hofburg in it. He lived in a small palace for an emperor. He was a hard-working, thrifty, "Frederick the Great" type, but he was terribly impatient.

The playwright Gotthold Lessing, one of the cleverest men of the 18th century, and one of the most influential figures of the Enlightenment, observed him from close up and he wrote: "He often achieves very accurate insights into the future, but he cannot wait for the future to come. He wants to see the future accelerated, and also wants to do the accelerating himself." Now, of course, it's true that Joseph II, like other despots, believed that only he could do it, and therefore life is short so he was, of course, in a hurry. There's a sense in which Joseph II was very like Margaret Thatcher. He believed in a set of axiomatic principles which were to be carried out over any opposition. What did she used to say? "Are they with us or against us?" All human beings were equal except, of course, the emperor. Reason was to be the only guide to action; and the good of the state the only end.

It's a wonderfully clear program. We can all understand it. The combination, however, of his temperamental impatience, his extreme diligence, and his capacity for hard work, his royal intolerance, and his belief in certain axioms led to what his bureaucrats called *Vielregieren* (a lot of governing). Between 1780 and 1790, in 10 years, he issued no less than 6,000 decrees to his governmental servants. One of them complained, "We couldn't even read all these things, let alone carry them out."

The reforms fell into various groups. First, there were the humane reforms. Joseph abolished torture and put an end to witchcraft trials. He imposed toleration of Protestants and of Jews. His edict liberating the Jews of 1781 was the first in Europe. He founded homes for the deaf and dumb. He liberated peasants from serfdom in his own hereditary holdings, but not in the empire as a whole, and he tried to tax their lords. He founded hospitals and introduced street lighting. Nothing was too small for his attention or for him to improve.

Now, religious reforms are very interesting. He abolished what he called "useless monastic orders." What is a useless order? A useless order was a kind of order which prayed, a contemplative order. The only monastic orders he wanted in the kingdom were those that did something practical—they either taught or they were nursing—and the rest he got rid of.

He reorganized the diocese of bishops to correspond to the territorial borders of the empire. It bothered him that archbishops and bishops' dioceses were all over the map, sometimes in his domains and sometimes out. Well, of course they were that way because they were medieval feudal inheritances.

He reduced the pope's authority and had some terrific clashes with the pope. He clashed with the ecclesiastical princes in the empire who protested at his interventions in archiepiscopal dioceses, and in so doing, of course, he alienated three of the seven electors of the empire. He was, above all, determined to cleanse the church of what he called its "abuses."

It's also rational that everybody should speak the same language and so, in 1784, a standardization of language was decreed, and the language chosen was German. German was to be the official language of the empire. Unlike Frederick the Great, Joseph II did speak good German, and it was introduced at once, and public employees were to be competent in it within a fixed and limited time. Again, that's rational. Why shouldn't they all speak German? It's, I suppose, what English speakers think about the world. Why shouldn't they all speak English? If we find ourselves in a country and if we speak loudly to them in English, they will after all understand us.

It's not that Joseph was a nationalist. He was a rationalist. German was the language of the court; it was the most important literary language, it had the largest number of speakers, so let everybody else speak it.

Now, the Hungarian case is a perfect example of his methods. When the Hungarian parliament complained, and remember they were using Latin, he replied to Count Esterhazy, Hungarian chancellor, that it was absurd for the Hungarians to use a dead language, Latin, and a reproach: all civilized peoples had abandoned Latin except the backward Magyars and Poles.

It was no problem anyway, since Hungarians were a minority in the kingdom of Hungary, and he concluded the message with these words: "You can easily work out for yourself just how advantageous it will be when there is only one language for written communication in the monarchy, and how conducive that will be to binding all the different parts of the whole."

Now, every single statement was an insult to the Hungarian gentry and nobility. Every one of them reminded them that they were a minority in the kingdom and reminded them that they were backward—it insulted their use of Latin, etc. Yet, his policies had a paradoxical outcome. He insisted that schools be established to teach German to populations which were illiterate and mostly peasants, and that in turn required a small army of schoolmasters to teach German.

Now, these young Magyars, Czechs, Poles, and Croats had to go to teacher training college to learn German, but they also, of course, had to use the native dialect when they taught. They were in effect teaching Czech, Polish, Croat, and Magyar at the same time that they were teaching German, and thus the rational standardization produced its opposite: They became nationalists. Thus, a rigorous application of reason yielded exactly the opposite: anti-reason in the cult of the nation. He attempted to suppress the ancient noble privileges and: "to humble and impoverish the grandees, for I do not believe it is very beneficial that there should be little kings and great subjects who live at their ease, not caring what becomes of the state."

Here we can see a really interesting and sharp contrast with Frederick the Great of Prussia, whom we discussed in Lecture Four. Frederick believed that: "a sovereign should regard it as his duty to protect the nobility, who form the finest jewel in his crown and the luster of the army." Of course, what Frederick the Great did was to give his nobility a kind of deal. They had a monopoly of high commands and officer commissions in the army and of high posts in the civil service. In that way, because they were not a rich nobility, they were bound to the well-being of the king and therefore loyal.

You can see the program that I've put before you was going to be opposed, and the result was indeed revolution. The whole monarchy began to bubble with unrest, and increasingly there were votes against what came to be called "Joseph's Tyranny." In 1784, there was a peasant revolt in the Tyrol. In 1787, riots broke out in the then Austrian Netherlands, today's Belgium. In 1788, Hungarian dissidents began to negotiate a secret alliance with Prussia to declare independence and, as it were, to fight against the Habsburgs. In 1789, a real revolution broke out in the Austrian Netherlands and, as a matter of fact, if you had asked an intelligent observer on the first of January, 1789, which is the country most likely to have a revolution in the next two or three years, nobody would have said France. They would certainly have said the Habsburg monarchy, because the Austrian Netherlands were just about to burst out in revolution. In January of 1790, the Bavarian ambassador reported to Munich that: "The unanimous opinion here is that only his death can save the monarchy."

I haven't got time to talk about Joseph's wars which, unlike those of Frederick the Great, were not successful. But by 1790, Joseph was exhausted, increasingly disappointed, and probably disillusioned. He fell ill and on February 20, 1790, the Emperor Joseph died. When the old adviser to Maria Theresa heard that Joseph had died, he said cynically, "Well, that was very nice of him." Joseph's brother, Leopold, took over as new emperor and repealed instantly most of the reforms.

I want to stop and think at slightly greater length than I normally do in these lectures about what are the lessons we need to draw from this exemplary life. There's a legend that Joseph wanted to have his grave: Here lies Joseph II, Holy Roman Emperor, who failed in all his enterprises. The contemporaries, I think, on the whole, believed that, and many historians claim that Joseph was convinced of his failure in all his endeavors, but they were not all failures. He had gained deep affection among the poor, the peasants, the Jews, and the Protestants. He had made real improvements in the laws and city government and in bureaucracy, but he had earned the hatred of the great nobles and of the privileged.

It is the fact that when the French Revolution spread, as we shall see in Lecture 16 on Robespierre and Lecture 18 on Napoleon, when the French Revolution spread and when Napoleon brought the new doctrines of democracy and liberty to the Austrian Empire, the Austrian Empire survived. It did not disintegrate, and I think a lot of it has to do with the fact that Joseph's reforms had really taken, but his reign raises some, I think, profound problems for us. We've seen now three examples of enlightened despotism: that of Frederick the Great, that of Catherine the Great, and that of Joseph II.

There is, I think, in Joseph's case a real set of problems that we need to consider. The first is that Joseph's authority, as we've seen, rested on non-rational structures. He was king, emperor, by birth, not by competitive examination or by any other rational system of selection. So he was already in some sense caught up in a dilemma which was inherent in his own position. It could be argued that to say enlightened and despotism in the same phrase is itself a contradiction in terms, that despotism can never be enlightened. Second, the nobility had a profound case against him, and here is a perfect statement of that noble position. We don't, alas, have time in this course to look at the parallel period of Prussian reform between 1806 and 1819, but during that period, when reforms were being carried out by King Frederick William III, General Count Yorck von Wartenburg said to the Prince of Prussia: "If your Royal Highness removes my rights and those of my children, who will defend yours?" This is, of course, absolutely right.

The attempt to reduce and eliminate noble privilege to get rid of the little kings in the empire ended in a paradoxical dilemma, because the emperor was the most privileged of the privileged. He was in fact the most noble of the nobles. When Emperor Joseph attempted to crush the rights of the Belgian nobles, he was actually attacking the whole Old Regime of which he was the most prominent representative.

The Austrian Netherlands were, as one historian has called them, "a museum-piece of medieval corporate liberties." And they were liberties, rights, and privileges precisely against the threat of a rational despot like Joseph. Joseph simply saw them as a nuisance, tried to eliminate and crush them on the grounds that they were irrational and, of course, they were irrational. They were historic. That's what these people had grown up with. That's what they felt protected them. Then Joseph was caught in another paradox, the dilemma of all reform from above. How do you write a decree to make people citizens and brothers? How can you reform human nature from above?

The final paradox was that Joseph II did everything for the greater good of the state. The glorification of the state was his palladium, but what was the state? There was no state. It was either a complete abstraction or it was simply another name for the emperor's unlimited power, and this he was never willing to see. His rationality always stopped at the point at which he should have looked in the mirror and said, "Wait a minute. Is it rational for me to claim that the state benefits here when the state is entirely represented by one individual?"

Here, we face for the first time, though we'll come to it again in the French Revolution, the final dilemma of all reformers who want to practice despotic reason by forcing human beings to be free. Joseph ordered his subjects to behave reasonably and become uniform and identical citizens. He denied them their collective identities and recognized no groups. There was the state and there was the individual. Joseph was an extreme, but not the most extreme, example of the attempt to make us better by reason, and thus he marks another stage on the way from the Old Regime to the rational modern state. But we shall see in Lecture 16, when we look at Robespierre, that this program is far more dangerous when it's carried out not by a despot but by the democratic will of the people. Once Rousseau's *Volonté générale* is liberated and allowed to carry out a reasonable program, some very odd things happen.

Lecture Twelve
Goethe—The Artist as Work of Art

Scope:

Johann Wolfgang von Goethe (1749–1832) is to German literature what Shakespeare is to English. Goethe could do everything well. He painted, sketched, designed, and wrote poetry and plays. He had a large private income and could afford to travel, never having to slave as a tutor to some minor German prince. Goethe knew everybody worth knowing, and they found him fascinating. Two of his greatest novels are autobiographical, and he wrote an explicit autobiography. Here, we consider that astonishing moment when Goethe had his "revelation," as a student in 1770, that marked the beginning of Romanticism. We ask what causes a generation to change its values and habits so suddenly? The 1960s in the United States serves as a comparison in trying to understand the mysterious changes that mark great cultural breaks.

Outline

I. Our journey from the Old Regime to modernity takes an important step in this lecture. In Lecture Five on Rousseau, we saw the emergence of a new bourgeois self, but in Goethe, this change takes place in a "normal" person and a German. Here, we can study the sudden rise of Germany to cultural importance.

   A. The peculiar career of Goethe shows that he was, in many ways, the subject of his own art. The odd thing is how interesting he is. His prose has a unique, ironic charm.

   B. Goethe was a European "star" at the age of 25; the publication of *The Sorrows of Young Werther* (1774), the first German novel, was the start of a new movement: *Sturm und Drang* ("Storm and Stress").

      1. Storm and Stress was a movement of German writers in the 1770s and 1780s who rebelled against the existing artistic model, proclaimed their dedication to art, and preached a return to nature.

      2. Our problem is to explain the emergence of this new, more modern self. What accounts for the rise of the cult of youth, the worship of the "genius"? There seems to have been a sudden break in the conception of a person. For what reasons, and why then and there?

II. We will use the young Goethe as a test case to address these questions.

    A. Goethe's achievements were gigantic. He wrote several of the world's greatest literary masterpieces (including novels, poems, plays, and nonfiction), painted, drew, acted as a minister for Duke Carl August of Saxe-Weimar, founded the National Theater, and experimented in science and studied the physics of color.

    B. In this lecture, we will examine the really interesting issue of Goethe's personality and the new type of person that Goethe represents: the student as hero, the young as the ideal type.

        1. The idea of the young as an ideal is now taken for granted, but in Goethe's age, it was a kind of revolution. Hitherto, the young were suppressed and bound to the established hierarchy.

        2. With Goethe and Storm and Stress, the young were important cultural trendsetters. *Sturm und Drang* might be compared to the impact of the Beatles and their generation in the 1960s.

    C. *Sturm und Drang* also marked the birth of the Romantic movement in the early 1770s. Goethe was not the sole agent of this movement, but for Germany, he was an emblem of it. In the end, he came to dislike Romanticism, an irony of history.

III. The birth of Storm and Stress took place in the context of an explosion of German culture after 1750.

    A. Sudden bursts of cultural development in history present a puzzle. Such a flourishing took place in parts of Greece in the fifth and fourth centuries B.C. Similarly, during the Italian Renaissance, Dante, Petrarch, Boccaccio, and other artists were clustered in Florence. In the age of George Washington, the colony of Virginia had dozens of statesmen-philosophers. Why in certain locations, but not others?

B. The sudden emergence of a German culture after 1750 was unexpected. The terrible destruction of the Thirty Years' War (1618–1648) had left Germany in poverty and provincialism. Music was the only really great art in Germany before 1750, but many of the nation's great composers had to go to Italy to learn technique.

    1. The prevalence of French culture and the prestige of the Palace of Versailles, Louis XIV, and later, the *philosophes* in Paris (Voltaire, Rousseau, Diderot) swamped the poor, provincial German states with the French language, manners, styles of art and literature, and architecture. Indeed, Frederick the Great, the greatest German king, spoke only French in society.

    2. In 1755, Gotthold Ephraim Lessing (1729–1781), the first serious German playwright, put on a bourgeois tragedy, *Miss Sara Simpson*. It was a revolutionary break, because the English middle classes had become the model, not the French aristocracy.

C. Things began to change in Germany after 1750, beginning with a transformation of the reading public between 1750 and 1800. The number of new journals founded in this period was nearly four times higher than in the previous 50 years. By 1800, Leipzig had 18 printing presses, each employing 17 to 20 workers. Literature replaced theology as the main type of book published.

D. Cultural institutions for the public began to emerge. The court theater had been the prince's private activity, and no tickets were sold. Frederick the Great's symphony orchestra existed for his use, not to give concerts. In 1767–1769, when Lessing tried to experiment with a public theater in Hamburg, it failed. By comparison, London and Paris had dozens of commercial theaters.

E. By the 1770s, German culture could boast Immanuel Kant (1724–1804) and others in philosophy, along with Goethe and Schiller (1759–1805) in literature.

IV. Johann Wolfgang von Goethe was born in Frankfurt am Main, Germany, on August 28, 1749.

A. His father was a wealthy lawyer and city magistrate. Wolfgang and his sister were taught at home by their father and private tutors. Wolfgang wrote his first plays for a small puppet theater.

B. When Goethe was 16, he entered the University of Leipzig as a law student. He completed his studies at the University of Strasbourg and was awarded a doctor of laws degree in 1771.

C. Goethe returned to Frankfurt to practice law but turned to writing almost at once. In 1773, his drama *Goetz von Berlichingen* was published; the following year, he wrote *The Sorrows of Young Werther*. *Werther* was a sensation and made the young Goethe famous.

D. There are several things to notice in this story. The Goethe family was rich on both sides and belonged to the urban elite in Frankfurt, though, of course, without a claim to noble status. The young Goethe had no formal schooling and was allowed to do what he wanted. His puppet theater and youthful plays eventually became the subject of an autobiographical novel: *Wilhelm Meister: The Years of Apprenticeship*.

E. Because Goethe was independently wealthy, he never had to serve as a house tutor to some noble's child, nor was he forced to become a pastor or civil servant; *all* the other German artists were unable to make a living from their art and had to bow and scrape to their lords.

V. Goethe's celebrity at age 25 was a sign of two changes: First, that there was a literate public in Germany that could and would buy books and, second, that there was a new sensibility or a new kind of person.

A. *The Sorrows of Young Werther* was the bible of the new type of man. The book begins with a tone of overblown emotions and borrows the *epistolary* form from Samuel Richardson's *Clarissa* (1748).

B. The plot is simple: Werther, a student, goes off to study at a university (not unlike the experience of the author) and meets Charlotte. He is ecstatic.

C. But Werther has to learn that genius and sensibility cannot make up for rank in society. Werther may be the man of passion, but he is only middle class, as he learns to his cost.

D. In one of the most humiliating passages in literature, Werther learns that genius is not enough to overcome the limits of social inferiority. Goethe was rich, handsome, and gifted but still a middle-class man. The Old Regime was still in place; the new Romantic hero was subordinate to the old nobility.

E. Werther's tragic end comes when Charlotte marries another man, and Werther borrows his dueling pistols to commit suicide. At the end, the Romantic hero is born. The book was a sensation, and Goethe became internationally famous.

VI. When a new type of person appears, we have to ask why. It is clear that such changes occur in history, but they are hard to explain.

A. For Goethe, the change came as a revelation he had in looking at a cathedral of Gothic architecture. The moment is described in *Autobiography: Truth and Fiction Relating to My Life*.

B. This "revelation" was the key moment of a new sense of the individual and national identity—Goethe was a "German" writer, who had a "German" self and was a Romantic. He then describes the subsequent rejection of the French style and manners in favor of more natural manners and emotions.

VII. The 1960s and 1770s were both periods when new generations emerged. The rejection of prevailing mores was common to both, and the changes in culture took on wider meanings in politics and society.

Essential Reading:

Johann Wolfgang von Goethe, *The Sorrows of Young Werther*.

Supplementary Reading:

T.C.W. Blanning, *The Culture of Power and the Power of Culture.*

Nicholas Boyle, *Goethe: The Poet and the Age: The Poetry of Desire, 1749–1790.*

Questions to Consider:

1. How do you react to the Romantic text of *Werther*? If you find it ridiculous or overdone, ask yourself why it was such a huge success in the 1770s.

2. Do you think there is such a thing as "genius"?

Lecture Twelve—Transcript
Goethe—The Artist as Work of Art

Our journey from the Old Regime to modernity takes a big and important step in this lecture. We saw in Lecture Five, on Rousseau, the emergence of a new kind of bourgeois-self, but in Goethe it takes the form of what I guess is a normal person (because whatever one thinks about Rousseau, one could hardly call him normal), and moreover, a German. Besides, in Goethe we can study the sudden rise of Germany to cultural importance.

Johann Wolfgang von Goethe, who was born in 1749 and died in 1832, is to German literature what Shakespeare is to English. But the peculiar career of Goethe shows that he was in many ways the main subject of his own art, and the odd thing is how extraordinarily interesting he is. I've read in German an original one of his two autobiographical novels, *Wilhelm Meister*, 600 pages, and his *Autobiography*, equally large, and I came away wanting more. His prose has a unique, ironic charm, just wonderful, wonderful writing.

Goethe became a European megastar at the age of 25 with the publication of his book, *The Sorrows of the Young Werther* in 1774. It was the first major German novel, and was the start of a new cultural movement called *Sturm und Drang*, "Storm and Stress." Storm and Stress was a literary movement of young German writers in the 1770s and the 1780s who rebelled against the existing artistic model, which was French, and who proclaimed their own dedication to art, and preached a return to a more natural form of expression and a more natural way of living.

One of the problems I want to try to think about in this lecture is to explain the emergence of this new more modern, more recognizably modern self. What accounts for the rise of this new cult of youth, the worship of the genius? There seems to have been a sort of sudden break in how it was to be a person. There was a change. What accounts for such changes, and why did they occur then and why there? I want to use the young Goethe as a kind of test case to see if we can get somewhere in thinking about that particular problem.

Goethe's achievements are much, much too elaborate and grand for a 30-minute lecture. He wrote several of the world's greatest literary masterpieces: His *Faust*, his plays, his novels, his poems and his non-fiction. He painted, he drew, he was a Minister of State for Duke

Carl August of Saxe-Weimar, he founded the National Theater, he experimented in science, and read extensively on the physics of color. What I want to examine in this lecture, though, is the interesting issue of Goethe's personality, and examine the new type of person that Goethe comes to represent, the student as hero, the young as the ideal type.

Now we take for granted, I suppose, that the young are some kind of an ideal, but in Goethe's age it was really a cultural revolution. Hitherto, to be young was simply to be in apprenticeship; you weren't allowed to speak up; children were to be seen and not heard; and they were bound to an established hierarchy of values. With Goethe and *Sturm und Drang* (Storm and Stress), the young suddenly became important and, I think for the first time in history, became cultural trendsetters.

I know this may sound like a silly comparison, but I'm going to develop it. *Sturm und Drang* might be compared, in the generation of the 1770s, to the impact of the Beatles and the Stones on the generation of the 1960s. The music represented a symbolic break with the morays of the past. *Sturm und Drang* also marked the birth of the Romantic movement in the early 1770s, and Romanticism is one of the most important fundamental changes which takes place in the way people think about themselves, in culture, art, the world, in the period that we're looking at, between 1715 and 1914.

It is a real break, and it, I think, starts with the experience that Goethe represents. Obviously, he's not the sole agent of it and he's not the sole cause, but for Germany he became an emblem of it, and it's ironic that, as an old man in the 1820s and '30s, he looked back on his role in the foundation of Romanticism with extreme distaste, and in old age he returned to the classicism which he had rejected as a youth.

What was the context for the birth of "Storm and Stress"? After 1750, there was an explosion of German culture, and this is a mysterious process. This is a process for which I have no flip or easy explanation. There's a real puzzle about why certain places at certain times suddenly show this cultural flowering. There was one in Greece in fifth and fourth centuries B.C., but not in all the Greek city states. Why was Athens the leader and not Corinth? During the Italian renaissance, they were the so-called *cento citta,* the hundred cities, like Florence, Siena and Venice, in which a new culture developed. Why was Florence, though, with Dante, Petrarch, Boccaccio, Machiavelli, Leonardo da Vinci, the capital of this particular movement?

Take your case nearer at home; let's take the case of the colony of Virginia in the 18th century, in the age of George Washington. There were dozens of statesmen philosophers: Washington, Jefferson, Madison, George Mason, Patrick Henry, Richard Henry Lee, Thomas Nelson, and so on. They weren't equaled in the 19th century, nor were they as prominent in South Carolina or Maryland, something about Virginia culture at that time? Who knows? What is clear, even though I can't explain it, is that after 1750 there was a kind of explosion of German culture.

For more than 100 years, from the end of the Thirty Years' War, which raged between 1618 and 1648, Germany was still suffering from the impact of this disastrous war, its terrible destructiveness. I think something like a third of the population of Mecklenburg, one of the northern German provinces, died as a result of the war. It left Germany impoverished and rather provincial. Between 1648 and 1748, as we saw in Lecture Nine, music was the one really great art in Germany, and there were many great composers, Schuetz, Buxtehude, Biber, the Bach family, Telemann, Georg Friedrich Handel, but many of them, indeed practically all of them except the Bach family, had to go to Italy to learn their techniques.

In addition, German culture was under the influence of the French. The prevalence of French culture and the prestige of the palace of Versailles of the Sun King Louis XIV and later the *philosophes* in Paris (Voltaire, Rousseau, Diderot, people we've looked at in thinking about Rousseau), swamped the poor provincial German states with the French language, French manner, French styles of art, French styles of literature, and French styles of architecture.

In 1750, Frederick the Great, king of Prussia as we saw in Lecture Four, published his *Oeuvres de Philosophe de Sanssouci (The Works of the Philosopher of Sanssouci)*, which was his residence, and became a *philosophe* in his own right. Frederick, however, only spoke, as we saw, French in society. He spoke German to his servants but not to his dogs, to whom he spoke French (they were too noble to be spoken to in that barbarous language). Thus, the greatest German king was a French speaker.

In 1755, Gotthold Ephraim Lessing, the first serious German playwright, put on a bourgeois tragedy, *Miss Sara Simpson*. It was a revolutionary break, because in this case the English middle classes had become the model, not the French aristocracy. A theatrical infrastructure was almost non-existent in Germany outside of princely courts, and Lessing was unable to make a living in the 1750s as a playwright. There was still no real public sphere. Compare that situation to Lecture Six on Johnson. When, in 1755 Samuel Johnson published his *Dictionary*, there was a flourishing public fear, a big market for literature, and his friend David Garrick, the actor, was starring in commercial theaters all up and down London. Fielding worked *Tom Jones*. Richardson was publishing *Clarissa* and *Pamela*. That was not there yet for Lessing. He couldn't make a go in the theater.

Things began to change in Germany after 1750, however. There was a transformation of the reading public, and we've got numbers. The number of new journals founded in the period was nearly four times larger (2,684) than in the first half of the century (752). By 1800, Latzig had 18 printing presses, each employing 17 to 20 workers. Goethe called the city "a little Paris that educates her people." Literature replaced theology as the main type of book. In 1750, 31 percent of all books published were in theology and only 8.7 percent in literature. By 1800, the ratio had reversed, with 6 percent in theology and 27.3 percent in literature. Cultural institutions for the public began to emerge. You will recall from Lecture Nine on C.P.E. Bach, that he began to sell his music.

The court theater, which had been the prince's private activity, and had no tickets sold, was just slowly giving way to other kinds of institutions. Frederick the Great's symphony orchestra, of course, existed for him and not to give concerts. When, for example, in the years 1767–1769 Lessing tried to experiment with a public theater in Hamburg, it failed. By comparison, London and Paris had dozens of commercial theaters. In the German realm, only kings and princes could found theaters, and many did. Joseph II founded one in Vienna in 1776, Grand Duke Karl Theodor in Mannheim in 1779, and Duke Carl August of Weimar in 1791. All these founded theaters, and it is in Weimar where Goethe actually lived for many years under the Duke Carl August. By the 1770s, there was a real who's-who of German culture. In philosophy: Immanuel Kant, Johann Georg

Hamann, the famous Moses Mendelssohn, the first Jew to emerge from the ghetto and become an international literary figure; in literature, Klopstock, Lessing, Winckelmann, the first modern art historian; and then there was a younger generation: Among Goethe's contemporaries there was the great Friedrich Schiller and there was Johann Gottfried Herder, who was really the father of modern nationalism.

Thus, after 1750, something big happens. Germany suddenly becomes a place in which literature and the arts begin to flourish. Now, the special life for Johann Wolfgang von Goethe needs some background. He was born in Frankfurt-am-Main in Germany on August 28, 1749. His father was a wealthy lawyer and city magistrate. Wolfgang and his sister never went to school. They were taught at home by their father and private tutors. He wrote his first plays for a small puppet theater, which was a gift from his grandmother, which he describes vividly in his autobiography, *Poetry and Truth*.

When Goethe was 16, he entered the University of Leipzig as a law student and completed his studies at the University of Strasbourg and was awarded a Doctor of Laws Degree in 1771. The critic Herder introduced him to old German folktales and to the best of English literature in German translation. Folktales are a very important element in the spread of Romanticism, not French models of reason but the naturalness of the fairytale.

In the 19th century, Grimm's fairytales become, of course, best sellers. Goethe returned to Frankfurt to practice law, but he turned to writing almost at once. In 1773, he published his drama, called *Goetz von Berlichingen* and in the following year, 1774, he published *The Sorrows of the Young Werther*. *Werther* was a sensation, a bestseller, and made Goethe famous throughout the whole of Europe.

There are a few things that we need to notice in the story of Goethe's life which may not be obvious. The Goethe family was rich on both sides, and they belonged to a urban elite group in one of the main German trading cities, though of course they had no claim to noble status: They were commoners. Goethe had no formal schooling and was simply allowed to do what he wanted. His puppet theater and his youthful plays eventually became the subject of his wonderful autobiographical novel, *Wilhelm Meister: The Years of*

Apprenticeship. The novel gives a beautiful description of this charmed and happy childhood.

Because Goethe was independently wealthy, he never had to serve as a house tutor to some noble's child, nor was he forced to become a protestant pastor or a civil servant. All the other German artists were unable to make a living from their art until quite late on, and they had to bow and scrape to their lords. In the lecture on C.P.E. Bach, I quoted Friedrich Schiller writing in 1784, "Ecstatically there is now a public, and I am a servant of the public, and I have no other master"—but that is quite late in the century.

With Goethe, we get the birth of the romantic hero. Goethe was a European celebrity at the age of 25 with his novel *Werther*. He was a sign, I think, of two things which matter in the analysis that we're trying to carry out in this course: First, that there was now for the first time in Germany a new literary public which could and would buy books; and secondly, that there was a new sensibility or perhaps even a new kind of person. *The Sorrows of the Young Werther* became the bible of this new type of man, and I'd like to quote some passages from it for you to give you an idea of its flavor.

Here is how the book begins:

> Preface: I have carefully collected whatever I have been able to learn of the story of poor Werther, and here present it to you, knowing that you will thank me for it. To his spirit and character you cannot refuse your admiration and love; to his fate, you will not deny your tears. And thou, good soul, who suff'rest the same distress as he endured once, may now draw comfort from his sorrows; and let this little book be thy friend, if, owing to fortune or through thine own fault, thou can'st not find a dearer companion.

Note the tone, the tears, what to us sound like over-blown emotions. Goethe borrowed the form again from an English model, not from the French. Samuel Richardson, the novelist and printer, had published *Clarissa* in 1748, and *Clarissa* was a huge, 1,000 pages long, epistolary novel. It tells the story in the form of letters, and the English epistolary novel, the novel based on imaginary letters, became the model which Goethe used.

The text is composed of letters from Werther to a friend, and there is no other text. Now England, of course, provided the model of a bourgeois society which was actually much more striking and much more attractive to young Germans (like Goethe and Lessing), than the French aristocratic model with its hierarchy of society and its salience.

The plot of the young Werther is very simple: Werther, a student, goes off to study at a university, which is exactly like the experience of its author, and there he meets Charlotte. As he writes to his friend Wilhelm, June 21: "My days are as happy as those reserved by God for his elect, and, whatever be my fate hereafter, I can never say that I have not tasted joy—the purest joy of life. You know, Wilhelm, I am now completely settled there. In that spot I am only half a league from Charlotte; and there I enjoy myself, and taste all the pleasure which can befall the lot of man."

He fell in love, and he was ecstatic. July 18: "Wilhelm, what is the world to our hearts without love? What is a magic lantern without light? You have but to kindle the flame within, and the brightest figures shine on the white wall; and if love only shows us fleeting shadows, we are yet happy, when, like mere children, we behold them, and are transported with the splendid phantoms." It's a beautiful image, that of the magic lantern, love being the magic lantern which projects images on to the wall.

Werther, though, has to learn that genius and sensibility cannot make up for rank in society. Werther may be the man of passion, but he is only middleclass, as he learns to his cost, and this is a passage which I really must read to you because it captures the clash between the Old Regime's values and the new genius of literature. I quote:

> The Count of O--- likes and distinguishes me. It is well known, and I have mentioned this to you a hundred times. Yesterday I dined with him. It is the day on which the nobility are accustomed to assemble at his house in the evening. I never once thought of the assembly, nor that we subalterns did not belong to such society. Well, I dined with the count; and, after dinner, we adjourned to the large hall…The rest of the company now arrived. There was the Baron F---, in an entire suit that dated from the coronation of Francis I; the Chancellor N---, with his deaf wife; the shabbily-dressed I---, whose old-fashioned coat bore

evidence of modern repairs: this crowned the whole. I conversed with some of my acquaintances, but they answered me laconically. I was engaged in observing Miss B---, and did not notice that the women were whispering at the end of the room, that the murmurs extended by degrees to the men, that Madam S--- addressed the count with much warmth (this was all related to me subsequently by Miss B---); till at length the count came up to me, and took me to the window. 'Ah, you know our ridiculous customs,' he said. 'I perceive the company is rather displeased that you are being here. I would not on any account--' 'I beg your excellency's pardon,' I exclaimed. 'I ought to have thought of this before, but I know you will forgive this little inattention. I was going some time ago, but my evil genius detained me.' And I smiled and bowed, to take my leave. He shook me by the hand, in a manner which expressed everything. I hastened at once from the illustrious assembly, sprang into the carriage, drove to M--. I contemplated the setting sun from on top of the hill, and read the beautiful passage in Homer, where Ulysses is entertained by the hospitable herdsman. This was indeed delightful.

Now, I actually think this is one of the most humiliating passages in all of literature. The young genius is driven from the count's reception chamber because he's just a commoner and the nobles don't want him there. The great composer Franz Joseph Haydn was a servant and wore livery until 1790, when the huge success of his London symphonies moved Prince Esterhazy, his employer, to invite him to dine.

Mozart was a transitional figure, part servant of the archbishop of Salzburg and part touring genius as composer/performer. Johann Wolfgang Goethe was very rich, very handsome, very gifted, but just a middleclass man, and the Old Regime was still in place; the new Romantic hero was still subordinate to the old nobility.

Now, Werther's end was tragic. Charlotte married Albert, and Werther borrowed Albert's dueling pistols to commit suicide. I quote:

> I wish, Charlotte to be buried in the dress I wear at present: it has been rendered sacred by your touch. I have begged this

favour of your father. My spirit soars above my sepulchre. I do not wish my pockets to be searched. The knot of pink ribbon which you wore on your bosom the first time I saw you, surrounded by the children -- Oh, kiss them a thousand times for me, and tell them the fate of their unhappy friend! I think I see them playing around me. The dear children! How warmly have I been attached to you, Charlotte! Since the first hour I saw you, how impossible have I found it to leave you. This ribbon must be buried with me: it was a present from you on my birthday. How confused it all appears! Little did I then think that I should journey this road. But peace! I pray you, peace! 'They are loaded -- the clock strikes twelve. I say amen. Charlotte, Charlotte! farewell, farewell!'

That's the way the book ends. The romantic hero was born in death, dies for love, and the book was a sensation. Goethe was now internationally famous. I think when you listen to that passage, nothing that I've read to you before sounds like this. Dr. Johnson doesn't sound like this, "Of the exultations and depressions of your heart, you like to speak, I hate to hear." Frederick the Great doesn't talk like this. We're actually listening to the voice a new kind of human being.

The question that poses itself for the historian is: How do these changes occur in history?

They're hard to explain, but I'd like to give you an example from my own experience. I recall vividly, when I was a tutor at Cambridge College, Trinity Hall, in 1967 the arrival of Nick M. Now, I had been teaching in that college for about two years at that stage, and my students were English types, the kind of people you see in the old 1950s Boulting Brothers comedies. They wore tweed jackets; they wore tan cavalry twills; they wore ties, and they were frightfully English. They didn't tell you anything; you didn't find out about their private life. They were very amusing, but they were very reserved.

Nick M. was something all together different. He came in wearing jeans; he had long, shoulder-length curly hair; he had round Granny Smith glasses; he was extremely emotional, and perfectly prepared to burst out in tears when so moved. And I sat there and I looked at this freshman, and I said to myself, "Son, you are seeing a genuine break in sensibility. This is exactly like the thing that you read in Goethe's

Autobiography." I went back to the autobiography to pick it up, and sure enough, Goethe describes it. In 1770, Goethe was completing his law studies at the University of Strasbourg, and there is in Strasbourg a remarkable cathedral. I don't know if you've ever seen it, but I went and made a special pilgrimage to stand in front of it to see the place where Romanticism, so to speak, was born. It's a Gothic cathedral, and the main entrance has one of these Gothic arches, and in the Gothic arches there are rather narrow round columns, and in between the columns, a bit like peas in the pod, there are lots and lots and lots of carved heads, several hundred carved heads. The little heads go up to the top of the arch and go down the other side, just lots of them. It's at that point that Goethe had his great revelation. He describes it in his *Autobiography: Truth and Fiction Relating to My Life.*

In addition to his other talents, he was a very gifted artist. He did a lot of drawing. He was out there sketching the west portal of Strasbourg Cathedral, and this is what he wrote in his *Autobiography*:

> Having grown up among those who found fault with Gothic architecture, I cherished my aversion from the abundantly overloaded, complicated ornaments which, by their capriciousness, made a religious, gloomy character highly adverse. I strengthened myself in this repugnance, since I had only met with spiritless works of this kind, in which one could perceive neither good proportions nor a pure consistency. But here I thought I saw a new revelation of it, since what was objectionable by no means appeared, but the contrary opinion rather forced itself upon my mind.

This is not a beautiful translation; it's a 19th century translation, but what he's saying is: I grew up with French style, with the idea that things should be balanced, good proportions, right regulations, and this was medieval. These were the dark ages, the Goths were savage. Gothic art is savage art, and we reject this. We now live in the age of light, the age of Enlightenment, and they lived in the age of darkness, the age of medieval barbarism. The "revelation," the *Offenbarung* which Goethe describes, was the key moment, I think, in the emergence of this new sense of the individual and, indeed, of national identity. He goes on to say, "Finding that this building had been based on old German ground, and grown thus far in genuine

German times, and that the name of the master, on his modest gravestone, was likewise of native sound and origin, I ventured, being incited by the worth of this work of art, to change the hitherto decried appellation of 'Gothic architecture' and to claim it for our nation as 'German architecture.'"

In other words, what happened here is that Goethe actually began to see the same building in a completely transformed way. Whereas, as he says in *Autobiography*, he'd been brought up to worship the French style, to look for the principles of the Enlightenment, length twice width, rational proportions, the kind of thing we actually saw in the previous lecture on Joseph II, the idea there's a rational way of organizing things.

Art, too, had to reflect this. If you think about the classical architecture of the 18th century, this Greek temple with its perfect proportions, or the balanced prose of a Dr. Johnson, or the way in which certain kinds of courts are balanced and have a rather faceless classical façade. That's what Goethe's taste was. He approached a medieval cathedral with all the prejudices of that taste.

Now, what does he see? He doesn't see something which lacks reason; he sees something which has history. And this history is a particular history: It's the history of them being Germans. What had been called goatish, Gothic, primitive, uncivilized is now German.

His first important work was *Über Deutscher Baukunst*, concerning German architecture. It's that moment of revelation. How can one describe it? You can see it in front of you. He has changed his way of looking at the world. He substituted one set of criteria for another. Now this new self and this new nationalism revealed in that moment. Goethe suddenly realized: "I am a German writer. I have a German self. I am looking at German art."

It is also the beginning, I think, of Romanticism. In *Autobiography* he then describes the way his group of friends and students began to behave. They stopped wearing powdered wigs; they took off their fancy French coats; they began to wear loose clothing; they wore open-necked shirts; they let their hair grow naturally. They became physically different people because they were now no longer in the thrall of this particular old practice.

The Romantic movement, as I say, was perhaps the greatest break in culture of the entire period of 1715–1914. We are all, in all sorts of ways, the product of the Romantic conception of self. The 1770s and the 1960s were, I think, both periods when a new generation emerged. The rejection of the prevailing morays is common to both. Where the 1950s had been an era of conformity, stable gender roles and sharp racial divisions, the 1960s changed all that.

I am so old that I can still remember the conformity of my generation; it was perfectly self-evident. That's the way things were. But when Nick M. and his generation arrived, the Beatles were their spokesmen, their young Werther, the Beatles, the Rolling Stones and the new culture of protest gave their music, their style, their new gender roles a political meaning. It seems to me that the parallel with Goethe is obvious. It was obvious to me at the time, and it's still obvious to me nearly 40 years later. But at the time and now, I'm simply unable to explain it. What is it that suddenly makes a young human being snap from one way of looking at the world to a completely different one, with a whole series of consequences for his way of life and, indeed, in the case of Goethe, for the rest of European history?

Timeline

1713 .... Peace of Utrecht (June 13); end of the War of the Spanish Succession.

1714 .... George, the German elector of Hanover, becomes King George I of Britain (Aug. 1); Henry Mill receives patent in England for a typewriter.

1715 .... Five-year-old Louis XV of France succeeds his great grandfather, with the duke of Orleans as regent (Sept. 1). Jacobite nobles (trying to put James Stuart back on the British throne) defeated at Preston and Sheriffmuir (Nov. 13).

1716 .... The first group of black slaves is brought to the Louisiana territory. John Law founds joint-stock bank in Paris.

1717 .... Prince Eugene captures Belgrade (Aug. 18).

1718 .... Smallpox vaccination introduced in England. Halley discovers independent movement of fixed stars.

1719 .... Reaumur proposes using wood to make paper. Defoe publishes *Robinson Crusoe*.

1720 .... Peter the Great of Russia signs treaty with the Chinese permitting trade. South Sea Bubble bursts, and France is bankrupt (Dec.).

1721 .... Robert Walpole appointed First Lord of the Treasury and Chancellor of the Exchequer (April 3). Peter the Great proclaimed tsar of all of

Russia (Oct. 22). Montesquieu, *Letteres Persanes*.

1722 ...................................J.S. Bach, *Wohltemperietes Klavier* ("*Well-Tempered Clavier*").

1723 ....Russia gains control of southern shore of Caspian Sea (u.1732).

1724 ....Russia and Sweden sign treaty of mutual assistance (Feb. 24).

1725 ....Peter the Great dies (Feb. 8). G.B. Vico, *Scienza nuova intorna alla Natura*. Academy of Science founded at St. Petersburg.

1726 ....Jonathan Swift publishes *Gulliver's Travels*. Allan Ramsay opens first circulating library at Edinburgh.

1727 ....Isaac Newton dies (March 31). George I of Britain dies (June 12); succeeded by George II (–1760).

1728 ....John Gay, *Beggar's Opera*. Alexander Pope, *Dunciad*.

1729 ...................................J.S. Bach, *St. Matthew Passion*. Hall constructs achromatic lens.

1730 ....Peter II of Russia dies of smallpox (Feb. 11). Anne succeeds (–1747). Senate House completed in Cambridge by J.S. Gibb.

1731 ....*Gentleman's Magazine* appears (April 26). Harley invents quadrant for use at sea.

1732 ....Boerhaave, *Elements of Chemistry*, founds organic chemistry.

1733	War of Polish Succession (–1735). Austria and Russia recognize Augustus the Strong of Saxony. Bach, *B-minor Mass*.
1734	Voltaire, *Lettres sur les Anglais*. Bach, *Christmas Oratorio*.
1735	Peace of Vienna (Oct. 3); Stanislas obtains Lorraine; duke of Lorraine to obtain Tuscany on grand duke's death; Austria obtains Parma and Piacenza; Don Carlos, Naples and Sicily.
1736	Maria Theresa marries Francis Stephen of Lorraine (Feb. 12). Russo-Turkish War (May). Euler establishes analytical mechanics.
1737	Death of last Medici grand duke (July 9); Francis Stephen inherits duchy.
1738	Clement XII bull against freemasonry (*In Eminenti*) (April 18). John Wesley starts Methodist revival. First spinning machine patented in England. Daniel Bernoulli's kinetic theory of gases.
1739	Treaty of Belgrade between Russia and Turkey (Sept. 23). England declares war on Spain (War of Jenkin's Ear) (Oct. 19). David Hume, *Treatise of Human Nature*.
1740	Frederick William I of Prussia dies (May 31); succeeded by Frederick II (–1786). Charles VI, last Habsburg emperor dies (Oct. 20); succeeded by Maria Theresa, queen of Bohemia and Hungary (–1780).

Frederick II invades Silesia (Dec. 16). Richardson, *Pamela*.

1741 .... Frederick II defeats Austrians at Möllwitz and conquers Silesia (April 10). Treaty between France and Prussia against Austria (June 5). French invade South Germany, Austria, and Bohemia (Aug. 15). Handel, *Messiah*. First German translation of a Shakespeare play (*Julius Caesar* by von Borcke).

1742 .... Charles Albert of Bavaria elected emperor (Charles VII) (Jan. 24). Peace of Berlin between Austria and Prussia, which obtains Silesia and Glatz (July 28). Anglo-Prussian alliance (Nov. 29). Celsius's thermometer scale.

1743 .... George II defeats French at Dettingen (June 27). Voltaire, *Mérope*. Balthasar Neumann builds Vierzehnheiligen Church (1743–1772).

1744 .... France declares war on England (March 15). Prussia acquires East Friesland on death of last prince (May 25). Alliance between France and Prussia (June 5). Frederick II invades Saxony and enters Bohemia (Aug. 15).

1745 .... Charles VII, Habsburg emperor, dies (Jan. 20). Frederick II defeats Austrians at Hohenfriedberg (June 4). Francis Stephen of Lorraine elected (Sept. 13) Holy Roman Emperor (–1765). Frederick victorious at Kesseldorf (Dec. 15). Peace of Dresden; Prussia keeps

Silesia but recognizes the Pragmatic Sanction (Dec. 25). Knobelsdorff builds Sanssouci Palace, Potsdam (1745–1747).

1746 ....Charles Stuart and Jacobites finally defeated at Culloden (April 16). Scottish clan organization abolished by "Butcher" Cumberland. Austro-Russian alliance against Prussia (June 2).

1748 ....Peace of Aix-la-Chapelle; general recognition of Pragmatic Sanction and conquest of Silesia (Oct. 18). Richardson, *Clarissa*. Montesquieu, *Esprit des Lois*.

1749–1753 ....Drainage of the Oder moorlands.

1754 ....Anglo-French war breaks out in North America.

1756 ....Treaty of Westminster between England and Prussia (Jan. 16). Alliance of Versailles between France and Austria, reverses French policy (May 1). England declares war on France (May 15). Frederick II invades Saxony; outbreak of Seven Years' War (Aug. 29). Frederick defeats Austrians at Lobositz (Oct. 1). Saxon army capitulates at Pirna (Oct. 15).

1757 ....Empire declares war on Prussia (Jan. 10). Russia, Poland, and Sweden join war against Prussia. Second treaty between France and Austria; Prussia to be divided (May 1). Frederick II victory at Prague (May 10). Austrians defeat Frederick at Kolin (June 18). Russians defeat Prussians at Gross

Jägersdorf and occupy East Prussia; Swedes invade Pomerania (Aug. 30). Frederick defeats French and imperial troops at Rossbach (Nov. 5). Frederick defeats Austrians at Leuthen (Dec. 5).

1758 .... London Convention; English subsidies for Prussia (April 11). British take Louisburg, Quebec (July 24). Frederick defeats Russians at Zorndorf (Aug. 25). Austrian victory at Hochkirch (Oct. 14).

1759 .... Russians and Austrians defeat Frederick at Kunnersdorf (Aug. 12). Prussian army capitulates at Maxen (Nov. 12).

1760 .... Prussian defeat at Landshut (June 23). Frederick defeats Austrians at Liegnitz (Aug. 15). George II dies (Oct. 25); succeeded by George III (–1820).

1761 .... Austrians take Schweidnitz and blockade Frederick at Bunzelwitz (Oct. 1). Russians take Kolberg (Dec. 16).

1762 .... Elizabeth of Russia dies (Jan. 5); succeeded by Peter III ("the miracle of the House of Brandenburg"). English cease subsidies to Prussia (April). Peace between Russia and Prussia (May 5). Peace between Prussia and Sweden (May 22). Peter III assassinated (July 17); succeeded by Catherine II (–1796). Frederick defeats Austrians at Burkersdorf (July 21). Truce among Prussia, Austria, and Saxony (Nov. 24).

1763	Peace of Paris among England, France, Spain, and Portugal (Feb. 10). Peace of Hubertusberg between Austria and Prussia, which definitely cedes Silesia (Feb. 15).
1764	Treaty between Russia and Prussia to control Poland (April 11).
1765	Emperor Francis I dies (Aug. 18); succeeded by Joseph II (–1790).
1769	Joseph II and Frederick meet at Neisse, Silesia (Aug.).
1772	First partition of Poland (Aug. 5): Russia obtains territory east of the Duna and Neiper; Austria, eastern Galicia and Lodomeria; Prussia, west Prussia, except Danzig and Ermland.
1773	Clement XIV suppresses the Jesuit order (July 21).
1774	Peace of Kutschuk-Kainardi between Russia and Turkey, which cedes mouth of Dneiper and Crimea (July 21).
1776	Declaration of Independence of British North American colonies (July 4). Adam Smith publishes *The Wealth of Nations*.
1777	Maximilian III of Bavaria dies; Joseph II claims the succession (Dec. 30).
1778	Prussia declares war on Austria on behalf of Bavaria (July 3).
1779	Peace of Teschen (May 13). Austria receives Inn Quarter; Prussia gets reversionary rights to Ansbach and Bayreuth.

1780 .... Maria Theresa dies (Nov. 29).

1781 .... Prussia joins League of Armed Neutrality (May).

1783 .... Peace of Versailles: England recognizes independence of United States of America (Sept. 3).

1784 .... Joseph II proposes to exchange Bavaria for Belgium (April 1).

1785 .... North German League against Joseph II (July 23).

1786 .... Frederick II dies (Aug. 17); succeeded by Frederick William II (–1797).

1787 .... Prussia intervenes in Holland in favor of William V against the Patriot Party.

1787-1792 .... Russia and Austria at war against Turkey.

1788 .... Alliance among England, Holland and Prussia.

1789 .... Russo-Austrian alliance renewed (April 7). Estates-General meet at Versailles (May 5). Third Estate declares itself National Assembly (June 17). Fall of the Bastille (July 14). Austrians and Russians defeat Turks at Foksani (July 31). Austrians enter Belgrade (Oct. 9). Revolution in the Austrian Netherlands (Oct.).

1790 .... Organization of France into 83 departments (Feb. 26). Sections of Paris established (May 21). Civil Constitution of the Clergy (July 12).

1791 .... Guilds and corporations dissolved (March 2). Flight of Louis XVI and the royal family to Varennes (June 20). Declaration of Pillnitz; Austria and Prussia threaten intervention (Aug. 27).

1792 .... War declared on Austria (April 20). Storming of Tuileries; overthrow of the monarchy (Aug. 10). Massacres in Paris, murder of more than 1,000 prisoners (Sept. 2–6). Convention meets (Sept. 20). Republic proclaimed (Sept. 22).

1793 .... Execution of Louis XVI (Jan. 21). Second partition of Poland (Jan. 23). Revolutionary tribunal created (March 10). Committee of Public Safety created (April 6). Death penalty for hoarding (July 26). Robespierre joins Committee of Public Safety (July 27). Decree of *levée en masse* (Aug. 23). Revolutionary government declared (Oct. 10). Marie Antoinette executed (Oct. 16). Festival of Reason in Notre Dame (Nov. 10).

1794 .... Danton and Desmoulins executed (April 5, 16 germinal year I). Law of 22 prairial year II: Great Terror begins (June 10). Fall of Robespierre (July 27, 9 thermidor year II). Jacobin Club closed (Nov. 12).

1795 .... Treaty of Basle concluded with Prussia (April 5). Directory constituted (Nov. 2).

1796 .... Bonaparte appointed commander in Italy (March 2). Battle of Lodi (May

10); Bonaparte defeats the Austrians.

1797	Peace of Campo Formio (Oct. 17). Austria cedes Belgium and Lombardy to France.
1798	Nelson destroys French fleet at Aboukir (Aug. 1).
1799	Bonaparte's *coup d'etat* (Nov. 9). Directory overthrown and Bonaparte becomes first consul.
1800	Act of Union of Great Britain and Ireland (July 2).
1801	Concordat restores Roman Catholic Church in France (July 15).
1802	Peace of Amiens between Britain and France (March 27). Bonaparte appointed consul for life (Aug. 2)
1803	Britain declares war on France (May 18).
1804	Diet of Ratisbon abolishes German ecclesiastic principalities and imperial free cities (Feb. 25). End of Holy Roman Empire. Bonaparte crowned Emperor Napoleon I (Dec. 2).
1805	Nelson destroys French-Spanish fleet at Trafalgar (Oct. 21). Napoleon defeats Austrians and Russians at Austerlitz (Dec. 2).
1806	Napoleon defeats Prussians and Saxons at Jena (Oct. 14).
1807	Napoleon defeats Russians at Eylau (Feb. 7–8). Peasants in Prussia emancipated (Oct. 9).

1808	Insurrection against French begins in Spain (May 2).
1809	Napoleon annexes Papal States (May 1). Napoleon defeats Austrians at Wagram (July 5–6).
1810	Andreas Hofer leads insurrection in Tyrol (Feb. 10).
1811	State bankruptcy in Austria (Feb. 20).
1812	Spanish Cortes in Cadiz passes liberal constitution (March 18). Napoleon defeats Russians at Borodino (Sept. 7). Napoleon takes Moscow (Sept. 14); holds it until Oct. 18. Convention of Tauroggen (Dec. 30): Prussia switches sides in war and joins Russia against France.
1813	Austria declares war on France (Aug. 12). Battle of Leipzig: Allies defeat Napoleon (Oct. 16–18).
1814	Allies enter Paris (March 30). Napoleon abdicates and becomes Prince of Elba (April 11). Ferdinand VII abolishes liberal constitution in Spain (May 4). First Peace of Paris (May 30): France granted frontiers of 1792; Louis XVIII, king of France. Congress of Vienna opens (Nov. 1).
1815	Napoleon lands in France (March 1). Empire restored. Louis XVIII flees. Congress of Vienna closes (June 8). Wellington and Blücher defeat Napoleon at Waterloo (June 18). Napoleon abdicates and is banished to St. Helena (June 22).

1816	Carl-August of Saxe-Weimar grants first German constitution (May 5).
1817	German student festival at Wartburg condemns reactionary politics (Oct. 18). David Ricardo publishes *Principles of Political Economy and Taxation*.
1818	Liberal constitution in Baden (Aug. 29). Mary Wollstonecraft-Shelley publishes *Frankenstein*.
1819	Princess Alexandrina Victoria (Queen Victoria) born (May 24). Peterloo demonstrators fired on, causing "massacre" (Aug. 16). Metternich imposes Carlsbad decrees on German states, putting an end to constitutions and other freedoms (Sept. 20).
1820	Revolt in Spain and constitution restored (Jan. 1–March 7). Revolt in Portugal (Aug. 24). First iron steamship in England.
1821	Bank of England resumes cash payments (May 1). Death of Napoleon (May 5).
1822	Congress of Verona meets (Oct. 20); Metternich guides powers against the revolutionary movements.
1823	War between France and Spain to restore Ferdinand VII (April 7). French storm Trocadero and restore Ferdinand VII (Aug. 30).
1824	Louis XVIII dies (Sept. 16); Charles X succeeds (–1830). Beethoven finishes Ninth Symphony.

1825 ....Nicholas I succeeds Alexander I as tsar of Russia (Dec. 1). First steam locomotive between Stockton and Darlington.

1826 ....First German gas works at Hannover.

1827 ....Manzoni publishes *I Promessi Sposi*.

1828 ....Wellington forms Conservative government in Britain (Jan. 25).

1829 ....Catholic Emancipation Act allows Catholics to enter the House of Commons (April 13). Sir Robert Peel remodels London police force ("bobbies") (Sept. 29).

1830 ...."Three Glorious Days," overthrow of Bourbon monarch in France (July 27–29). Louis-Philippe (Orleans branch), king of the French (Aug. 7). Wellington resigns; Earl Grey forms Liberal government (Nov. 16). Charles Lyell, *Principles of Geology*.

1831 ....Austria suppresses revolutions in Modena and the Papal States (Feb.). Russian army suppresses Polish revolution and takes Warsaw (Sept. 8).

1832 ....Goethe dies (March 22). Great Reform Bill passes House of Lords and becomes law (June 4).

1833 ....German *Zollverein* (Customs Union) established (March 22). Keble publishes *National Apostasy*, and Oxford movement to reform the Church of England begins (July 14).

1834	Slavery ends in the British Empire (Aug. 1).
1835	First German railroad between Fürth and Nuremberg (Dec. 7).
1836	Louis Napoleon Bonaparte fails to seize Strasbourg, is exiled to the United States (Oct. 29).
1837	Accession of Queen Victoria to the throne of Great Britain, and Crowns of Britain and Hannover separated (June 20).
1838	Anti-Corn Law League founded (Sept. 24).
1839	First prohibition of child labor in Prussia (March 9).
1840	Penny postage introduced in Britain (Jan. 10). Queen Victoria marries Prince Albert of Saxe-Coburg-Gotha (Feb. 10). Frederick William III dies (June 7). Frederick William IV, king of Prussia.
1841	*Punch* started (July 17). Hoffman von Fallersleben publishes *Deutschland über Alles* (Aug. 16).
1842	Chartist riots in manufacturing districts (Aug.).
1843	Disruption of Scottish church; Free Church of Scotland started (May 18). Richard Wagner's *Flying Dutchman*.
1844	Bank Charter Act passed (July 19).
1845	First potato blight signs found in Ireland (Sept. 9). Friedrich Engels publishes *The Condition of the Working Class in England*.

1846	Pius IX elected Pope (June 16) (– 1878). Corn Laws repealed in Great Britain (June 26).
1847	United Diet summoned in Prussia (Feb. 3). *Sonderbundkrieg* ("Swiss Civil War") (Oct. 21–Nov. 19).
1848	Revolution in Sicily (Jan. 12). Revolution breaks out in Paris; Louis-Philippe abdicates and the Republic is proclaimed (Feb. 22). Revolution breaks out in Vienna (March 13). Revolution breaks out in Berlin (March 18). Louis Pasteur presents his first scientific discovery in crystallography (May 28). Cavaignac suppresses Paris rising (June 23). Louis Napoleon elected president of French Republic (Dec. 10).
1849	Rome proclaimed a republic under Mazzini (Feb. 9). Austrians defeat Piedmontese; Charles Albert abdicates (March 23). Hungary declares independence from Habsburg Empire (April 14). Street fighting and revolt in Dresden (May 3–8). Prussia adopts three-class suffrage (May 30) (–1918).
1850	Prussian Constitution granted (Jan. 31) (–1918). Pope Pius IX makes his return to Rome under the protection of French troops (April 12). The constitution of 1848 is revoked. Wagner's *Lohengrin* produced, conducted by Liszt (Aug. 28). Roman Catholic Church recognized in England (Sept. 24).

1851 ....Louis Napoleon's *coup d'etat.* Republic overthrown (Dec. 2).

1852 ....Cavour forms government in Piedmont (Feb. 2).

1853 ....Turkey declares war on Russia (Oct. 4).

1854 ....Britain and France declare war on Russia (March 27). Dogma of the Immaculate Conception made an article of faith (Dec. 8).

1855 ....Piedmont-Sardinia signs alliance with France and Britain to send troops to fight Russia in the Crimean War (Jan. 26). Nicholas I of Russia dies (March 2); Alexander II, tsar of Russia (–1881).

1856 ....Congress of Paris (Feb. 25–March 30) opens to settle peace in the Crimean War. Louis Pasteur becomes professor at the University of Paris.

1857 ....Atlantic cable completed (Aug. 5).

1858 ....Italian republican, Felice Orsini, attempts to assassinate Emperor Napoleon III (Jan. 14). James Stephens founds Irish Republican Brotherhood in Dublin (March 17). Napoleon III and Cavour meet at Plombières (July 20); the emperor agrees to join Piedmont in a future war against Austria, provided that Austria is the aggressor.

1859 ....French and Piedmontese defeat the Austrians at Palestro (May 30). Austrians defeated at Magenta. Napoleon III and Victor Emanuel enter Milan (June 4). Napoleon III concludes armistice with Austria without consulting Piedmont (June 8). Charles Darwin's *The Origin of Species by means of natural selection* is published in London (Nov. 24).

1860 ....In Palermo, an insurrection against the Bourbons is suppressed, but the rising continues in the countryside and small towns (April 4). Garibaldi sets sail from Quarto, near Genoa, with 1,000 volunteers (May 5). Garibaldi lands at Marsala and, at Salemi, assumes the dictatorship in the name of Victor Emanuel II (May 11). Battle of Calatafimi, Garibaldi: "*Bixio, qui o si fa l'Italia o si muore!* [Bixio, either we make Italy here or we die!]" (May 15). Bourbon troops are defeated at Milazzo and are forced to abandon Sicily (July 20). Garibaldi enters Naples; received as a national hero (Sept. 7). Garibaldi and Victor Emanuel II meet at Teano and reach an accord about a peaceful transfer of power (Oct. 26).

1861 ....Frederick William IV dies (Jan. 2); William, king of Prussia (–1888). The new Italian parliament meets at Turin and ratifies the unification of the country (Feb. 18). Victor Emanuel, king of Italy. Alexander II grants emancipation of serfs in Russia (March 3). Wagner's *Tannhäuser* produced in Paris (March 13). Prince Albert, prince consort of Great Britain, dies (Dec. 14).

1862	Otto von Bismarck appointed Prussian minister-president (Sept. 23). Bismarck's "blood and iron speech" (Oct. 13).
1863	Insurrection in Poland (Jan. 22). Frederick VII of Denmark dies (Nov. 15); Christian IX succeeds (– 1906). First underground railway (Metropolitan Line) in London.
1864	Prussians defeat Danes at Düppel (April 18). Geneva Convention for Protection of Wounded ("Red Cross") (Aug. 22). Peace of Vienna (Oct. 30): Denmark cedes Schleswig, Holstein, and Lauenberg jointly to Austria and Prussia. Pius IX issues the Syllabus of Errors (Dec. 8).
1865	Convention of Gastein (Aug. 18): Austria gets Holstein; Prussia gets Schleswig. Tolstoy's *War and Peace* published.
1866	Prussia defeats Austria at Königgrätz-Sadowa (July 3). Peace of Nikolsburg between Austria and Prussia (July 26). Prussia annexes Hanover, Hesse-Cassel, Homburg, Nassau, and Frankfurt (Sept. 7).
1867	North German Confederation established (April 17). *Ausgleich* ("compromise") between Austria and Hungary establishes dual monarchy with common foreign, military, and economic policies (June 12). Second Reform Act in Britain enlarges voting franchise (Aug. 15). Karl Marx, *Das Kapital*, Part 1.

1868 .... Wagner's *Der Meistersinger* produced at Munich (June 28). Gladstone forms Liberal ministry after great election victory (Dec. 9).

1869 .... Disestablishment of the Irish Church (March 1). Vatican Council meets (Dec. 8).

1870 .... Doctrine of papal infallibility declared by Vatican Council (July 18). France declares war on Prussia (July 19). Prussia defeats France at Sedan; Napoleon III captured (Sept. 3). Siege of Paris begins (Sept. 19). Roman Catholic Center Party founded in Germany (Dec. 30).

1871 .... William I of Prussia proclaimed German emperor (Jan. 18). Italian kingdom issues Law of Guarantees for the Pope (May 13). Communard revolution begins in Paris (May 18–28). Trade unions legalized in Great Britain (June 29).

1872 .... Jesuits expelled from Germany (June 19).

1873 .... Austrian stock market crashes (May 9); beginning of "Great Depression." "May Laws" against Catholic Church passed in Prussia (May 11). French pretender (Henry V, comte de Chambord) refuses to accept tricolor as national flag (Oct. 27); destroys hopes of monarchical restoration.

1874 .... Swiss constitution revised with stronger central government (May 29). *Union génerale des postes* ("World Postal Union") established at Berne (Oct. 9).

1875 ....Britain buys Suez Canal (Nov. 25).

1876 ....Turks massacre Bulgarian civilians (May 9–16). Serbia and Montenegro declare war on Turkey (July 2). Bayreuth *Festspielhaus* opens with *Ring of the Nibelungen*.

1877 ....Russia declares war on Turkey (April 24).

1878 ....Pius IX dies (Feb. 7); Leo XIII, new pope (–1903). Berlin Congress on peace between Russia and Turkey (June 12–July 13).

1879 ....Germany abandons "free trade"; introduces tariffs (July 12). Austro-German "dual alliance" signed (Oct. 7).

1880 ....Gladstone forms second Liberal ministry (April 28).

1881 ....Alexander II assassinated by populists March 13); Alexander III (–1894) succeeds. League of Three Emperors (Germany, Austria, Russia) (June 18). Irish Land Law Act passed (Aug. 22).

1882 ....Phoenix Park murders: Irish nationalists murder Lord Frederick Cavendish and T.H. Burke (May 2).

1883 ....Friedrich Nietzsche, *Zarathustra*.

1884 ....*Oxford English Dictionary* begins to appear (Feb. 1). Three Emperor's League renewed (March 27). St. Gotthard tunnel opened.

1885 ....Revolt breaks out in eastern Rumelia, joins Bulgaria (Sept. 18). *Dictionary of National Biography* begins to appear.

1886	Gladstone defeated on Irish Home Rule (June 7).
1887	Reinsurance Treaty between Germany and Russia (June 18). Golden Jubilee of Queen Victoria (June 21).
1888	Emperor William dies (March 9); Emperor Frederick III dies (June 15); William II becomes emperor of Germany (–1918). Pasteur Institute established in Paris.
1889	London dock workers strike (Aug. 9–Sept. 14).
1890	Bismarck dismissed as Reich Chancellor (March 20).
1891	*Rerum Novarum*: Leo XIII's encyclical on the rights of labor (May 15). Erfurt Congress of German Social Democrats adopts Marxist program (Oct. 21).
1892	France and Russia sign military convention (Aug. 17). Pan-Slav Congress meets at Krakow (Dec. 12).
1893	First meeting of Independent Labor Party (Jan. 13).
1894	Captain Alfred Dreyfus arrested and charged with spying (Oct. 15). Alexander III dies (Nov. 1); Nicholas II, tsar of Russia (–1917).
1895	Russia, France, Germany intervene against Japan in Sino-Japanese War (April 22).
1896	Emperor William II sends encouraging telegram to President Krueger of the Boer Republic (Jan.

3); English public outraged. Anatolian railway begins operations (July 28).

1897 ....Czech language granted equal rights with German in Bohemia (April 5). Admiral Alfred Tirpitz appointed German navy minister (June 15). Queen Victoria's Diamond Jubilee (June 22).

1898 ....Émile Zola publishes "*J'accuse*" article against French army cover-up in the Dreyfus trial (Jan. 13). First German navy bill passed (March 28).

1899 ....International Working Men's Congress in London (June 26). Dreyfus found guilty "with attenuating circumstances" at re-trial (Aug. 7).

1900 ....Second German navy bill passed (July 14).

1901 ....Queen Victoria dies (Jan. 22); Edward VII (–1910) succeeds. First wireless communication between America and Europe (Dec. 13).

1902 ....Anglo-Japanese treaty (Jan. 30). Fritz Krupp commits suicide (Nov. 23).

1903 ....Pope Leo XIII dies (July 20); succeeded by Pius X (–1910).

1904 ....Anglo-French *Entente Cordiale* (April 8). Plehve, Russian minister of the interior, murdered (July 28).

1905 ....Revolution breaks out in St. Petersburg (Jan. 22). Japanese defeat Russians at Mukden (March 1–9).

1906 ....Russian constitution promulgated (May 6). Dreyfus formally rehabilitated (July 12). Russian village communities (*mir*) abolished (Nov. 22).

1907 ....Universal male suffrage introduced in Austrian "half" of Austro-Hungarian Empire (Jan. 10).

1908 ....Asquith forms Liberal government (April 8); Lloyd George, Chancellor of the Exchequer.

1909 ....Franco-German agreement on Morocco (Feb. 9). Young Turk rebellion deposes sultan (April 27). Lords reject Lloyd George's finance bill; Parliament dissolved (Nov. 30).

1910 ....Edward VII dies (May 6); George V succeeds him (–1936).

1911 ....Second Hague peace conference begins (June 15). Parliament Act reduces power of the House of Lords (July 6). Stolypin, Russia premier, murdered (Sept. 14). Italy declares war on Turkey and seizes Tripoli (Sept. 29).

1912 ....German army and navy bills passed (May 21). First Balkan War begins (Oct. 17–Dec. 3).

1913 ....Irish Home Rule passes Commons (Jan. 16); Lords reject it (Jan. 30). Second Balkan War (Feb. 3–April 23). Irish Home Rule passes Commons (July 7); Lords reject it (July 15).

1914 ....Suffragette riots in London (March 10). Curragh mutiny in Northern Ireland (March 20). Commons passes Home Rule for the third time (May 25). Archduke Franz Ferdinand murdered in Sarajevo (June 28).

Glossary

absolutism: The political doctrine and practice of unlimited, centralized authority and absolute sovereignty, as vested especially in a monarch. The essence of such a system is that the ruling power is not subject to regularized challenge or check by any other agency, be it judicial, legislative, religious, economic, **or electoral**.

Ashkenazi: The Hebrew word for "German"; applied to all Jews who used a German dialect written in Hebrew characters and, by extension, all Jews north of the Alps and east of the Rhine.

assignat: Paper money issued in France as currency during the revolution. Its security rested on the value of seized royal, noble, and church property, but it depreciated because too much was issued and too few sales of land took place to redeem it.

Bonapartism: A political movement in 19th-century France that looked to the model of Napoleon I, strong executive power, and glory abroad as a counter to Jacobinism on the left and reaction and the Church on the right. It has been called the "dictatorship of the center."

concordat: A pact, with the force of international law, concluded between the ecclesiastical authority and the secular authority on matters of mutual concern; most especially a pact between the pope and a temporal head of state for the regulation of ecclesiastical affairs in the territory of the latter.

deism: Deists believed that God and nature were essentially the same. They rejected revelation and the supernatural doctrines of Christianity in the name of *natural religion*.

département: The new units of provincial France after the revolution. The whole country was divided into 83 equal squares of territory.

dialectic: G. W. F. Hegel applied the term *dialectic* to the logical method of his philosophy, which proceeds from thesis through antithesis to synthesis. Hegel's method was appropriated by Karl Marx and Friedrich Engels in their philosophy of dialectical materialism.

division of labor: A central idea in Adam Smith's *The Wealth of Nations* (1776), which attributes the great expansion in production to the rational and consecutive assignment of limited but specialized productive tasks in the modern machine-based industrial system.

dvorianstvo: The Russian term for nobility, which comes from the word for "house" or "court." It expresses the dependence of nobles in Russia on the tsar.

Elector: One of the seven electoral princes (three of whom were archbishops) who had the right to "elect" the Holy Roman Emperor of the German nation.

Encyclopédie; ou, Dictionnaire raisonné des sciences, des arts, et des métiers: Edited by Denis Diderot and Jean le Rond d'Alembert, the *Encyclopédie* was rational and secular and expressed the new systematic view of reality.

Enlightenment: A movement of ideas that is difficult to define easily. Dictionaries start with the image receiving mental or spiritual "light." The "light" in the 18th century was no longer the light of revealed truth but the light of human reason. This development was unique to Europe and is an essential element in the evolution of modern society.

Estate: The nearest equivalent in English to *stand* or *ordre*, which described corporate identities in Old Regime Europe. Its most famous application was in the name *Estates General*, the recall of which by a frightened Louis XVI of France marked a crucial stage in the fall of the French absolute monarchy.

feudalism: A system by which land was held by tenants from lords. As developed in medieval England and France, the king was the supreme lord with numerous levels of lesser lords, down to the occupying tenant. The system represented the disintegration of central authority.

gentry: The lower English nobility, often without any titles but with ancient lineages, country houses, and a distinct sense of their place in society.

ghetto: An enclosed quarter in European cities in which Jews were forced to live.

hwyl: A Welsh word for "passion" or "fervor," used about oratory.

ilustrado: A Spanish term for a disciple of the Enlightenment.

intelligentsia: A Russian term to describe the class composed of writers, artists, musicians, and others involved as readers or critics in intellectual life.

invisible hand: Attributed to Adam Smith; the idea that market mechanisms operate to convert the individual search for profit into public benefits by a kind of invisible providence of which the individual is unaware.

Jacobin: The most famous political group of the French Revolution, which became identified with extreme egalitarianism and violence and led the revolutionary government from mid-1793 to mid-1794.

Junker: Term used to describe the Prussian country squires from the old German term for a "young lord."

Kondratieff cycles: The so-called "long waves" of business and economic activity, generally reckoned to be 50 years in duration, named after the Russian economic historian N. D. Kondratieff (1892–1938).

labor theory of value: The value of a good derives from the effort of production, based on supply. Ricardo asserted that the cost of production can be reduced to the cost of labor, either paid in wages or used as capital.

Latifundia: A great estate owned by a landlord, found in Spain and Italy

leitmotif: A leading musical theme in a Wagner opera, often connected to a character or an idea.

levée en masse: Total mobilization of French society for war, according to the decree of August 23, 1793, which declared that all French men, women. and children were "in a permanent state of requisition for service in the armies."

magazine: The original idea was a metaphor, because the meaning of the word is "a place where goods are stored." In 1731, Edward Cave founded *The Gentleman's Magazine*, as he wrote, "to treasure up, as in a Magazine, the most remarkable Pieces" from the many newspapers then circulating.

Magyar: A name for Hungarian as a nationality and the language known as Hungarian, which is member of the Finno-Ugric family. The Magyar language has affinities with Finnish and Turkish but is not an Indo-European tongue.

Malthusian: The adjective taken from the name of the Rev. T. R. Malthus (1766–1834), whose theory that human population would be limited only by the limits of the food supply became an essential part of the thought of 19th-century economists and politicians.

mir: The peasant commune in Russia under serfdom and afterward, in which land was communally held and, in some places, regularly reallotted to families that had more or fewer mouths to feed.

natural selection: The central principle used by Charles Darwin to explain the variety of plants and animals. It rests on the idea that the struggle for survival "selects" over time certain adaptations of form, color, behavior, or structure that have proved themselves.

nonconformist: All Protestant churches and sects in Britain that were not part of the established Church of England and would not "conform" to the 39 articles of dogma of the Church of England.

non-expedit: A papal or episcopal injunction against certain activities by faithful Roman Catholics; most famous as a prohibition on taking part in the politics of the Italian kingdom in the 19th century.

Old Regime: The English version of the French *l'ancien régime*, which describes the world before 1789 of particular, not general, rights; of *Estates*; and of irregular, overlapping administrative jurisdictions, weights, and measures.

parlement: A French court, descended from the medieval supreme court, which by the 18th century, had developed into a semi-parliamentary body with the right to register the king's edicts. The *parlements* were the embodiment of privileges. Thirteen of these sovereign, quasi-judicial bodies operated in different places with different traditions and legal bases.

philosophes: The term used to describe the leading figures of the French Enlightenment.

Pietism: The name for the movement (originated by Philipp Jakob Spener late in the 17th century) for the revival and advancement of piety in the Lutheran Church by emphasizing conversion experience in the soul rather than external worship.

plane polarized light: A technique by which crystallographic structures in substances can be analyzed by placing a specimen between two glass planes and shining light through the two planes and the material. Used in the 19th century and still used today.

proletariat: In Marxian theory, the class of exploited workers and wage earners who depend on the sale of their labor for their means of existence

public sphere: A term coined by the German philosopher Jürgen Habermas to describe the new "public spaces" in the 18th century, such as coffeehouses or literary journals, in which people could gather for "conversation," irrespective of rank or class.

Realpolitik: A completely unemotional or ethical attitude to practical politics; policy is determined by considerations of power and national interest, rather than by moral or ideological considerations.

remonstrance: The "right" or the power of the 13 French sovereign *parlements* to block royal decrees and register laws, which allowed them to point out any breach of monarchic tradition. It was a sort of veto power that the king could override if he wished.

Restoration: The attempt to restore monarchy, divine right of kings, religious observance, and social conservatism after the defeat of Napoleon; also the name for the period 1815–1848.

Risorgimento: Literally, "resurgence"; used generally to describe the rise of the national idea in Italy in the 19th century.

Roman law: The law of ancient Rome, which became the legal system in most Western countries except England, where common law based on precedent and adversarial proceedings continued. It formed the basis of the law codes of most countries of continental Europe west of the Russian border. It is frequently called civil law.

Romanticism: A powerful movement in art, literature, and sensibility that began just before 1789 but swelled in reaction to the French Revolution and Napoleonic Empire. Romanticism can be seen as a rejection of the precepts of order, calm, harmony, balance, idealization, and rationality that typified Classicism in general and late 18th-century Neoclassicism in particular. It was also, to some extent, a reaction against the Enlightenment and against 18th-century rationalism and physical materialism in general. Romanticism emphasized the individual, the subjective, the irrational, the imaginative, the personal, the spontaneous, the emotional, the visionary, and the transcendental.

section: One of the 48 electoral districts into which the city of Paris was divided and that sent representatives to the city government, known as the *Commune de Paris*.

Sephardim: The Hebrew word for "Spanish"; applied to those expelled from the Spanish and Portuguese Empires after 1492 who used Ladino as their native tongue. Castilian Spanish written in Hebrew letters.

Slavophile: A term for certain Russian intellectuals who rejected Western ways of life and praised the differences of the Russian way.

South Sea Bubble: The speculation mania that ruined many British investors in 1720. The bubble, or hoax, centered on the fortunes of the South Sea Company, founded in 1711 to trade (mainly in slaves) with Spanish America.

suffragette: A woman who campaigned with militancy and civil disobedience in the United Kingdom in the years before 1914 to gain the right to vote.

take-off: The term used in economic history to describe the "spurt" in growth rates that many developing economies experience as industrialization reaches a certain stage.

temperament: A musical term to describe a system of tuning instruments by equal intervals made up of semitone units, each of which is set exactly at a 12th of an octave. As a result, some intervals are a little flat and some are a little sharp in relation to their absolute harmonic relations.

temporal power: The doctrine that the pope, in order to guarantee his spiritual freedom, must be a sovereign ruler in the world of states.

Tory: A term used from the 18th century on to describe the main British conservative party, as well as attitudes of mind.

Whig: The slang term for the more liberal, progressive group in 18th- and 19th-century English politics.

Zollverein: The German word for "customs union," but in particular, the one led by Prussia that developed between 1819 and 1834.

Biographical Notes

Albert, Prince Consort (Franz Albrecht August Karl Emanuel, Prince of Saxe-Coburg-Gotha) (1819–1861). The much-loved husband of Queen Victoria. He was an active reformer of stern principles and the organizer and guiding spirit of the Great Exhibition at the Crystal Palace in 1851.

Alembert, Jean le Rond d' (1717–1783). French mathematician and philosopher. Diderot made him co-editor of the *Encyclopédie*, for which he wrote the "preliminary discourse" (1751) and mathematical, philosophical, and literary articles.

Alexander II (1818–1881) (Tsar of Russia, 1855–1881). After Russia's defeat in the Crimean War in 1856, Alexander began an era of reforms, especially the emancipation of the serfs in 1861. He reformed municipal government and introduced a limited self-government in the countryside.

Augustus the Strong (1670–1733). Duke of Saxony and king of Poland, he built palaces, collected art, and founded the famous Meissen china works. He ruled the richest of the German states and nearly exhausted the royal treasury.

Bach, Carl Philipp Emanuel (1714–1788). C.P.E. Bach was the most distinguished son of the great Johann Sebastian Bach (1685–1750) and himself a great composer. He said, "I never had a teacher other than my father," yet their styles could not have been more different. The younger Bach developed an expressive style that reflects a change in the social reality and in the listening public, the beginnings of the market for art.

Bach, Johann Sebastian (1685–1750). J.S. Bach was, for much of his life, organist and choir master at St. Thomas Church in Leipzig. A pious and mystical Lutheran, Bach composed dozens of church cantatas and the towering musical representations of the Passions according to St. Matthew and St. John, as well as a Mass in B Minor. The greatest musical intellect of all time.

Bismarck, Otto von (1815–1898). The "Iron Chancellor," he unified Germany in three wars and came to embody everything brutal and ruthless about Prussian culture. The real Bismarck had a different character: He was a hypochondriac, a brilliant and well-read man, a convert to an extreme form of Protestant mysticism, and one of the few Prussians who never served in the king's army.

Boswell, James (1740–1795). The alter ego in Samuel Johnson's life. Boswell, a Scottish gentleman of questionable character, arrived in London in 1762. He was a toady, a name-dropper, and a sexually irrepressible rake. His *London Journal, 1762–1763* reveals that he was an anxious depressive, who suffered from mood swings, hypochondria, and fears of venereal disease, but he was, perhaps, the greatest biographer in the English language.

Burke, Edmund (1729–1797). One of the greatest orators, stylists, and political figures of the late 18th century. An Irishman with a Protestant father and a Catholic mother, he rose to high office in the corrupt politics of Georgian England without wealth or connections because of his extraordinary intellectual power. He "invented" modern conservative ideology in his book *Reflections on the Revolution in France of 1790*.

Butler, Bishop Joseph (1692–1752). Butler was an Anglican bishop. His sermons and *The Analogy of Religion* (1726) were attempts to construct a science of man but one compatible with the Christian faith. Hume was impressed by Butler's philosophy but cut the ground from under it by his skepticism.

Calonne, Charles Alexandre de (1734–1802). Controller general of the finances in France from 1783 to 1787. He had to deal with the bankruptcy, which he knew had occurred but which he dared not admit. His problem was to find a way around the parlements and raise taxes.

Catherine II, the Great (1729–1796). A German princess from Anhalt-Zerbst, a minor principality. She became empress of Russia in a military coup that toppled her husband, Tsar Peter III, and began a campaign to Westernize Russia. She opened the country to foreigners, reformed the legal system, and waged a series of wars to establish Russian prestige as a great power.

Cavour, Camillo Benso Count di (1810–1861). Prime minister of the kingdom of Piedmont-Sardinia, Cavour was responsible for the unification of Italy. He was a liberal in politics and economics but also anticlerical. Under his government, Piedmontese legislation grew increasingly hostile to the Church, and after the unification of Italy, his legacy was a stalemate in church-state relations that lasted until Mussolini signed the Lateran Treaties with Pius XI in 1929, which established the Vatican as a separate state.

Churchill, Sir Winston Leonard Spencer (1874–1965). Grandson of the duke of Marlborough and son of Lord Randolph Churchill, Winston Churchill was born into the Conservative Party's elite leadership. He made a name for himself as a soldier and war correspondent in the Boer War and was elected to Parliament as a Conservative. When the Conservatives became committed to "tariff reform," that is, ending free trade, Churchill "crossed the aisle" in 1904 and joined the Liberals, where he became a friend of Lloyd George. In 1905, the Liberals formed a government and Churchill was appointed undersecretary for the colonies in the cabinet of Sir Henry Campbell-Bannerman. Under Asquith, he was initially (1908–1910) president of the Board of Trade, then home secretary (1910–1911), and championed innovative labor exchange and old-age pension acts.

Darwin, Charles (1809–1882). A member of a prominent Cambridge academic family, Darwin studied medicine at Edinburgh and for the ministry at Cambridge but lost interest in both. A botanist friend, J. S. Henslow, got him a job as official naturalist on a five-year cruise (1831–1836) aboard HMS *Beagle*. What Darwin saw, especially on the Galapagos Islands, started him on work that resulted in the formulation of his concept of evolution. In 1859, Darwin set forth the structure and evidence for his theory in *The Origin of Species*.

Disraeli, Benjamin, the first Earl of Beaconsfield (1804–1881). The elegant Jewish leader of the Conservative Party who was also a successful popular novelist and a great wit, Disraeli extended the mass base of the Conservatives and introduced the Reform Bill of 1867. Queen Victoria's favorite prime minister.

Dreyfus, Captain Alfred (1859–1935). A French general staff officer, he became famous as the victim of the most notorious miscarriage of justice in the 19th century. Dreyfus was falsely accused of passing secrets to the Germans, convicted by court martial, and sent to Devils Island in solitary confinement. Dreyfus was an Alsatian and a Jew and, hence, obviously guilty. The secrets continued to be passed. The French army covered up the fact that they had convicted an innocent man.

Drumont, Edouard (1844–1917). The most brilliant and violent of the French anti-Semitic journalists, he used his paper, *La Libre Parole* ("*The Free Word*"), to blame the Jews for all the ills of modern society and to insist that Dreyfus was guilty, whatever the evidence might say.

Eliot, George (1819–1880). The pseudonym of Mary Ann or Marian Evans. Three novels of provincial life made her reputation—*Adam Bede* (1859), *The Mill on the Floss* (1860), and *Silas Marner* (1861). Thackeray's *Cornhill Magazine* published her historical romance *Romola*, a story of Savonarola. *Felix Holt* (1866), a political novel, was followed by *The Spanish Gypsy* (1868), a dramatic poem, *Middlemarch* (1871–1872), and *Daniel Deronda* (1876).

Engels, Friedrich (1820–1895). One of the two founders of Communism, Engels was the son of a rich manufacturer from Barmen in the Rhineland. In 1842, he went to take a position in a factory near Manchester, England, in which his father had an interest and to learn the latest machine technology. In 1844, while passing through Paris, he met Marx, and their lifelong association began. Engels wrote *The Condition of the Working Class in England* and was the most important interpreter of Karl Marx's thought.

Fontane, Theodor (1819–1898). A German novelist, Fontane, who grew up in Berlin Huguenot community, was the Jane Austen of the Bismarck era. His novels provide wonderful portraits of life in Bismarck's Prussia, and several are available in English, such as *Effi Briest*, *Cecile*, and *Delusions and Confusions*. Fontane was a contemporary of Bismarck, who appears in several of the novels.

Frederick II, the Great (1712–1786). King of Prussia from 1740 to 1786, he embodied the principle of a rational autocracy. He wanted his state to hum like a well-oiled machine. All the parts had specific functions, but only the king could see the whole. Wit, philosopher, expert musician, brilliant general, tireless administrator, he called himself "the first servant of the state," and for 46 years, he served the state with no family, no close friends, no advisors, and no confidantes—only his six beautiful greyhounds and a few silent servants.

Garibaldi, Giuseppe (1807–1882). Garibaldi was an Italian patriot and a guerrilla leader in the Mazzinian mold. Under the influence of Mazzini, he became involved in an unsuccessful republican plot and fled to South America. There, he gained his first experience in guerrilla warfare. Garibaldi was the perfect Romantic hero and a noble leader. His expedition to Sicily in 1860 triggered the events that led to the unification of Italy under the Piedmontese monarchy, not to Mazzini's radical republic.

George I (1660–1727). King of Great Britain and Ireland, he was a German prince. In 1698, he became elector of Hanover. He was exactly like Augustus the Strong. As the heir of the last Stuart, Queen Anne, who died in 1714, he suddenly found himself king of England, unable to speak a word of English.

George II (1683–1760). King of Great Britain and Ireland, his long reign (from 1727 to 1760) coincided with the establishment of a two-party system in Great Britain. He is the monarch who most benefited from the economic growth of the 18th century. Under him, the last serious Scottish revolt on behalf of the Stuarts was crushed, and the Highlands were "ethnically cleansed."

George III (1738–1820). King of Great Britain and Ireland (1760–1820), his long reign falls into two unequal parts; in the first, he tried to root out corruption in British politics and to assert royal authority. His policies and his ministers provoked the conflict with the North American colonies that resulted in the independence of the United States. He gradually succumbed to porphyry, a viral disease that made him insane and took him out of active life.

George IV (1762–1830). King of Great Britain and Ireland (1820–1830), eldest son and successor of George III. He spent much of his life as prince regent for his father, trying to gain the full powers of a king. Utterly dissolute, cynical, and fat, he is one of the "old royals" against whom the young Princess Victoria reacted when she became queen.

Gladstone, William Ewart (1809–1898). The stern moralizing leader of the Liberal Party under Queen Victoria, he espoused extreme Liberal views and wished to reduce the power of the state, reduce expenditure, and give home rule to the Irish.

Goethe, Johann Wolfgang von (1749–1832). Goethe is to German literature what Shakespeare is to English. Goethe could do everything well. He painted, sketched, designed, and wrote poetry and plays. He had a large private income and could afford to travel.

He wrote *The Sorrows of Young Werther*, which became a bestseller in 1774 and made Goethe famous everywhere in Europe.

Goya, Francisco de (1746–1828). A Spanish painter, he is often called "the first of the moderns" because of his bold paintings and satirical etchings, and his belief in the priority of the artist's vision over tradition. He was also a traditional court painter who made his living painting kings and queens.

Habermas, Jürgen (1929–). Habermas is German philosopher and emeritus professor at the University of Frankfurt. He developed the idea of the bourgeois public sphere. Habermas thought that the 18th century was a period in which a new space emerged, beyond and alongside the court, the closed corporation, and the family, which he called *Öffentlichkeit*, or the "public sphere."

Heine, Heinrich (1797–1856). Germany's greatest lyric poet, he was also born a Jew in the ghetto. He had to flee Germany in the reactionary period after the Napoleonic War and lived most of the rest of his life in Paris. He predicted with uncanny accuracy the explosion of German nationalism.

Herder, Johann Gottfried (1744–1803). A German philosopher, critic, and clergyman, he was a leader in the *Sturm und Drang* movement and an early Romantic. His most influential ideas are to be found in a pamphlet entitled "*Über den Ursprung der Sprache*" ("On the Origin of Language") of 1772. It is the founding charter of Romantic nationalism.

Herzl, Theodor (1860–1904). The founder of Zionism, he was a German-speaking Hungarian Jew who worked as a theater correspondent for the Vienna *Neue Freie Presse*, the *New York Times* of the Habsburg Empire. His paper sent him to Paris, where he was appalled by the vicious anti-Semitism he observed during the public reaction to Dreyfus's trial. Herzl decided that Jewish assimilation in Europe was impossible and that the only solution to the Jewish problem was the establishment of a Jewish national state.

Hobbes, Thomas (1588–1679). The philosopher of the English Civil War. Hobbes saw the religious wars as chaotic and dangerous to orderly rule. His *Leviathan* (1651) is a reflection of the chaos of civil war. It rested on a mechanistic view that life is simply the motions of the organism and that man is by nature a selfishly individualistic animal at constant war with all other men.

Holbach, Paul Henri Thiry, Baron d' (1723–1789). A leading figure in the French Enlightenment. d'Holbach's estate was a meeting place for the most important French radical thinkers (the *philosophes*) of the late 18th century. He was an atheist, a determinist, and a materialist. d'Holbach was protected in his extreme views by his high aristocratic rank and wealth.

Hume, David (1711–1776). The greatest British philosopher. The publication in 1739 of Hume's *A Treatise of Human Nature: Being an Attempt to introduce the experimental method of reasoning in Moral Subjects* was a revolution. Hume's application of the experimental method to ideas broke the continuity of human affairs and demolished existing rules of thought.

Johnson, Samuel (1709–1784). Johnson became the most famous literary figure in England during the 18th century. In 1755, he published his two-volume dictionary, the biggest commercial publication of its time. It became an immediate success, because Johnson's definitions sparkled with wit, yet he is most famous as the subject of James Boswell's *Life of Johnson*.

Joseph II (1741–1790). Holy Roman emperor (1765–1790) and king of Bohemia and Hungary (1780–1790), he was the son of Maria Theresa and Holy Roman Emperor Francis I, whom he succeeded. Joseph attempted to rule his immense and quarrelsome territories by pure reason. He tried to rationalize the mess of royal possessions that Maria Theresa had ruled by common sense.

Krupp, Alfred (1812–1887). Krupp built up the great firm of Friedrich Krupp Essen, which he took over at the age of 14 when his father, the founder, died. Known as the "Cannon King," Krupp introduced new methods for producing large quantities of cast steel. After the Franco-Prussian War, he specialized more and more in armaments and acquired mines all over Germany.

Krupp, Friedrich-Alfred "Fritz" (1854–1902). The son of Alfred. Under Fritz, the Krupp family vastly extended its operations. Fritz, a fat, bespectacled, shy man, had to keep his true nature "in the closet." He bought a villa on Capri, where he pursued his hobby of oceanography and set up a homosexual cult in a temple he built for the purpose. He kept it liberally staffed with compliant Neapolitan boys until the local Socialist paper found out about it and published a series of exposés. Fritz committed suicide.

Lessing, Gotthold Ephraim (1729–1781). One of the most influential figures of the German Enlightenment, he wrote the first plays about the middle classes and tried to create a German national theater.

Lloyd, Sir Nathaniel (1669–1741). Master of Trinity Hall, Cambridge, from 1710 to 1735. He was an exact contemporary of Walpole. Lloyd's was a perfect example of an 18th-century life: A wealthy civil lawyer, he held the mastership at Trinity Hall without giving up his fellowship at All Souls College, Oxford, or his London legal practice. The fact that he had three jobs presented no problems for him.

Lloyd George, David, First Earl Lloyd-George of Dwyfor (1863–1945). He was a brilliantly eloquent, forceful, and creative statesman who became famous as the British prime minister during the First World War. Elected (1890) to Parliament as a Liberal, the young Lloyd George soon became known as a radical. When the Liberals won an overwhelming victory in the election of 1905, Lloyd George became a cabinet minister and, in 1908, chancellor of the exchequer (the equivalent of secretary of the treasury). Lloyd George was the architect of the "Peoples Budget" of 1909, which introduced social security for the first time. The battle that ensued and his ultimate victory led to curbing the power of the House of Lords.

Macaulay, Thomas Babington, Lord Macaulay (1800–1859). English writer and politician, he expressed Liberal views most brilliantly in his essays and speeches in Parliament. He defended the rights of non-baptized Jews to be elected to the House of Commons in a famous article of 1829. He wrote a *History of England*, as well as many nonpolitical essays. A contemporary said, "I wish I were as certain of anything as Macaulay is of everything."

Malthus, the Reverend Thomas Robert (1766–1834). An Anglican clergyman and the inventor of modern demography, he was as influential as Adam Smith. In his famous "Essay on the Principle of Population," he contended that poverty and distress are unavoidable, because population increases by geometrical ratio and the means of subsistence by arithmetical ratio.

Maria Theresa (1717–1780). Maria Theresa ruled over a complex of states and territories that had no overall name. She was archduchess of Austria above and below the Enns; queen of

Bohemia, Hungary, Dalmatia, and Slavonia; and duchess of Burgundy and held many other titles. The most important title, Holy Roman Empress, could not be hers, because the Salic Law forbade female succession. She was the mother of Joseph II and Marie Antoinette.

Marie Antoinette (1755–1793). A Habsburg princess, she was the youngest daughter of Maria Theresa and the sister of Emperor Joseph II. She married a Bourbon, thus uniting the two greatest European royal families, and became queen of France when her husband took the throne as Louis XVI. She was beheaded during the French Revolution.

Marwitz, Friedrich August Ludwig von der (1777–1837). von der Marwitz was a Prussian landlord who resisted Prussian government reforms to liberalize society, free serfs, and introduce constitutional protections and representative government. His intellectual position reflected the influence of Edmund Burke.

Marx, Karl (1818–1883). The founder of Communism. Marx was the greatest theorist of society in modern times. His work is largely a criticism of the consequences of the new commercial society and capitalist markets. Marx's most famous book, *Das Kapital* (1867), has as its subtitle: *A Critique of Political Economy*.

Mazzini, Giuseppe (1805–1872). He dedicated his life to the revival of the Italian "nation" and to the establishment of a republic of free citizens. He believed passionately in the so-called *Risorgimento*, or "resurgence," of the Italian people. A purist, an idealist, and a Romantic, he used violence and even terror to achieve his aims but failed in the end, defeated by the backwardness of Italian society and its economy.

Metternich, Clemens Wenzel Nepomuk Lothar Prince von (1773–1859). Napoleon's great adversary, not on the field of battle, but over the lacquered tables of diplomacy. His family had been independent rulers of a small principality until the French Revolution wiped the tiny states away. He became foreign minister of Austria in 1809 and put Europe back together in 1814 and 1815 after the French Revolution and Napoleon had twisted it to their purposes. He then ruled Europe by persuasion, by suppression of liberties, and by maintaining the balance of power until 1848.

Moser, Johann Jakob (1701–1785). The greatest constitutional expert of the 18th century in Germany, Moser explained the historical messiness of the old Holy Roman Empire in several works and defended the historic rights of its 3,000 separate sovereign units. He was twice jailed for his opposition to the duke of Württemberg, who was trying to turn his duchy into an absolute monarchy.

Napoleon I (Napoleon Bonaparte) (1769–1821). He was born into a provincial gentleman's family in Ajaccio, Corsica, and rose to be emperor of France and lord of the greatest empire since the days of the Romans. A brilliant general and a canny politician, he converted the gains of the French Republic, turned it into a monarchy, and installed his Corsican clan as kings and queens.

Napoleon III, Louis Napoleon Bonaparte (1808–1873). The son of Louis Bonaparte and Hortense de Beauharnais, the daughter of Napoleon's lover, and the nephew of Napoleon I. After the collapse of his uncle's empire, the family was driven from France. Obsessed with Napoleon I, Louis planned unsuccessful coups, until the revolution of 1848 gave him his opportunity. His reign, known as the Second Empire, was a glorious chapter in French history, which saw the rebuilding of Paris, but it came to a miserable end in the Franco-Prussian War in 1870.

Newman, John Henry Cardinal (1801–1890). A Catholic theologian who wrote "Lead, Kindly Light" and other hymns. In 1841, Newman published Tract 90, demonstrating that the Thirty-Nine Articles, the formulary of faith of the Church of England, was consistent with Catholicism, and in 1845, he was received into the Roman Catholic Church. Newman published the *Apologia pro vita sua* in 1864, a masterpiece of religious autobiography.

Newton, Sir Isaac (1642–1727). The greatest scientist of all time, Newton created a new relationship between man and nature. He discovered the law of universal gravitation, began to develop the calculus, and discovered that white light is composed of all the colors of the spectrum.

Nietzsche, Friedrich (1844–1900). The most important philosopher of the irrational, he was the prophet of a boundless attack on enlightened rationality, God, and conventional thought and morality. His cult of the "Superman" raised the great creative soul beyond good and evil. The new Superman with his "will to power" was to be the savior of decadent humanity.

Pasteur, Louis (1822–1895). A French chemist and microbiologist, he made numerous and varied contributions to science and industry. His experiments with bacteria showed conclusively that the theory of spontaneous generation was not valid and gave rise to the germ theory of infection. He was able to trace the cause of fermentation and specific diseases to specific micoorganisms and created and used the first vaccines for rabies, anthrax, and chicken cholera. He was responsible for pioneering work in the area of stereochemistry, and his name has become forever linked with the process he invented, *pasteurization*.

Pius IX (Giovanni Maria Mastai-Ferretti) (1792–1878; pope, 1846–1878). By far, the most important pope of the 19th century. Elected in 1846 as a young cardinal, for two years he pursued a progressive policy in governing the Papal States and granted a constitution. However, the revolution of 1848 embittered him by its excesses of liberalism and nationalism. In *The Syllabus of Errors* of 1864, he declared freedoms of speech, the press, and religion, indeed all freedoms, to be errors. In 1869, he convoked the First Vatican Council, at which the enunciation of papal infallibility was proclaimed.

Ricardo, David (1772–1823). An English "classical" economist, Ricardo put Smith and Malthus together in *The Principles of Political Economy and Taxation* of 1817. Ricardo stated the *iron law of wages*, according to which wages tend to stabilize around the subsistence level. Any rise in wage rates above subsistence will cause the working population to increase to the point that heightened competition among the glut of laborers will merely cause their wages to fall back to the subsistence level.

Robespierre, Maximilien (1758–1794). A provincial French lawyer who rose to head the French revolutionary Committee of Public Safety, in effect, the government at the most violent and radical stage of the French Revolution. Under Robespierre, terror first became a modern political concept. While he was in power, some 40,000 "enemies of the people," including King Louis XVI and Queen Marie Antoinette, were beheaded by guillotine or shot.

Rothschild, Nathan Mayer (1777–1836). The "English" Rothschild, one of five remarkable brothers whose father sent them to five European capitals to found banks. In the 1820s, this Jew from the ghetto of Frankfurt, who spoke broken English all his life, was probably richer, relative to his times, than Bill Gates is today.

Rousseau, Jean-Jacques (1712–1778). He wrote the first French bestseller, *Julie ou La Nouvelle Héloïse*, a story of passion across the lines of class. He also wrote works of philosophy in the 18th century, and his *Social Contract* remains one of the most important accounts of democracy ever written. He argued against the prevailing optimism about the progress of civilization and believed that the "noble savage" represented humanity's highest form of morality.

Smith, Adam (1723–1790). Scottish moral philosopher. A Prussian aristocrat said in 1806, "Adam Smith is the uncrowned king of Europe." His work *The Wealth of Nations* was published in 1776, the year of the American Declaration of Independence, and can be said to be equally revolutionary. It explained the way a capitalist market-based economy works. It is the most important work of economic theory ever written.

Stephen, Leslie (1832–1904). Founder of *The Dictionary of National Biography* and father of Virginia Woolf, he wrote countless books and magazine articles and was one of the most influential Victorian essayists and thinkers. His *History of English Thought in the Eighteenth Century* is a forgotten masterpiece.

Strauss, David Friedrich (1808–1874). A German theologian, his *Das Leben Jesu* ("*The Life of Jesus*") (2 vol., 1835–1836) applied the "myth theory" to the life of Jesus, treated the Gospel narrative like any other historical work, and denied all supernatural elements in the Gospels. The book caused an uproar and, in Zurich, led to a serious revolt against the government. George Eliot began her literary career when she translated it into English.

Tocqueville, Alexis de (1805–1859). Author of two of the wisest books of the 19th century: *Democracy in America* (4 vol., 1835–1840) and *The Old Regime and the French Revolution* (1856). de Tocqueville saw things few understood at the time but are now clear.

Tolstoy, Leo Nikolayevich (1828–1910). A Russian noble and novelist, Tolstoy wrote *The Cossacks* (1863) and the masterpieces *War and Peace* (1862–1869) and *Anna Karenina* (1873–1876).

Tolstoy had a "conversion" in 1878 and, for the rest of his life, was a kind of prophet of nonviolence and moral reform. He exchanged letters with Gandhi.

Turgot, Anne-Robert-Jacques (1727–1781). A French economist and *philosophe*, he was a member of the Enlightenment circles in Paris. He was also a civil servant and a reformer who served as comptroller general of finances from 1774 to 1776 and tried unsuccessfully to introduce free trade in grain.

Victoria, Queen of Great Britain and Ireland (1819–1901). She gave her name to an entire epoch, the *Victorian Era*. Her importance as a symbol and in practice as the head of state of the greatest empire the world had known played a great part in the era, but in a deeper sense, she represented a new kind of monarch, the monarch as the ideal of the respectable middle classes.

Wagner, Richard (1813–1883). A revolutionary in politics and music. He fought on the barricades in Dresden in the revolution of 1848 against the king of Saxony and the repressive regime of Metternich. In exile, he conceived an equally gigantic revolution in music that would create the "total work of art." Its grandest expression is the *Der Ring des Nibelungen* (1853–1874), his tetralogy based on the *Nibelungenlied*. Here, he carried out his new ideas of opera and drama, which embodied large-scale quasi-religious myths.

Walpole, Sir Robert (1676–1745). Walpole served as prime minister for more than 20 years and created the first "modern" party government in the world. He made his reputation in dealing with the South Sea Bubble of 1720, a very modern stock exchange collapse, and protected his position with skilled use of corruption.

William II (1859–1941). German emperor and King of Prussia from 1888–1918. A difficult and bombastic man, Emperor William devoted his considerable energies to expanding German military and naval power and to increasing German prestige in the world. Many contemporaries blamed him for the catastrophe of the First World War.

William IV (1765–1837). King of Great Britain and Ireland (1830–1837), he was the third son of George III and the last of the "old royals." His best achievement was not to oppose the reforms brought in by the Whigs during his reign and grudgingly to consent to create enough peers to allow the reforms to get through the House of Lords. He was about as dissolute as his brother, George IV, but the times were changing. His behavior was no longer as tolerable.

Wollstonecraft, Mary (1759–1797). Wollstonecraft can be considered the first feminist. Her *Thoughts on the Education of Daughters* (1786) and *A Vindication of the Rights of Woman* (1792) were the first feminist manifestos. After all, if "all men are created equal" and if the French Revolution declared the "rights of man and the citizen," the logical consequences of that must lead to the equality of "the second sex."

Young, Arthur (1741–1820). An English agricultural expert, whose *Travels in France* (1788–1789) and *Travels in Ireland* (1776) offer a unique eyewitness account of life at that time. Young was one of the great pioneers of modern farming practice.

Zola, Emile (1840–1902). France's most popular novelist, he used literature to expose the social evils of his time. In January 1898, he published an article in *L'Aurore*, a left-wing Republican newspaper, entitled "*J'accuse*" ("I accuse"), in which he told the story of the miscarriage of justice in the Dreyfus case and accused the entire French establishment of injustice, lies, and cover-up. Within 24 hours, 200,000 copies were sold.

Bibliography

General Reference for the Course:

Merriman, John. *A History of Modern Europe, from the French Revolution to the Present.* New York: W.W. Norton & Company, 1996. Because this course of lectures is unique, no textbook is available for the period. I use this source in my university classes.

Essential Reading:

Blanning T. C. W. *The Culture of Power and the Power of Culture: Old Regime Europe, 1660–1789.* Oxford/New York: Oxford University Press, 2002. A brilliant study of the interaction of art and the context in which it is created. An inspiration for much of this course.

————. *Joseph II.* Profiles in Power. London/New York: Longman, 1994. As perfect and delightful a short biography as can be imagined.

Boswell, James. *Life of Johnson.* R. W. Chapman and J. D. Fleeman, eds. Oxford: Oxford University Press, 1998. The best biography ever written.

————. *Boswell's London Journal: 1762-1763.* Frederick A. Pottle, ed. New Haven: Yale University Press, 1992. A wonderful insight into London life, high and low, in the middle of the 18th century.

Boyle, Nicholas. *Goethe: The Poet and the Age: The Poetry of Desire, 1749–1790.* Oxford/New York: Oxford University Press 1992. This is an absolutely masterly biography of Goethe and his times.

Burke, Edmund. *Reflections on the Revolution in France And on the Proceeding in Certain Societies in London Relative to That Event in a Letter Intended to Have Been Sent to a Gentleman in Paris. 1790.* L. G. Mitchell, ed. Oxford/New York: Oxford University Press, 1999. This explosion of political fury turned into one of the greatest critical assessments of politics ever written and shows why Burke enjoyed the reputation of the greatest stylist of his age.

Burns, Martin. *France and the Dreyfus Affair.* New York: Bedford/St. Martin's, 2000. A new and useful attempt to set Dreyfus in context.

Darwin, Charles. *The Origin of Species by means of Natural Selection or the Preservation of Favoured Races in the Struggle for Life*. London/New York: Penguin USA,1985. This great work is also wonderful to read, with astonishing descriptive passages. Easy to see why it became an instant bestseller in 1859.

————. *The Autobiography of Charles Darwin, 1809–1882*. Nora Barlow, ed. New York: W.W. Norton & Company, 1993. These delightful reminiscences tell the story of the great Darwin in his own words.

Dixon, Simon. *Catherine the Great*. Profiles in Power. New York/London: Longman, 2001. A compact and readable biography by a real historian of Russia who knows the archives.

Duffy, Eamon. *Saints and Sinners: A History of the Popes*. New Haven/London: Yale University Press, 2002. Duffy makes the popes come alive.

Eliot, George. *Middlemarch*. Rosemary Ashton, ed. New York: Penguin USA, 1994. This is Eliot's masterpiece. If you have not done so, read it.

Engels, Friedrich. *The Condition of the Working Class in England*. New York: Penguin USA, 1987. A work that changed the world; it described to a horrified public what conditions were really like in the "dark satanic mills."

Ferguson, Niall. *The House of Rothschild: Money's Prophets 1798–1848*. New York: Penguin USA, 1999. This is the only work to use the Rothschild family archive and is essential for anyone interested in their extraordinary success.

Fontane, Theodor. *Effi Briest*. Hugh Rorrison and Helen Chambers, trans. New York: Penguin, 2001. This is the novel of Bismarck's Germany by its most perceptive observer, who was Bismarck's direct contemporary.

Fraser, Antonia. *Marie Antoinette: The Journey*. New York: Anchor Books, 2002. Lady Antonia Fraser has written more than 30 biographies and is one of the most successful biographers of our time.

Fulbrook, Mary. *Historical Theory: Ways of Imagining the Past* . New York: Routledge, 2002. There is no good piece of theory that explores the relationship between biography and history, but this new book by an excellent historian discusses the issues and does not use fancy jargon.

Geison, Gerald L. *The Private Science of Louis Pasteur*. Princeton, NJ: Princeton University Press, 1996. This fine study makes it possible for a layperson to understand how Pasteur managed to do the experiments he did. It uses his original lab notes to do so.

Goethe, Johann Wolfgang von. *The Sorrows of Young Werther and Selected Writings*. Catherine Hutter, trans. New York: Penguin USA, Inc., 1987. The first great text of continental Romanticism and a wonderful read.

Ingrao, Charles W. *The Habsburg Monarchy, 1618–1815*. Cambridge: Cambridge University Press, 2000. A handy and readable guide to the intricacies of the Habsburg domains; there's no really good work on the Holy Roman Empire in paperback.

Kissinger, Henry Alfred. *The World Restored: Metternich, Castlereagh, and the Problems of Peace, 1812–22*. Boston: Houghton Mifflin Co., 1973. This is where America's master diplomat learned his principles.

Lampedusa, Giuseppe Tomasi di. *The Leopard*. Amherst, NY: Pantheon Books, 1991. One of the great novels of the 20th century; recreates the world of Sicily at the time of unification and provides good reasons for Mazzini's failure.

Magee, Bryan. *Aspects of Wagner*. Oxford/New York: Oxford University Press, 1988. Magee, who is both a philosopher and a music critic, finds a middle ground between the violent schools of interpretation about Wagner.

Manchester, William. *The Arms of Krupp: The Rise and Fall of the Industrial Dynasty That Armed Germany at War*. Boston: Back Bay Books, 2003. A large, well-written, popular history by the biographer of John F. Kennedy.

Marx, Karl, and Engels, Friedrich. *The Communist Manifesto*. New York: Penguin Putnam, 1998. This is the founding document of world Communism and another work that changed history.

Palmer, R. R. *Twelve Who Ruled*. Princeton, NJ: Princeton University Press, 1970. A study of the 12 members of the Committee of Public Safety during the French Revolution and of Maximilien Robespierre, who led them.

Plessis, Alain. *The Rise and Fall of the Second Empire, 1852–1871*. Jonathan Mandelbaum, trans. Cambridge/New York: Cambridge University Press, 1988. One of the few histories of the second Napoleonic Empire in print.

Plumb, J. H. *Sir Robert Walpole: The Making of a Statesman*. London: Cresset Press, 1956. There is nothing in print, hardback or paperback, on Walpole. This is the book to read, if you can find it.

Ritter, Gerhard A. *Frederick the Great: A Historical Profile*. Berkeley, CA: University of California Press, 1968. A short biography by one of Germany's most famous historians.

Rousseau, Jean-Jacques. *"The Social Contract" and Other Later Political Writings*. Victor Gourevitch, ed. Cambridge: Cambridge University Press, 1997. Read the original. It is better than anything written about him.

Sked, Alan. *The Decline and Fall of the Habsburg Empire, 1815–1918*. New York: Longman, 2001. Sked writes a short and readable account of the problems that the multinational Habsburg Empire faced in the 19th century, which led to the First World War and its destruction.

Smith, Adam. *An Inquiry into the Nature and Causes of the Wealth of Nations*. Amherst, NY: Prometheus Books, 1991. Smith wrote beautifully, and his classic deserves reading and rereading. It is a superb piece of observation of human nature, as well as the most important work ever written in economic theory.

Smith, Denis Mack. *Mazzini*. New Haven/London: Yale University Press, 1996. The most distinguished historian of Italy writing in English turns his hand to the biography of the founder of Italian nationalism.

Strachey, Lytton. *Queen Victoria*. London/New York: Penguin, 2003. This biography of Victoria may not correspond to the latest academic research but it cannot be beaten as a work of art in its own right.

Symmons, Sarah. *Goya: Art and Ideas*. London/Boston: Phaidon Press, Inc., 1998. An elegant and neatly illustrated account of Goya's life and work.

Taylor, Alan John Percivale. *Bismarck, the Man and the Statesman*. New York: Random House Trade Paperbacks, 1975. A. J. P. Taylor never wrote a dull line. His reading of Bismarck is controversial, but you will not be bored.

Tolstoy, Leo. *War and Peace*. Rosemary Edmonds, trans. New York: Viking Press, 1982. Simply the greatest novel ever written.

Wollstonecraft, Mary. *Vindication of the Rights of Woman: An Authoritative Text*. Carol H. Poston, ed. New York: W.W. Norton & Co., 1988. The first serious feminist text; it demanded equal rights for women based on the general rights of human beings.

Wrigley, Chris. *Lloyd George* (Historical Association Studies). Oxford/Malden, MA: Blackwell Publishing, 2002. If you have time to read one brief life of Lloyd George, make this it. It allows you to hear Lloyd George speak.

Supplementary Reading:

Blake, Robert (Lord). *Disraeli*. London: Prion Books, 1998. Lord Blake, the historian of the British Conservative Party, also wrote the classic biography of Queen Victoria's favorite prime minister, Benjamin Disraeli, Lord Beaconsfield.

Bredin, Jean-Denis. *The Affair: The Case of Alfred Dreyfus*. This is an ingenious study by a French lawyer who looks at the case with a professional eye. He also pays attention to the role of Theodore Herzl and the foundation of modern Zionism.

Burke, Edmund. *The Portable Edmund Burke*. Isaac Kramnick, ed. A useful selection of Burke's main writings; helpful for readers who want to see connections between Burke and the early American Republic.

Deathridge, John. *Wagner: New Grove*. New York: W.W. Norton & Company, 1997. Deathridge served as one of the editors of the official edition of Wagner's works; he provides the musical expertise to understand Wagner's technique.

Ellis, Geoffrey. *Napoleon*. Profiles in Power. London/New York: Longman, 2000. Essays examining various aspects of Napoleon's rise to power, his impact on Europe, and his contributions to the arts.

Endelman, Todd. *The Jews of Georgian England, 1714–1830: Tradition and Change in a Liberal Society*. Ann Arbor, MI: University of Michigan Press, 1999. An excellent account of how Jews were readmitted to English society in the 18th century.

Fontane Theodor. *Effi Briest*, Hugh Rorrison and Helen Chambers, trans. Theodor Fontane (1819-1898) was a direct contemporary of Bismarck and the finest social novelist of his generation. *Effi Briest*, like many of his works, explores the inner world of the *Junker* aristocracy and the wider context of the empire Bismarck created.

Foster, Roy F. *Modern Ireland, 1600–1972*. London/New York: Penguin USA, 1990. A fine and fluent, if controversial, history of Ireland from the Middle Ages to the present.

Fraser David. *Frederick the Great*. London: Penguin Books 2002. An up-to-date popular biography of the "great" Frederick.

Garrioch, David. *The Making of Revolutionary Paris*. Berkeley, CA: University of California Press, 2002. Paris was an actor in the French Revolution, and David Garrioch describes what it was like to be there.

Gilligan, Carol. *In a Different Voice: Psychological Theory and Women's Development*. Cambridge, MA: Harvard University Press, 1993. One of the most influential modern works to claim that women see the world fundamentally differently from men.

Grigg, John. *Lloyd George: The Young Lloyd George*. London/New York: Penguin Books, 2002. This is a wonderful biography that covers the period before the lecture, but the book we need, *The People's Champion*, is out of print. This one will have to do.

Habermas, Jürgen. *Structural Transformation of the Public Sphere : An Inquiry into a Category of Bourgeois Society*. Cambridge, MA: MIT Press, 1991. A hard but rewarding study of the way culture became a commodity and the effects on society that such a change brought. It has become a cult book.

Hardman, John. *Robespierre*. Profiles in Power. London/New York: Longman, 2000. A neat, short biography of Robespierre.

Hibbert, Christopher. *The Days of the French Revolution*. Quill, 1999. Focuses on the famous days of the revolution, including July 14, 1789, when the Bastille fell, and others.

Jenkins, Roy (Lord). *Gladstone: A Biography*. New York: Random House Trade Paperbacks, 2002. Jenkins held every high office in the British government except prime minister and writes with a unique practitioner's perspective. Here, he gives us the life of Queen Victoria's least favorite prime minister.

Johnson, Paul. *Napoleon: A Penguin Life*. New York: Viking Press, 2002. A fine writer, biographer, and journalist turns his skilled hand to Napoleon.

Jordan, David P. *Transforming Paris: The Life and Labors of Baron Haussmann*. Chicago: University of Chicago Press, 1996. An account of the greatest city-planning enterprise of the 19th century and Napoleon III's greatest monument.

Mayr, Ernst. *What Evolution Is*. New York: Basic Books, 2002. The greatest living evolutionist published this astonishing work at the age of 97. It is an excellent introduction to evolution as we now understand it, a century and a half after the publication of *The Origin of Species*.

Norton, David Fate. *The Cambridge Companion to Hume*. Cambridge and New York: Cambridge University Press, 1993. A handy guide to everything you need to know about Hume and his philosophy.

O'Brien, Conor Cruise. *The Great Melody: A Thematic Biography and Commented Anthology of Edmund Burke*. Chicago: University of Chicago Press, 1994. The famous Irish politician and writer offers his reading of Burke's life and works.

O'Grada, Cormack. *Black '47 and Beyond*. Princeton, NJ: Princeton University Press, 2000. The latest research on the Irish famine and its consequences.

Pierenkemper, Toni and Tilly, Richard H. *The German Economy during the Nineteenth Century*. A short, readable history of German economic development during the period when the Krupp concern grew to world status.

Quinton, Anthony. *Hume: The Great Philosophers* (The Great Philosophers Series). London/New York: Routledge, 1999. Quinton selects and explains Hume's basic philosophy, then gives extensive citations.

Reddick, Allen. *The Making of Johnson's Dictionary, 1746–1773*. Cambridge and New York: Cambridge University Press, 1996. The inside story of how Johnson's great dictionary was compiled and published.

Rothschild, Emma. *Economic Sentiments: Adam Smith, Condorcet, and the Enlightenment*. Cambridge, MA: Harvard

University Press, 2002. Looks at the way the great economists of the 18th century thought about their world.

Steinberg, Jonathan, *Yesterday's Deterrent: Tirpitz and the Birth of the German Battle*, Modern Revivals in History. An attempt to trace the way in which naval expasnsion came to dominate German politics in the 1890s. It sheds light on the "military-industrial complex" which gave Imperial Germany its special character.

Steinberg, Jonathan. *Why Switzerland?* Cambridge/New York: Cambridge University Press, 1996. This is the only general study of Switzerland and should help to offer background to Rousseau.

Stokes,Donald E. *Pasteur's Quadrant: Basic Science and Technological Innovation.* A recent study of the interrelation between science and its applications as seen in the career of Pasteur, who made—unusually—great contributions in both fields.

Todd, Janet. *Mary Wollstonecraft.* New York: Columbia University Press, 2002. A sensitive biography of the first feminist.

Tomlinson, Janis. *From El Greco to Goya: Painting in Spain, 1561–1828.* New York: Prentice Hall Press, 1997. Traces the development of art from the mid-16th century to Goya's time, placing the art and artists in the context of Spanish history.

Watanabe-O'Kelly, Helen. *Court Culture in Dresden.* London: Palgrave Macmillan, 2002. A chance to see how Augustus the Strong spent his money.

Wheatcroft, Andrew. *The Habsburgs: Embodying Empire.* New York: Penguin USA, Inc. 1997. This charming, lively, and beautifully illustrated book brings the individual Habsburg monarchs and their families to life.

Wheen Francis. *Karl Marx: A Life.* New York: W.W. Norton & Company, 2001. A well-known English journalist and broadcaster writes a popular biography of Marx.

Wills, Gary. *Why I Am a Catholic.* Boston: Houghton Mifflin Co., 2002. One of America's leading Catholic intellectuals confronts the problems of ecclesiastical authority and freedom of conscience.

Wilson, A.N. *Tolstoy: A Biography.* New York: Publisher: W.W. Norton & Company, 2001. A famous British novelist writes a biography of the most famous of all novelists, a great combination.

285